Praise for *A Child's Journey Out of Autism*

"Leeann Whiffen's fight for her ...)f
perseverance and love—a remin ... ie
greatest ally a child with autism ' ... ut
of Autism shines a heartfelt light ...
—**Jenny McCarthy**, *New York Times* ... ier
Warriors and *Louder than Words*

"I have heard so many stories like Clay's that I thought I could no longer be moved by them; I was wrong. This is an important book to read if your family has *not* been touched by autism, because it's important to understand the disorder that has affected so many all over the world. If someone you love is on the autism spectrum, read it because it will allow you to see that autism is treatable. While not all children make a complete recovery, improvements in their quality of life are possible at any age. I strongly recommend this moving and intelligent book."
—**Jane Johnson**, executive director, Defeat Autism Now!

"Leeann Whiffen takes the reader onto the rollercoaster ride that is autism from the first chapter to the last. *A Child's Journey Out of Autism* is a field guide on how an average family can grow in love as they take on autism, refusing to accept the mainstream doom and gloom pronouncement that there is no hope or treatment. This is an important, really powerful book. If you know a child with autism, read this book for them."
—**Kim Stagliano**, managing editor, Age of Autism, and mother of three girls with autism

"This uplifting and positive book gives parents of newly diagnosed children hope for the future. There is no easy fix or magic bullet for recovering a child from autism, but as Leeann so skillfully shows us, with perseverance and determination, the possibilities and rewards are endless. Thank you, Leeann, for sharing your story and empowering parents to make that journey to rediscover their child."
—**Chantal Sicile-Kira**, author of *Autism Life Skills*, *Adolescents on the Autism Spectrum*, and *Autism Spectrum Disorders*

"The journey from diagnosis to recovery is filled with obstacles and setbacks. The financial and emotional burdens families endure are heartbreaking. Yet, like the Whiffen family demonstrates, there is power in hope and determination. Parents like Leeann and Sean demonstrate that autism doesn't have to be a lifelong struggle. This book shows that there is a pathway to recovery.

With effective treatments, a supportive network, and unwavering parents, recovery is indeed possible. We have had the opportunity to see this many times at CARD. These success stories are what keep us going. The successes Leeann facilitated for her son are what kept her going. I commend her commitment to her child and willingness to share her personal story and private struggles so others can benefit from her knowledge and experience.

Leeann's determination, drive, and hope are inspirational. Her story is unique, yet it mirrors what so many families encounter, the stress of inadequate funding options, the frustration of misdiagnosis, the confusion associated with learning about the best treatments. Her ability to tell her story with heart mixed with concrete information will no doubt help many families."

—Doreen Granpeesheh, PhD, BCBA, founder and executive director, Center for Autism & Related Disorders, Inc. (CARD)

"The Autism club is not one that we choose to join. Sadly, many of us are welcomed to this club by medical professionals who offer little hope for our children. But as the Whiffen family and thousands of others have discovered, our children can get better and in many cases, even recover from autism. In *A Child's Journey Out of Autism*, Leeann Whiffen welcomes us to the club with the gift of hope. This book is a must-read for parents with a newly diagnosed child with autism."

—Wendy Fournier, president, National Autism Association

LEEANN WHIFFEN

A Child's Journey Out of Autism

*One Family's Story of Living in
Hope and Finding a Cure*

SOURCEBOOKS, INC.®
NAPERVILLE, ILLINOIS

Published by Sourcebooks, Inc.
P.O. Box 4410, Naperville, Illinois 60567–4410
(630) 961–3900
Fax: (630) 961–2168
www.sourcebooks.com

Library of Congress Cataloging-in-Publication Data
Whiffen, Leeann.
A child's journey out of autism : one family's story of living in hope and finding a cure / Leeann Whiffen.
p. cm.

1. Whiffen, Leeann. 2. Whiffen, Clay. 3. Parents of autistic children—United States—Biography. 4. Autistic children—United States—Biography. 5. Autistic children—Family relationships—United States. 6. Autistic children—Rehabilitation—United States. I. Title.
RJ506.A9W457 2008
618.92'858820092—dc22
[B]
                                    2008034036

Printed and bound in the United States of America.
VP 10 9 8 7 6 5 4 3 2 1

To Drew, Clay, Judd, and Sean. You make every day my lucky day.

To those who love someone with autism —*Numquam Cede.*
"Never Give Up"

Author's Note

The names of certain individuals in the text have been changed, except for the following who appear under their real names:

Sean; Leeann; Clay; Drew; Judd; Bryan Jepson, MD; Jennifer Gale, PsyD; Sam Coates, MD; Andrea; Sarah; Andy/ Anndalyn; Natalie; Trisha; Brooke; Kimber; Susan; Kim; Gretchen; and Mary.

A portion from the proceeds of this book will go to the National Autism Association to help support families affected by autism.

Foreword

My own journey into the world of autism started in 2001, when my second son, Aaron, was diagnosed with the disorder. As an emergency medicine physician, one-third of my training and my patient contacts had been with pediatric patients. Yet, I knew virtually nothing about autism. It wasn't talked about in medical school, nor in the pediatrics rotations during my residency. My previous exposure to autism was the two hours spent watching the movie *Rain Man.* Then, suddenly it seemed, my family was thrust into this strange new world. Unfortunately, it seemed that this was a world as foreign to everyone else as it was to us. There were no maps, no GPS systems. No one in the medical profession seemed to have any answers to our questions about cause or treatments. They just gave us the diagnosis and sent us on our way, intentionally trying to lower our expectations of any meaningful future for our son.

Surprisingly, the autism world was becoming increasingly populated with children and families just like ours who were also struggling to blindly navigate the terrain. The rates of autism diagnoses had risen from a rare condition before the mid-1980s (1 in 5000) to the most common developmental disability in children by the mid-1990s (1 in 150). No one had any explanation for that, either. If autism was a rare genetic disease like everybody thought, why was there a several thousand percent increase in a decade? That rate of change in such a short period does not happen with a genetic illness. So, if it is not genetic, then it must be environmental, at least in part. And if it is environmental, it means that something is causing it. If we can figure out what is causing it, we might be able to treat it or even prevent it. So why was this research not being done? Almost overnight, something was stealing the future of at least 1 in 150 of our children. Why weren't people noticing? Why was it not on the front page of the newspaper? The media talks all the time about epidemics like West Nile Virus, SARS, Hantavirus, and others, in spite of only a handful of individuals being diagnosed in the entire country. If Al Qaeda were stealing these children, we would stop at nothing to get them back. One in 150 children means 500,000 children in the United States. Even during the biggest polio epidemic in the United States in 1952, the rate of those affected with paralysis was 1.4 per 10,000. Deaths were 0.2 per 10,000. These numbers pale in comparison to this silent epidemic of autism.

As we began searching for answers for my son, I began reading the existing medical literature about autism. What I found surprised me. There were many studies from independent researchers, published in peer-reviewed medical journals, that talked about medical conditions associated with autism. Many of these talked about the involvement of the immune system and the gastrointestinal system. My son had symptoms consistent with problems in these areas. Why was this not discussed with me by the psychiatrist who diagnosed him? To the contrary, he had dismissed the notion that autism involved anything besides behavior, and in fact, he discouraged us from looking further at things like diets and medical treatment, stating that there was no research that backed up the theories. Yet, a simple search on PubMed, an online medical database, brought up dozens of articles from reputable research institutions.

Other research pointed to metabolic problems and detoxification problems in autism. Is this why these children are more susceptible to environmental exposures? The more I learned, the more convinced I became that autism is much more than just a behavior disorder. It is, in fact, a metabolic disorder that is affecting multiple organ systems in the body. And the problems with the immune system are affecting the gastrointestinal tract and the brain. Is it not sensible that in addition to behavioral treatments, individuals with autism need treatment for the underlying medical issues?

After becoming sufficiently educated in therapeutic interventions, I began treating children on the autism spectrum. The stories I hear are hauntingly similar. The tired and frightened looks on the faces of the parents are universal. These parents are not crazy. They are not just looking for excuses or someone to blame. They are just desperate to help their children and are forced by circumstances to battle for every bit of assistance they can get.

Leeann Whiffen tells her story of the heartache that all parents of autistic children feel when they realize that their child has been taken. Leeann and I first met when she brought her young son, Clay, to me soon after he was diagnosed with autism. Over the next three years, I was able to partner with Leeann and her husband, Sean, in caring for their son's multiple and complex medical problems. Correcting these issues requires intense parental effort over many years. Leeann has taken on this challenge with a true fighting spirit that has helped her to persevere through the difficult challenges this illness presents. She fought back, and Clay responded beautifully. To date, I have treated 1,500 children like Clay. We still have a long way to go before we truly understand this disorder completely and can predict a response as profound as Clay's. But, his story shows us that it is possible. Autism is treatable. Children can recover. This gives us all, parents and practitioners alike, the hope and the courage to keep fighting.

Bryan Jepson, MD
Medical Director
Thoughtful House Center for Children
Austin, Texas
Author, *Changing the Course of Autism*

Prologue

I see fear and terror in Clay's eyes, as if he's a wild animal being chased by a predator. But the hallway he is running through is empty. He screeches. Suddenly his stubby, two-year-old legs trip over one another, and his head strikes the hard floor with such force that the sound echoes in the narrow corridor of the church. Then he springs to his feet and continues charging around a corner, oblivious to any pain. I finally catch up to him, scooping him up to cradle him in my arms. But he madly fights my grip with his adrenaline-boosted strength and wriggles free, bursting back around the corner and easily outrunning me in my dress and high heels.

He barrels up to a young man standing against the wall with his hands jammed in his pockets, and Clay grabs the stranger's pant legs and yanks with desperation. He looks up at the man and screams as if to say, "Help me." The man stares in confusion while Clay beats on his legs. Finally, he bends down and gathers him into his arms. Clay burrows his head into the man's shoulder.

I meet up with them, my chest heaving, bending down with outstretched arms. "Clay, come with me. Come on…come to Mom."

He looks at me, but his eyes seem to look right through me. The blood pumps in my chest. Questions hammer my mind as loud and hard as the rhythm of my heartbeat. I try to make sense of what is happening. A two-year-old clings to his mother, not some stranger. I don't understand. Why is he running from me? Why is he so out of control? And why doesn't he call me Mom anymore? He acts like he doesn't even know who I am.

I pry his digging fingers from the man's shoulders and unwrap his arms and legs, embracing him in a firm grasp so he can't escape. "I'm sorry," I mutter to the man, then leave the church and scurry through the parking lot, my toddler clenched tightly to my chest. The sides of the earth fold in on me with unbearable pressure. I wipe my sleeve on my forehead to absorb the damp sweat beads. Those nagging feelings…they are becoming stronger, louder…steadily pulsating.

There is something terribly wrong with my son.

Jyl Read Photography

Chapter 1

I amble out into the balmy June morning with a pregnant swagger. The fog is still heavy in the air at 6:00 a.m. My hospital bag clutched under my arm, I maneuver my awkward body up and into the car. I hear the thumping of Sean's fingers and turn to see him tapping the keys of an imaginary piano on the steering wheel. As we drive to the hospital, I think about Drew, our two-year-old son, who can't wait to meet his brother. I envision the boys growing up together as best friends, sticking up for each other amidst trouble, playing sports together, sharing a room, double dating. It is then I remember why we chose to have our babies so close together.

Just as I'm settling into my room at John Muir Hospital, gentle music begins pouring through the hallways. I look at Sean, puzzled. He points up at the intercom in the ceiling. As it plays longer, I recognize the familiar melody. Brahms' "Lullaby."

"What's this?" I ask, looking upward.

"Another baby was just born," my nurse says, like she has answered the same question over a hundred times this week.

"Oh, how nice," I say.

I think about how lucky I am that I'm even here on this day, June 20, 2000. I'm overdue. Consuming slice after slice of "prego pizza," a specialty pie with every topping in the house that Skipolini's claims will kick-start labor, didn't deliver anything but severe intestinal distress. When my OB/GYN offered to induce, I instantly took him up on it.

I squeeze Sean's hand, noting his boyish hairline and dark chocolate eyes. His masculine, geometric jawline beckons my gaze. I mouth the words, "I love you." Holding up his hand he grins slightly to one side and flashes me the "I love you" sign.

The entire labor process blurs, setting itself apart from my grueling first delivery. I clench Sean's hand again, this time so hard he pretends to grimace dramatically. I shoot him the look that says, *you are silly to try and tease me now.*

"Push," the doctor says again. "He's almost there."

"One more time!" Sean says excitedly, leaning in closer.

I bear down with all the energy I can marshal. I feel the blood rush to my face and the veins pop out of my head and neck as I strain to deliver this new life into our world.

"There he is," I hear the doctor say in a calm low voice.

A tiny, shrill cry penetrates the air. I lift my head off the pillow and smile, seeing his wet, curly hair matted to his head. His scrawny reddish-purple body swims in the hands of the doctor.

A feeling of peace and reverence fills the room.

The doctor hands the scissors to Sean and shows him where to cut the umbilical cord. The nurses take our son to the sink and wash him. They wrap him tightly in a thin blanket and put a beanie on his head. The room is quiet except for his tiny cries. The doctor takes him from the nurse and places him in my arms. I brush my lips against his face and inhale his sweet smell. I kiss his soft, warm head and nestle him close to me. Brahms "Lullaby" softly plays above.

I hold him only for a brief moment before one of the nurses whisks him away to weigh him and check his vitals.

"He scored a 9 on his Apgar test and his measurements were right on target," the nurse says.

She hands him back to me and places him on my chest. His warm body relaxes me. He stretches and squeaks so much he sounds like a dry hinge. I quickly glance at his hands and feet to ensure he has all five fingers and toes. I pull down the front of his diaper. "Everything is there," I whisper, easing my new mom jitters. I exhale a mental sigh of relief as I look at his tiny hand clasped over my first finger.

"So far so good," I say, looking over at Sean.

"Our baby boy is a healthy, normal little newborn. He's beautiful, and so are you," Sean says.

"I'm so happy, sweetie."

"Me too," he says, stroking my face and hair.

At that moment I realize that I love him more than I ever have.

At a few days old, Clay seems to be the perfect baby. I revel in his mild temperament and wonder how I got so lucky—Drew had colic, and I was dreading it again. He only wakes twice in the night to breast-feed, and rarely cries. I'm thrilled with his disposition.

Clay's first week goes by, and we take him into the pediatrician for his first well-child visit. She highly recommends he receive the hepatitis B shot at this visit.

"You'll need to sign this first," she says, handing me a clipboard with a consent form.

I scrawl my signature at the bottom of the paper without looking it over.

"What mother who cares at all about her child would refuse to vaccinate them?" I ask her as I mentally pat myself on the back for being so conscientious.

"Oh," she chuckles, "You'd be surprised."

"We are so fortunate to have two healthy boys. I could never live with myself if they were to get sick with a preventable disease."

She hands me an immunization schedule. "In order to keep Clay healthy, you'll need to make sure to bring him in for all of his well-child visits."

"Of course. We won't forget."

Four weeks pass and Clay seems less happy. He cries a little more, sleeps a little less. By his sixth week, he cries incessantly and hardly sleeps at all. His behavior evolves into days and nights filled with piercing screams, an arching back, and inconsolable crying. Soon Clay rarely sleeps for longer than thirty minutes at a time. He jerks awake, screaming frantically as if someone is pinching him. The area surrounding his eyes looks like a bull's-eye from lack of sleep. I'm frustrated because I don't know how to help him. His shrill screeches arouse every nerve in my body, wearing them raw. I get so attuned to hearing them, even everyday sounds like the running dishwasher mimic his cries.

I call the pediatrician, who says, "Oh, yes, it's probably just gas. Don't worry too much." She recommends some over-the-counter drops to help ease the "supposed pain" in his stomach. I hang up the phone, bolt to the drugstore, and purchase the drops that will hopefully solve all our problems. We begin using them right away, but it doesn't seem to help. As his crying becomes more intense, so too does the constant reminder that I'm failing to meet his needs. I spend entire days rocking him, cuddling him, talking to him. I play soft music, and Drew and I sing to him.

Yet nothing I do seems to comfort him.

Chapter 2

Sean's new job as an assistant to an estate-tax planner requires him to put in many extra hours. We live in Concord, California, only a thirty-minute commute to his office in Walnut Creek. But his early start and late finish make the days with Clay seem like months in our small condominium that lacks a yard. I often look out the glass doors at the pine trees that line our second-story patio, dreaming we live in the mountains surrounded by a thicket of lush trees. It passes the time and helps me endure the confining, endless days. I begin crossing the days off on the calendar. It signifies we've accomplished something, even if it is just getting through another twenty-four hours.

Drew's frustration flares with Clay's constant crying. He walks around the house with his hands covering his ears.

"Mom," he yells, "When will Clay stop crying?"

"I don't know, son," I yell loud enough for him to hear me over the noise.

"Make it stop!" he screams.

"I wish I could," I say, feeling invisible.

I encourage him to sing with me and help me rock Clay. Adjusting to being the big brother and not having my constant attention has been difficult for him. It's difficult for me too. I'm exhausted and would do anything to have a break from the constant chaos. I'm not sure what is worse, the crying that gnaws on my nerves, my upset toddler, or feeling completely inadequate in being able to help soothe my baby.

I answer the phone that evening and hear a good friend on the other line. She is crying.

"What's going on? Are you all right?" I ask, upset at the unknown.

"Kathy's husband just had a heart attack and passed away!" my friend says.

"No…no! I'm going to see her." I hang up the phone.

"I'll only be an hour or so," I tell Sean as I run out the door. "I just fed Clay. He should be fine."

As my car approaches Kathy's home, I see an ambulance with the lights still turning. A lanky man in a dark uniform is talking with Kathy between two black walnut trees. Her head is down, and her hands are over her mouth. I park the car and approach her, shocked that this entire scene is real. Her eyes show a hollow disbelief that her life is spinning out of control. We hug and cry together, then go inside and talk. More friends arrive.

About thirty minutes later, a friend comes to me and says, "Sean is on the phone for you." How strange he would call me at such a sensitive time. I take the phone.

"Is everything okay?"

"You need to come home. Clay has been screaming since you left, he doesn't even seem to take a breath. I'm really concerned about him. Please come home."

I quickly say good-bye and apologize for having to leave so abruptly. The dark car ride home is spent wondering what had happened to the sweet baby we brought home from the hospital. I question if this is really what motherhood is all about…colicky babies, long days with no end in sight, difficult two-year-olds. I want my life to be like the commercials in which the child looks into his mother's eyes, squeezes her cheeks, and giggles.

I whip into the closest parking space and shut off the engine. My heels click up the concrete stairs to our small condo in perfect rhythm. As I approach the door, Clay's screaming grows louder. I hesitate before turning the knob, scrambling for any thought of how I can help him. Nothing comes to me. I lean my head against the door briefly before turning the handle and stepping inside. I watch Sean pace around the living room, lightly bouncing Clay. As our eyes connect, his concerned expression slightly relaxes.

I take Clay from him.

I try to breast-feed him, but he refuses, his screams growing panic-like. I run the vacuum. I turn on soft classical music. I give him a bath. I talk to him. I talk to myself. I take him for a long car ride.

Nothing soothes him.

I cuddle him while he cries for two more hours before he finally drifts off. He jerks awake ten minutes later in full howl. I look up at the clock. It's 12:30 a.m. For the next four hours, I rock Clay, desperately searching for any inspiration. I wonder if it is possible to die from exhaustion. I wonder if it is possible for an infant to never sleep.

I try feeding him again. He falls asleep after three minutes. I'm careful not to move, breathing slightly. His screams still echo in my mind, threatening to interrupt any sleep I might steal. I wake at 5:00 a.m. to a squeal, and we start all over again.

Two weeks later, Sean bursts through the front door, throws his briefcase on the couch, and yells, "Lee, I have a surprise for you."

"What is it?" I call from the kitchen, pounding that night's meat with a tenderizer.

"Weelll…" He draws out the anticipation while yanking off his tie. "I got a job transfer to Utah."

"Utah?" I ask. I drop the mallet on the counter and face him. "What's in Utah?"

"What's in Utah? Are you kidding me?" He says, sweeping me up and into his arms. "Great skiing, less people, and all the outdoor recreation you can imagine!"

"Stop. You sound like an advertisement."

"Really, Lee, I think you're going to love it. There will be a shorter commute. I'll get the same salary but with a lower cost of living. And it's a great place to raise our family. Besides, your mom and dad's house in Idaho will only be two hours away."

"I'm sold. When do we leave?"

It is a prime time to sell a home in the San Francisco Bay Area. Recent sales show people bidding up to $100,000 over asking price. Buyers write essays describing why they deserve to be the new owners of the home. Some buyers even offer stock options or throw in cruises with their offers for the seller. We get lucky, but not that lucky. The day we list our property, we receive multiple offers. We sell our condominium for thousands more than the listing price. Within the week, we fly to Utah and purchase a home south of Salt Lake City.

As we settle into our new home together, I reflect on what an odd but perfect match we make. We were raised so differently, but dovetail one another as if designed by a master craftsman. I was born the youngest of five children on a large cattle ranch in Idaho. We were surrounded by 400 acres, a quarter alfalfa fields, with 300-head of cattle. As early as four years old, I helped my dad irrigate the expansive fields that were speckled with cow pies. Ranch life often provoked frustration, yet demanded resiliency. The first time I learned that "damn" and "shit" were swear words, and that "ass" wasn't just a donkey, was the last time I used them at school in front of my teacher in the second grade. Barely scraping by financially, our family managed to scavenge enough to eat between the ½-acre garden my mom nurtured like a sixth child, and by slaughtering sick or lame cows. I knew times were especially tough when I would see a cow's tongue curled and prepped in the refrigerator for that night's supper. If we had a family motto, it would have been, "There's no such thing as a free lunch."

Sean, on the other hand, was the youngest of six children, born in a suburb of Los Angeles. His dad was raised in the government projects of Oakland and bounced around in foster homes. He managed to maneuver his way from a deprived childhood, including brief stints in juvenile hall, to a successful businessman, working Saturdays and evenings to achieve his dreams of a better life. Sean's quiet, unassuming mother provided the silent support he needed to get there. His parents traveled the world experiencing Russia, China, Europe, and other exotic places. His dad would help him buy anything if he earned half the cost. Money was rarely scarce. Sean's family motto was "Never Quit."

Clay, four months old now, is becoming easier to manage. He still wakes several times in the night, but I'm relieved his crying has lessened. He smiles spontaneously, engaging others with a magnetic personality. He is drawn to music, bursting into giggling fits when we dance around the house together. Drew plays peek-a-boo with Clay for as long as he continues laughing, which can sometimes last through an entire meal. Drew shakes his bouncer up and down "giving him a ride" while Clay's laughing becomes so intense he can hardly catch a breath. My dreams are within reach as I watch them begin bonding together as brothers and friends.

As we settle into our home, we invite Sean's sister and her family over for a barbecue. In between bites, we laugh and tell "remember when" stories. Just as I'm coming off a good chuckle, I feel a tugging on my sleeve. It's Sean's ten-year-old niece. Her arms are locked, holding Clay two feet out in front of her, as if he is contaminated. "Aunt Leeann, Clay just pooped, and it's all up his back and in his hair." Her nose wrinkles and her cheeks puff out like she's holding her breath. I carefully take him from her and go to the closet to get a clean diaper. I lay him on the floor and strip him down for a head-to-toe cleaning. Just as I place the clean diaper underneath, he starts pooping again. It pours out steadily, like an erupting volcano. As it begins to fill up the first diaper, I send Sean's niece to grab a couple more. I switch to the second, and then the third clean diaper. I can hardly believe his small body can hold so much waste. I try to remember the last time he had a bowel movement. Since he had become irregular, over six weeks ago, I started keeping track. I go to the calendar and see that my last notation was two weeks ago. That can't be right! It has to be a mistake.

The next morning I immediately contact our new pediatrician and recount what happened. He listens carefully and says, "As long as it is soft, he isn't considered constipated. Give him more prunes and applesauce. That should take care of it."

As I hang up the phone, I question his advice. This isn't normal. It can't be healthy.

I talk to Sean about my concerns and finally conclude that the pediatrician surely knows what is best for our son. Over the next week or so, I feed him loads of prunes and applesauce, just like the pediatrician instructed. I wait two more weeks to see if anything changes. It takes eighteen days until he finally has another bowel movement. I watch in horror as he once again unloads massive amounts of stool. I pick up the telephone and punch in the pediatrician's number.

"I really need to talk to Dr. Keller, please."

"Dr. Keller is in with a patient right now," The nurse says. "Oh, hold on…actually, here he comes. Let me get him."

"Dr. Keller, Clay went two weeks again without a bowel movement," I say. "I did everything you told me to do. His stomach is swollen, and he's miserable!"

"Well," Dr. Keller replies, "next time, try giving him a glycerin suppository."

"Is that habit-forming?" I press.

"No, not if it's only used periodically. Mrs. Whiffen," he sighs, in a tired, condescending manner, "breast milk is highly absorbable. It's likely that his body just doesn't need to have consistent bowel movements. Everyone's body and metabolism are different and unique. There is no need to worry. Clay will be fine. Come and see me if the stool gets hard to pass, or pellet-like."

"But, Dr. Keller," I plead, "How can going two weeks in between bowel movements be normal? How can having waste built up inside anyone, let alone a small infant like him, be healthy?"

Silence on the line. Then a nasal-filled sigh.

"All right. Let's test him for Hirschprung's disease, just to be sure," he says, treating me like an annoying, yapping dog biting at his ankles. He seems willing to do anything just to shake me off.

The nurse at the hospital calls to tell us Clay needs to fast eight hours immediately before the procedure at 8:00 a.m. the next morning. He's only five months old, and usually eats in the middle of the night and again when he wakes up. Sean gets up with Clay in the night so that he doesn't smell me and expect to be fed. Withholding something as vital as food from a crying infant tests my willpower. I stay awake even after I hear Clay finally settle down. I try to avoid him that morning. But his pleading eyes melt my resolve, and I hold him close to me.

We arrive at the hospital and the nurse leads us down the hallway into a cool, dim room. The X-ray technician asks me to remove Clay's clothes and place him on his back on the table. I wince as I watch his little naked body quiver on the cold, flat examination table. His tiny cries echo through the quiet, spacious room as he is held down for the barium enema. I want to gather him in my arms and place his soft skin against mine.

A few days later, Dr. Keller calls me with the test results. "It's not Hirschprung's disease, but he does have a megacolon," he says. "You need to make sure he is having a bowel movement regularly so his colon will have time to shrink back to normal size. Try not to give him a large amount of bananas or cheese. Keep working on the prunes and applesauce."

I clutch the telephone so tightly I hear it crackle beneath my grasp. I want to scream back at him that the prunes and applesauce obviously aren't working.

I'm relieved it's finally Saturday. Sean is home, and this is my one day a week in which I can take a shower and fully enjoy it—no kids crying in the background or banging on the door for me. No wondering what they've smeared all over the floor or their faces when I'm lathering up.

I turn on the warm water and exhale slowly as the steam relaxes every part of my body. Then I'm jolted to reality by a shrill scream from downstairs. It's unlike any I have heard before. Sean bursts into the bathroom and says, "Lee, Clay fell out of his highchair and hit his head on the leg of the table." I frantically turn off the water and dry myself as fast as I can, running down the stairs still in my towel. Clay is throwing up and his eyes roll back into his head. I immediately grab the phone and call the pediatrician. The voice on the other line says, "You'll need to take him to the ER. He might have a concussion."

I run upstairs, hurriedly throw some clothes on, my hair still wet and take Clay in my arms. He vomits on my shirt and in my hair. I change my shirt, again, while Sean grabs some towels for the car. We hustle the boys into the car and drive as fast as we can to the hospital. I look back at Clay in his car seat next to Sean. He seems calm. Unusually calm, bordering docile. I long to hold him.

We call Sean's sister, who lives close to the hospital. She meets us at the emergency room entrance and takes Drew home with her. As we check in at the ER desk, they ask us a few questions. "Ma'am, can you tell me what happened?" At first, I'm unable to speak. "Ma'am?" I handled everything well up until this point. As the words begin to unravel out of my mouth, my throat swells, leaving me unable to finish. Sean picks up when I trail off.

They rush us back into a small room in which Clay's tiny eight-month-old body is overwhelmed by the vast examination table. He looks limp and lifeless. The doctor enters the room looking at his clipboard.

"Has he been unconscious at any point?" the ER physician asks.

"No," I reply.

He examines Clay's eyes and head.

"Wait here, please," he says, motioning us to the waiting room. "I am going to take your son to get a CAT scan. This will help us to know if there is any damage to his brain from the impact."

He wheels Clay down the hall and rounds the corner. Sean grabs my sweaty, cold hand and places it in his.

Eventually, I hear faint footsteps thump against the hard hospital floor, growing louder with each step. I look up and see the doctor rounding the corner with our baby in his arms. His long white lab coat folds into the floor as he hands Clay to me. I snuggle Clay against my body, kissing his soft, warm face.

"Mr. and Mrs. Whiffen, the CAT scan looks normal. It shows no evidence of brain trauma. Keep an eye on him, and wake him up every fifteen minutes or so during the day. He should be fine."

"Thank you," Sean says as he reaches out to shake the doctor's hand.

I take a deep breath, suddenly aware of the pounding pain within my head.

Three days later, Clay refuses to eat and hardly sleeps. He's lethargic, and his head burns at 103 degrees. I hurry him to the doctor's office. Dr. Keller examines him and finds he has ear infections in both ears. He sends me on my way with a prescription for Augmentin, a strong oral antibiotic. I'm instructed to give him the antibiotic as prescribed, and alternate Tylenol and Motrin as needed. The next morning Clay throws up again and his fever continues to run high, despite the antibiotic and over-the-counter meds. We head back to the pediatrician, who gives him a Rocephin shot, another antibiotic, and sends us home. Clay's symptoms finally subside a few days later.

Four weeks later, at nine months of age, Clay receives his diphtheria, tetanus, pertussis (DTaP), and hepatitis B (Hep B) vaccinations, resulting in the predictable high fever and irritability. But the doctor says to not worry about the fever, it will eventually go away. And yes, he may be irritable.

To me, his high fever and high-pitched screams seem anything but normal.

One month later, Clay becomes sick again with yet another

fever. This time he's inconsolable for almost three days. He won't let me out of his sight. I suspect another ear infection. Dr. Keller confirms my suspicions; this time the infection is in his right ear. He sends me home with a prescription for amoxicillin, an oral antibiotic. Antibiotics seem to be a permanent part of Clay's regular diet.

Regardless of how often he has been sick, Clay continues to be the happy, loving child we first saw at four months old. His toddler feet slap the floor as he runs around the house saying, "Mama, Mama." His smile lights up the room, and his laugh sends us to an exotic place. We dance together even more now that he's growing bigger. Some days we're in the mood for "Funkytown" and other days it's "One Night in Bangkok." We bob to the music, his right hand clasped in my left. Eventually we whirl around until we can't stop and fall on the couch while we watch the room spin around us. Sometimes Drew joins. Sometimes he'd rather carefully build a Lego structure, keeping a sharp eye on us to make sure we don't come within two feet of his masterpiece. He's verbally precocious, knowing the names of every construction vehicle ever made. Drew is three years old going on ten.

One day Clay and I sit across from each other on the family room floor and begin rolling the red playground ball back and forth. I tell Drew to come and play with us. He shakes his head.

"Here comes the ball, Clay!"

Clay looks at me with his blue eyes the size of silver dollars and says, "Ball."

"Clay! You just said your first real word! Ball!" I grab him and swing him around. We rub noses and giggle.

A few weeks later, he takes his first steps, then begins walking within that same week. He waves "bye-bye" and says "night-night." He calls Sean "Dada" and me "Mama." He squeals with delight when Sean throws him in the air, begging to go up again and again.

We celebrate his first birthday with the traditional cake and presents. He grins—the white frosting matches his hair and covers his face with a full beard. I smile and say a silent prayer of gratitude. *I'm so grateful for our two healthy, happy boys.* Clay strips the wrapping paper off each present in one brief stroke. Each item is greeted with a gleeful smile and clap. He flies his new Buzz Lightyear around the room, making spaceship noises as if he were the ranger in the spacesuit.

Sean puts his arms around my waist as he kisses my neck. "I love you," he says. I turn around and we embrace. Over his shoulder, I see Clay looking at the painting above our fireplace. He points at it and says, "Sheeshush." Then he looks up at me. He points to it again and says, "Sheeshush."

"Did you hear that, Sean?" I say, almost yelling. "He said, 'Jesus' while pointing to the picture of Christ."

"Is that what he said?"

"Yes! Yes, it is!"

"I don't ever remember telling him that was Jesus."

At twelve months old, Clay receives his Prevnar (pneumococcal) and Varivax (chicken pox) vaccines. Two days after that, he spikes another fever. I take him in again and this time he has an ear infection in his left ear. We are sent home with amoxicillin and Tylenol.

It isn't long before Dr. Keller's staff knows me by my first name, despite the hundreds of patients that funnel through their office daily. I am a regular.

Chapter 3

Two months after Clay's first birthday, his behavior gradually spirals downward, and he wants me to hold him constantly. He becomes a permanent appendage on my hip as I get used to doing everything with one hand. One afternoon, I plop him on my lap and open his favorite book, *The Very Busy Spider* by Eric Carle. But reading it once isn't enough. He demands that I read it again and again. He runs his fingers over the embossed web, following the lines to the spider, until it eventually wears off the page.

Clay vacillates from days of alienating everyone to days of demanding endless comfort and attention. He pounds on my legs and screams if I don't pick him up. He claws at my face and pinches my neck. His pacifier and blanket become an inseparable part of his being, sending him spiraling into fits of frustration if one or the other is missing.

Thomas the Tank Engine has taken over his mind. But he is especially fanatical about James, the red engine. He carries James in one hand, and Thomas, the blue engine, in the other at all times. If either go missing at any time, it throws Clay into fits until we find them.

One evening, I try getting him interested in playing with his trains so I can prepare dinner. He tantrums and wraps his arms and legs tightly around my right leg. I hobble around the kitchen doing as much as I can, but I don't want to hurt him, so I pry his hands from my leg and put on a new Thomas the Tank Engine video I purchased from the store earlier in the week. We already have several Thomas movies we rotate since they are the only ones he will watch for an extended period of time. I feel a pang of guilt each time I let him watch one, but sometimes it's the only way I can get anything done.

The movie begins, and the narrator begins to talk. Clay begins to scream, crying and pounding his fists against his thighs. *That's strange. These are his favorite videos to watch.* Baffled, I put a different Thomas video on for him and he watches it quietly. I tell Sean about the incident during dinner.

"Let's see," Sean says, "Hand me the case to the new Thomas video."

He checks the two covers. "The only difference I can see is that this new one has Ringo Starr as the narrator, instead of Alec Baldwin."

"That's got to be it!" I say, like we have just solved an impossible mystery. "He didn't scream until the narrator started talking."

"I wonder why he would care who was talking," Sean says. "He really seems to be rigid and obsessive about some things."

I know he is right. But I think it's probably just a phase. I remember my mom telling me that when I was his age, I used to gather rocks and carry them around in my bulging pockets. I turned out all right. I think.

Our grocery trips begin and end in a tantrum, and often have one somewhere in the middle. One day Clay starts to fuss as we pass the produce section. I chastise myself for not taking the alternate route, forgetting his recent obsession with round produce. He fixates on the circular fruits and vegetables, groping as many as he can grab from the front of the cart where he is buckled. Unexpectedly, the automatic water misters begin to spray—saturating not only the produce but also Clay's arm. In one panicked, sweeping motion he manages to knock an entire display of lettuce to the floor. He quickly bursts into an aggressive fit. I abandon my cart and bolt for the car with Clay fighting in my arms. People stop to watch. As I approach the car, his body stiffens, refusing to let me buckle him in his car seat. I eventually manage to force him into it, using all my strength. As I get into the driver's seat, I wipe the sweat from my forehead and notice a woman glaring at me in the car to my left side. I look in the rearview mirror and see someone else scrawling something on a scrap of paper while looking at the back of the car. Clay is still screaming in the back. I kick it in reverse and squeal out of the parking lot, vowing to never return.

The next day, after a grueling morning, I'm desperate to get out of the house. I load the kids in the car and drive with no particular destination in mind. If there is an outburst, at least it's contained inside the car. I can ignore it, or I can scream along too. And no one else is here to react. No dirty looks or rude comments. No one with the judgmental glare that says, "All that kid needs is a good spanking."

I become socially withdrawn, sinking deeper into myself. Clay's constant demands make it impossible to even talk on the phone, causing me to fall out of practice. My friends don't understand why I can't go with them on a walk or to the mall. They ask why we don't talk much anymore, but I can't adequately describe my pain and frustration. The more I retreat, the more awkward my attempts at conversation sound. I look out the window and see my neighbors outside their homes chatting, throwing their heads back in carefree laughter. Their children are playing happily alongside them. I crave to be out there with them. Two weeks pass without me talking to an adult not named Sean or Mom.

One night, in desperation, I get down on my knees and say, *Father in heaven, help me to know what to do for my son.*

Please, help me know what's wrong with him and how to take care of it. That night, I dream I know what I'm supposed to do. I wake up completely at peace with the answer. But what is it? It's right there, I just can't seem to access it. I remember dreaming about it, but....Ahhhh!...I can't remember what IT is! I groan as I roll out of bed, only to be met with another day of being housebound.

It's Saturday afternoon, and my parents are making the two-hour drive for a quick visit. The first prep item on my to-do list is to sterilize the bathroom because, from experience, I know that my mom uses it at least two times per hour. She's very tidy and cleans her bathrooms every other day. I have a phobia of disappointing people, and she's at the top of my list.

The doorbell rings and Drew runs to greet Nana and Papa with a big hug and kiss. He takes them by the hand to where he left his action figures and proudly tells them their names and what they do. Clay crouches in the corner of the living room and continues to stare at his trains seemingly unaware that anyone has come over to visit. My mom squats down in her usual gardening pose and embraces him. Clay sags like a rag doll in her arms—no return of affection, no gaze of curiosity, and no show of emotion. Her eyes drift down to see his Thomas the Tank Engine toys, lined up in a perfect row.

"Clay, did you get some new trains?" she asks. Clay doesn't answer or even act like he hears her speaking. She tries to pick him up, but he wriggles free so that he can remain focused on his trains.

She picks up a train and says, "Clay, is this the one...."

Clay squeals. He panics and snatches it from her hand and places it back in the exact spot where it had been. He never looks at her face—all attention is on the toy. I see hurt and rejection flicker across her face.

"Can I get either of you something to drink?" I jump in.

"No, we're fine." She waves me off, still staring at Clay.

"Mom," I say, putting my arm around her waist in our standard, family side hug, "He's just busy with his trains. He's glad you guys are here."

"Oh, I know. You just have busy little boys."

"He just hasn't seen you for a while. He'll warm up."

She turns and watches Clay. "Leeann, he doesn't seem to even notice we're here."

"What do you mean?"

"He used to love it when we would come to visit. Now I can't even get him to look at me."

I swallow. My throat sticks. I swallow again.

I know he's different.

It's September and time for Clay's fifteen-month well-child appointment. The nurse takes us back in the exam room and hands me a brief developmental checklist. Dr. Keller walks in several minutes later.

"I notice here that he should be saying a couple of words?" I ask, handing him the completed checklist.

"Boys usually don't pick up language as quickly as girls. He'll catch up."

"You know, he used to call me 'Mama,' and I've noticed that he doesn't do that anymore. He used to say a few other words too, but now he just squeals."

"Sometimes kids go through phases. He'll probably start saying 'Mama' again soon."

Dr. Keller claps his hands together.

"Okay, then, it looks like he's due for his MMR and…"

"That is something else I want to talk to you about." I pull out a worn, folded piece of paper from my purse. "My husband and I came across this article about a Dr. Andrew Wakefield, gastroenterologist in the UK, who had claimed to find Measles Virus in the guts of autistic children. We are very concerned about giving our son this vaccination, especially since we have a relative who was diagnosed with autism at age three and a half."

I unfold the piece of paper and hand it to him.

I watch his eyes move steadily through the first line, then jump to the next line like the movement of the carriage on an old typewriter. He doesn't say anything.

"Dr. Keller, are you familiar with this uh, Dr. Wakefield?"

"Who?"

"Andy Wakefield, the gastroenterologist from the UK."

"Oh," he chuckles. "You're going to ask me if autism is related to vaccinations, especially the MMR."

"Well, yes, you see, like I said, we have a relative…"

"That is completely unwarranted, and I am afraid you have been misinformed."

Trying to keep Clay occupied, I look up when I hear Dr. Keller's voice start to quiver with intensity. His face and the tips of his ears are now red, and I sense he is trying to hide his anger and disgust.

"Parents," he continues, clearing his throat, "are being deceived into thinking vaccinations are causing autism. This is simply not true. The American Academy of Pediatrics repeatedly assures us that vaccinations are safer than they have ever been and that you, as his parents, will be doing your child more harm by leaving him completely vulnerable and unprotected. You will be placing others at risk as well. Look, I go to a lot of these conferences. I was just at an AAP conference a few months ago addressing this same issue. This, Andy Wake... whatever, doesn't have a clue about what he is implying. They are doing so much harm by scaring parents into thinking that autism and vaccinations are linked. It's pseudoscience, that's all it is.

"Mrs. Whiffen," he continues, wheeling his stool in closer. His eyes narrow, and he pulls out his pointer finger, shaking it at me. "Clay is much more likely to get smallpox than autism."

I feel like a child who blurted out a bad word at school and is scolded by the teacher in front of the entire class. He looks at me like I'm this ignorant mother who would rather see her child die than get vaccinated. I doubt myself, allowing my farmgirl upbringing to bury my confidence. Dr. Keller, after earning his undergraduate degree, went to four years of medical school, followed by a one-year pediatric internship and a two-year pediatric residency. Of course he knows what he's talking about. I just found a couple of studies that may or may not be conclusive.

"Dr. Keller, I would never put Clay in that kind of danger. I could never forgive myself if he were to contract a preventable disease."

I can hear the flick of his pen tapping against his fingers as I contemplate the decision.

I feel trapped. I weigh my options.

"It is important that we vaccinate him," I finally admit.

Clay's face scrunches up and turns red as the needle slides into his upper thigh. He screams as big tears fall down his face.

I'm still not completely comfortable with my decision, though. I don't know what the truth is or how to find it. But this I do know—I don't want to be a negligent mother risking my son's life over a few studies that may or may not have merit.

A few days later, Clay breaks out into a rash, accompanied by a low-grade fever. Pencil head–sized red bumps dot his torso. I call Dr. Keller, and his nurse tells me he is unavailable to take my call. She tells me it is nothing to be concerned about. "If the fever persists, bring him in. Otherwise, he should be fine."

I hang up the phone.

"He doesn't seem fine." I whisper.

Chapter 4

Drew bursts into our bedroom at 6:00 a.m., whooping and hollering that Santa left presents for him and Clay. His small three-and-a-half-year-old body bounces with unbridled excitement, like a dog anticipating the throw in a game of fetch. He dashes into his little brother's room, eager to spread the good news. I groggily reach toward my nightstand to grab the camera, nearly knocking it to the floor. Sean and I trail the boys downstairs to capture the magic of the day.

Drew rips through his presents while shouting for joy. Spit spews from his lips as he flies his new airplane around the family room, as if his dream of being a pilot has already come true. "Today is my lucky day!" he shouts.

Clay sits cross-legged on the couch holding his favorite train in the air, studying it from all angles. He flicks a wheel with his fingers and watches it spin. I hand him a gift. "Open it, sweetie," I urge. With his train clutched tightly in his hand, Clay stares at the present. I tear off a piece of wrapping paper to reveal part of the toy, hoping to ignite some interest.

Still, nothing.

I take his hand from his lap, and with my hand over his, we tear off the paper and reveal a big dump truck. I place the truck on his lap. He throws it to the floor. He runs over, picks it up, and throws it again.

"No, Clay. Look, it's a truck!" I say excitedly. "Let me help you get it out of the box."

I rip open the box, pull out the truck, and push it along the floor making motor sounds. I hand it to Clay. He drops it. He picks up a piece of wrapping paper off the floor, holds it out in the air and twirls it through his fingers, seemingly mesmerized by the many colors. Then he finds his Thomas the Tank Engine toys on the floor and holds one in each hand. I give him another present.

"Here, Clay, open this one."

He drops it, uninterested. I pick it up off the floor and rip off part of the paper, hoping to get his attention.

"Look, Clay. What is it?"

He takes it from me and throws it across the room. I unwrap the gift to reveal a farm puzzle with lights and sounds. I place it on the table next to him pushing the sheep to make it "baa."

He doesn't even look over.

I lean over and say to Sean, "How strange that he isn't interested in any of the toys he got for Christmas. He doesn't even care to see what's inside the paper. He's eighteen months old." I glance up at a family photo hanging on the wall. It's from our recent family reunion in Idaho. Clay is in my arms, red-faced and screaming. His pacifier is hanging out of his mouth, and his blanket is pressed to his face.

Winter passes and the spring sun melts away the remaining crusted snow, revealing new growth in the yard. After a long day of relentless tantrums with Legos and action figures hurled at my head, I put the boys to bed and hurry outside for a desperate break. I clear my mind by pulling the weeds around the tulips that line the driveway. My thoughts are interrupted by the sound of footsteps crunching in the grass next to me. I look up and see my neighbor, Gretchen, who lives across the street.

"Looks like you're working hard," I hear her say. "How are things?"

"Great," I lie. "What's new?"

"Are you sure you're all right?" she probes. "I hardly ever see you come outside anymore. You never come to play-groups or the park with us. Everyone is wondering where you have been."

"It's hard to explain, Gretchen. Clay is going through a difficult stage right now. It's almost impossible to take him anywhere. If I bring him outside, I'm afraid he'll get hit by a car. He darts in and out of the street, totally unaware and with no fear. He's attached to my hip. My arms ache from constantly holding him. He screams and tantrums most of the day…I just…"

I can tell by the dull look on her face that she just can't relate. I chide myself for saying too much. This isn't the first time I have seen that look.

Gretchen's daughter, Maggie, runs to her and hugs her leg. Her head bobs out the side to peek at me, and then shyly goes behind again.

"Look, Gretchen, I really miss being able to do the things I used to do. But it's really hard with Clay right now. That's all."

"I know exactly what you're talking about. If Maggie doesn't get her way, she'll stamp her feet and yell. I just really don't know what I'm going to do with her if she doesn't…" Her words drum through my mind to a tune I don't recognize. My eyes drift down to her side to see Maggie looking up and smiling at me with a little mischievous grin.

When I go back inside the house later that night, I call my close friend, Kim, for advice. I can always count on her to make me feel better and validate my feelings. I recount to her the events that have taken place over the last several months.

"Oh, Leeann, really, you're paranoid. He's not even two years old. I have a friend whose little boy was four years old before he even said his first word; and you know what, he is a freshman in high school with a 4.0 GPA! Clay will be fine. Sometimes boys don't talk until later. Besides, look at Drew. He's a sharp little guy and does most of the talking for Clay. No wonder Clay never says a word. He doesn't have to!"

"Maybe you're right," I reply. I want to believe what she is saying. It feels good, like when a tired child is given her favorite blanket. I can see Clay growing out of this stage.

On the third Wednesday of each month the neighborhood moms get together and meet at the park to visit while the kids play. I remember what Gretchen told me in our conversation out in the yard. "Everyone is wondering where you are." Being confined to my home hangs over me, like a shadow dragging me into gloom. Gathering the resolve to break free, I load the diaper bag with all the tricks and bribes I can think of, and try to have a positive outlook on what might transpire. I buckle Drew and Clay in the double stroller and meet with the rest of the neighborhood moms at the end of the street. My friends greet me with surprise.

"We're so glad you could make it," says one.

"We've missed you," says another.

"Thanks," I reply. "It feels good to be back."

We walk a half mile to the park where the kids can play and the moms can talk. Having Clay in the stroller helps me to feel more confident and in control.

As we get to the park, most of the kids, including those younger than Clay, scatter on the grass toward the playground equipment. Some of the younger, more timid kids stay close to their mothers to assess the situation. I unbuckle Clay from the stroller, holding onto one of his arms. He manages to jerk free and runs full speed toward the road. I sprint after him, catching him just as his shoes slap the sidewalk. I carry him back to the playground and try visiting with a friend. Out of the corner of my eye, I see him by the road again. He darts in front of a car, narrowly beating the front bumper. I sprint after him.

I yell to a friend to keep an eye on Drew as I watch Clay head into a vacant lot. I can barely see his white hair bobbing above the lightly colored weeds. A couple of friends join the search, flanking my sides. Kim yells, "He's over here." She picks him up. He thrashes about in her arms shrieking; foamy spit seeps from his mouth. As I take him, he goes into a code-red meltdown, growling while he spastically jerks and writhes around. He chokes on his own saliva, bursting into a coughing fit. I put him into a firm hold and carry him back to the park.

Nobody says a word as we walk back to the playground together. Now my friends finally see a glimpse of what I have been telling them all along. I try to get him to swing, one of his favorite activities in our backyard. He slides out of the swing as quickly as I put him in and heads for the road again. I try getting him interested in playing with the other children and climbing on the equipment. Nothing. Feeling exhausted and defeated, I say good-bye and tell my friends we are heading home. Drew starts crying because he wants to stay, not understanding why we have to go so soon. Both boys cry all the way home.

That night Clay wakes nearly every hour, forcing me to take any sleep I can get next to his bed on the floor. As the night passes, I'm in and out of sleep and suddenly find myself annoyed by the sound of constant giggling. I finally open my eyes and look at the clock above his bed. The red numbers glow 2:45 a.m. in the blackness. I turn toward the giggles and see Clay sitting in the corner of the room. His giggles turn into light laughter. My eyes adjust, and I see he is looking at the wall in front of him. There is nothing. Nothing funny or silly…just nothing. He stops laughing and rises. He prances around the room on his toes but his eyes never leave the floor.

I convince myself I would just be happy if he would simply glance at my face. I get up from the floor to snatch him from his toe walking and set him on my lap facing me, determined to enter his world. He briefly plays with the logo on the left side of my shirt. Then he grabs my shirt with both hands, puts his head down, and smashes it against mine. The harder he hits, the more satisfaction he gets.

"No, Clay. Ouch," I whisper.

I put my hand on his forehead and stop him. His head is red from banging mine. He slips off my lap and takes my hand, leading me through the hallway and down the stairs to the TV in the family room where he places my hand on the screen and releases. I let my hand fall limp toward my side, pretending I don't understand. He repeats the process.

I drop to my knees and place my hand on his jaw, turning his head toward mine. His eyes continue looking at the floor.

"I want to see your eyes," I beg him through tears, as if my life were at stake.

Later that morning, I turn on music while cleaning up breakfast. A familiar song starts to play. I glance over and see Clay bobbing up and down to the beat. I watch him, then go and gather him in my arms. We dance together; the cadence of the music directing our movement. I dip him down and bounce him up while holding his right hand. We float across the room and back, flowing like ribbons in the wind. I see a smile flicker across his face. His teeth start to emerge as his lips part. I haven't seen him do this for months!

"Do you like this, Clay? Are you having fun?"

He squeals in delight. I spin him around the room, and for an instant our motion captivates us. His eyes drift up until they connect with mine. Our eyes lock. The objects around the room are a blur as we focus on each other's smiling faces. I become part of his world for an instant. A wave of enthusiasm rushes through me.

I can't remember the last time he looked at me.

Chapter 5

Sunday arrives and finds me in my usual spot in the church foyer with Clay. I wonder why I even bother to come. All I do is run after him as he screeches through the halls while the other children his age play together in the nursery. The rich vibrations of the organ hum through the chapel as the congregation erupts in song. Clay darts for the door, but I scoop him up before he escapes.

Someone approaches me from behind.

"Leeann," she says, gently touching my shoulder. I turn and face her. I can't recall her name, but I recognize her. I stare at her until I become uncomfortable. Then I remember—she's the neighbor who lives a street north of us and has an autistic boy.

"Oh. Hi, Brandie," I say, hoping I got her name right.

We exchange small talk.

"Hey, listen, I have been watching Clay for several weeks now," Brandie says, "and I wonder if you have considered having him evaluated?"

"Evaluated?" I ask, a little confused.

"Yes, I mean..." She rubs her forehead and looks at the ground. "I'm not sure how to put this...but...he seems like he could have autism."

"What?" I say. I feel the heat crawl up my neck and into my face. I suddenly remember a time a few years ago, when I went to the local adult developmental center to volunteer. There was a resident there with autism. He was nonverbal, didn't like to be touched or spoken to. He flapped his arms intensely while grunting like an animal.

Who the hell do you think you are! I want to shout. *Do you really think you can just come up to me and start blurting out a diagnosis for my son? I hardly know you!*

"That's an interesting observation," I manage to say. I know there is something not quite right, but how dare she suggest autism. Just because her son is autistic doesn't mean every kid she sees with behavior problems fits in that category.

"I've noticed how he screeches and walks on his toes. Is he talking yet?"

"Yes. Well, I mean no. He used to, but now—but that doesn't mean anything. There are lots of little boys his age that aren't talking. He'll catch up. His pediatrician thinks he'll be fine."

"I'm sorry if I've upset you. I just thought you might want to know from someone who has experience." She blushes.

"Oh, I'm sorry, I didn't realize you specialized in autism. What did you get your degree in?" I immediately regret being a jerk, letting my temper take over.

"Um, well, I don't actually have a…I'm his mom, and I know what…"

"I guess you just caught me off guard. It's certainly something I haven't considered," I say, hoping to pacify her enough that she will go away. But she doesn't. And Clay is now screeching so loud that bystanders flash the annoyed *will you take care of that kid?* stare.

"Excuse me. I need to go." I hoist Clay on my hip, take him outside, and buckle him in his car seat. As I turn the key in the ignition, I look up and see her standing in the doorway watching me.

The more I think about our conversation, the more defensive and angry I become. *It's not autism! It can't be!* Images of her son loudly repeating unintelligible phrases and flapping his hands out in the street, oblivious to traffic buzzing close to him, chug through my thoughts. It can't be! Besides, she seems grossly happy to think she has found some other child with autism, almost in an effort to help ease her own pain. I refuse to participate in her self-therapy.

For two weeks I cannot get Brandie out of my mind. Our conversation repeats like an annoying song stuck in my head. To prove her wrong, I schedule an appointment with our pediatrician to discuss Clay's development. As I check in at the front desk, the receptionist informs me that Dr. Keller had an emergency and can't see us, but that we can see the nurse practitioner.

"That's fine," I say, disappointed but realizing it would be another week or so to schedule with the pediatrician.

Just as we sit down, the nurse appears and calls us back into the room. As I wait for the nurse practitioner, I scan the walls plastered with "Immunize by 2" posters. Clay opens every drawer in the room and squeals the same sound repeatedly. I hear a quiet knock at the door and am met by a friendly face greeting me as she walks in. She quickly reviews Clay's medical history. I am surprised she is so thorough, and I feel at ease with her friendly yet professional demeanor.

"What brings you here today, Mrs. Whiffen?"

"I've talked to Dr. Keller about my son's behavioral and developmental regression, but he doesn't seem worried. He says Clay will eventually catch up. But I'm still very concerned. Something just isn't right. He's not talking anymore, and he rarely looks at me. He tantrums so much I can't take him out into public anymore. He doesn't seem to understand how to play with toys, and he is attached to certain objects. As you can hear, he makes this high-pitched squeal sound over and over. And why doesn't he look at me anymore? I think there is something wrong with my son. I need to know what I can do to help him."

"Well," she replies, glancing at his chart, "It looks like developmentally he's hit every milestone since birth until recently, at age eighteen months. Then I see notes here that you became concerned about his language development. Is that right?"

"Yes. And he was saying a few words, but now he doesn't say anything. And…he's just not there anymore. The lights are out."

Her smile fades.

"I think the best thing for you to do now is call the local Early Intervention Agency. In Utah County it is…let's see," she says, fumbling through a pile of papers. "Here it is. Kids On The Move. They can assess Clay and help you to know how to help him. Here's their number. If he qualifies, then he can receive their state-funded services."

She hands me a pink piece of paper with a GlaxoSmithKline logo at the top.

I look down to see Clay playing intently with a piece of string on the carpet.

Finally, someone who might be able to help us.

The next day at lunch Clay is happy with the usual staple—French toast. It is one of only two meals he'll eat, McDonald's chicken nuggets being the other. I watch him stuff bites into his mouth and wash them down with a big sippy cup of milk. Each mealtime I place a small portion of the family dinner on his plate, a tip I gleaned from a book I recently finished. Tonight it is hamburgers. I cut a piece with my fork and drop it on his plate. He instantly pushes it away with the back of his hand—careful not to touch it with his fingers. He squeals as he bobs up and down in his booster seat.

"One day, you're going to surprise me and eat that, won't you," I tell him as I hear someone knock at the front door.

"Drew, will you get the door?" I unbuckle Clay from his seat and hurry to the entryway, where I meet a young, blonde woman chewing wildly on her gum. She anxiously greets me by holding out her hand. "Hi, Mrs. Whiffen? I'm Andrea. I'm here to do your intake for Kids On The Move."

She looks about twenty years old, and like this is *totally* her first real job. I begin to regret making the call.

"Clay…Clay, where are you?" I ask, not seeing him behind me. I glance in back of the couch to see him hiding. This has become his normal reaction to any outsider coming into our home. "Someone is here to see you." I say.

Clay darts away, and when I try to stop him, he screeches. "Can you wave to Andrea?" I say as I hold onto his arm and prompt the gesture. Clay wriggles free and runs downstairs.

"Well, Andrea, let's get the questions I can answer out of the way first. Then we can tackle him together." I notice a perfect lineup of farm animals next to the chair Andrea is sitting in. The cows are grouped together, largest to smallest, then pigs and sheep, all manipulated in the same fashion.

She peppers me with questions about Clay's development as she scrawls the answers on a HELP Strands Curriculum-Based Developmental Assessment. Most of my answers begin with, "No, not yet." Clay interrupts several times, squealing and crying for me to hold him. At times I have to shout so Andrea can hear my answers.

Andrea concludes the interview by saying, "Mrs. Whiffen, I don't need to officially score this test to know that your son will definitely qualify for services at Kids On The Move. He is functioning right now at about the level of a nine- to twelve-month-old. At our next appointment, your advocate, Karen, and I will go over the Individualized Family Service Plan, or IFSP, and start intervention as soon as possible."

"Nine to twelve months?" It comes out in a raspy whisper, the fear wrapping around my throat, choking me and my child's entire future.

Chapter 6

The following Sunday we go to church as usual. Getting Clay to go to nursery is an outright war. Clothed in my wrinkle-free dress and flats, I force every step forward en route to the nursery. As I approach the room, small, chattering voices and squeals of excitement seep out. I open the door and step into the hullabaloo of ten busy toddlers playing with myriad toys. We are instantly greeted by nursery leaders like it is a surprise party. "Hello, Clay! We're so glad you're here!" Clay's whole body stiffens in my arms until I feel like I'm clutching a small ironing board. He grasps handfuls of my blouse and begins to scream. I feel a seam pop from under his grip. The noises, the children, the stimulation—he shakes his head repeatedly as if trying to rid himself of the sensory pollution. I try to comfort him by reading him a story. He beats his head against my arm. Tears stream down his red, rosy cheeks as he screams and claws at my face. I try every trick I know to calm him. The nursery leaders try to help, but it only makes Clay more agitated.

I want to take him and run. But I give myself a pep talk instead. *Don't give in. He needs the experience of being around other kids and adults besides our family. He'll never learn if you're not consistent. If you give up now, he will cry longer and louder the next time.*

I endure the rest of nursery with Clay thrashing about in my arms. The hallway bell rings, signifying the end of church. Round over. I have just won the wrestling match by default. Someone, come raise my arm.

Four weeks later, the doorbell rings, and Drew and I race to answer it. Clay is oblivious to the commotion and continues rubbing his hand back and forth along the back of the sofa. Drew beats me by an inch, flinging the door open so hard it hits the hall closet. The woman standing in front of me looks old enough to be my mother, yet gentle enough I want to be her friend. Her eyes welcome me as if she already knows me.

"Hello, Mrs. Whiffen?" she says, holding out her hand. "I'm Karen, your parent advocate from Kids On The Move. It's nice to meet you."

"It's nice to meet you, Karen. I'm anxious to get started."

"Well, great then, we have a lot to talk about."

"Is this Clay?" Karen asks, pointing to him. I nod as I watch him mouth the arm of the couch.

"Hi, Clay," she says, smiling.

Clay continues staring at the wall as if she isn't there.

"Clay…" She reaches out and touches him on the arm.

Clay shrieks and runs away. I note the seriousness in her face as her smile fades. Karen persists in her attempts to interact with him. We follow Clay as he runs into the backyard and gets into the swing.

"Okay, Leeann," she says, "You want to teach him to communicate his wants. Like this." She pushes him in the swing. She grabs the swing in midair and says, "Stop." She releases the swing and says, "Go."

"Do this over and over until he gets the idea. Pause before you say, 'go' and let go of the swing. Then eventually stop him in midair until he makes any sound at all. As soon as he does, let go of the swing and reinforce him by verbal praise or giving him a small piece of candy. He'll soon get the idea of what he's supposed to do."

Karen continues to play with Clay to get an overall idea of his development. As she continues talking, I notice a stench from Clay's diaper. I take him inside and lay him on the floor. Karen follows. He screams and flails his limbs in every direction, making it nearly impossible for me to take off his diaper. I try pinning down his arms and legs, but they eventually pop free. Karen watches me struggle with him for a minute or so. "Here, let me hold his legs so he's not kicking you." She cautiously offers her assistance, as if wanting to help, but also trying to keep her emotional distance. She holds his arms and legs while I put on a fresh diaper.

Karen stays for over an hour until she has to leave for another appointment. I surprise myself with disappointment that she can't stay longer. She knows how to handle Clay. She's not afraid of him, and wants to help him and our family—even beyond her job.

"Karen, what do you think is wrong with him? Do you think he just needs a little speech therapy? Is he just frustrated that he can't communicate? Why doesn't he respond to me—I'm his mom?" I pop off multiple questions like rounds of firecrackers.

"Well, Leeann, I can't really say. I mean, as a state-funded agency, we give families support and provide individualized early intervention services to benefit your child and his specific needs. We are not doctors, so we aren't authorized to diagnose your child. If you want a diagnosis, you should see a pediatric psychiatrist."

I'm dissatisfied with her evasive answer, and feel like she is using "company policy" as a shield to cover up what she really sees.

I move in closer and grab her arm.

"Karen, I am asking you, mother to mother, what do *you* think?"

There is hesitation in her eyes, which soften the longer she looks at me.

"Alright," she finally says, "But I can get in a lot of trouble for telling you this."

I look at her with pleading eyes.

"Leeann," she says in a low voice, "I think your son is showing signs of autism."

"Autism?" It trips off my tongue like a dirty word. "Autism." I say it again as if I need to get used to the way it sounds. I stare at the floor, tracing the diamond pattern in the tan carpet with my foot.

"Karen, are you sure? I mean, it can't be. I…I just don't think so."

Well it's a damn good thing they don't let her diagnose, because obviously she has no idea what she's talking about. How dare she tell me my child is autistic when she has only spent a couple of hours with him. After all, even the pediatrician said to give him time, boys usually talk later. Even my friends, who know him better, say he'll probably catch up.

"Thanks for your time, Karen."

"Uh, Leeann, what about our next meeting?"

"I'll call you to schedule," I say, opening the front door. She fumbles around in her notebook and pulls out a piece of paper and hands it to me.

"Please read this."

I read the heading: Signs and Symptoms of Autism

I close the door, tossing the paper aside since it doesn't apply to us, and grab the phone. My fingers tremble as I push the numbers on the keypad while dialing Sean's cell phone number.

"Can you believe she would suggest Clay has autism? I mean, how qualified is she to say such a thing?"

"Lee, you did ask for her personal opinion, didn't you?"

"Well, yeah, but…"

"She's probably worked with hundreds of kids with those types of issues. She has a lot more experience than we do. I think we should check it out."

"So you're taking her side?"

"What do you mean, sides? No, I'm just saying we can't discount it yet. We need to look into it some more."

"I just…I can't. Not yet anyway."

"We need to eventually, Lee, because things are getting worse."

"I know we do. I'm just not ready to accept something like that yet," I tell him.

I can't stop pacing around the house. Karen's words dominate my thoughts, which flit between her observations and my exchange with Brandie at church. I try to think of every reason why Clay doesn't have autism and grab the book I always use for answers to my toddler questions, *What to Expect the Toddler Years*. Thumbing through the bent pages to the developmental checklist for two-year-olds, I see Clay hasn't met any of the criteria. But I remind myself he still has a couple of months before he turns two years old. Eventually, after staring at the book for several minutes, I find it within myself to look up the dreaded "A-word" in the index.

I read a behavioral signs checklist for autism. Then, I start my own checklist for Clay, marking the behaviors he does and doesn't display. I anxiously wait for Sean to get home from work, and then proudly show him my list. "See, I knew it. He doesn't meet every symptom on the list. In fact, there are a few he doesn't have."

Sean takes the paper and glances through it.

"Look, Leeann, it says here at the bottom that this is just a general list. Even if the child meets the majority of the symptoms, he should be evaluated. Just glancing through it, I see he meets nearly all of the symptoms. Maybe we should obtain a professional diagnosis. And let's call Kids On The Move and at least get some services for what we do need."

"You're probably right. I just don't know if I can face Karen again. I just…kind of…feel like she thinks I'm in denial or something."

"Well…are you?" Sean asks.

"Are you kidding me?" I hide the pain from his frank question. "I'm his mom. I was the first one to notice that there was something wrong with him, even when the pediatrician disagreed."

"Then, why can't the 'something wrong with him' be autism?"

"Because. He's just not autistic. Is he? He can't be. Aggh, I just don't know. I'll let the doctor decide. Then we can go from there."

I call my mom and tell her everything that has happened over the last couple of days. After I finish passionately refuting every shred of evidence that my baby has autism, I stop. There is silence.

"Hello? Are you there?" I ask.

"Leeann, what if he does?" she asks quietly, almost in a whisper. "What are you going to do?"

I open my mouth, and then close it again.

"I've got to run, Mom, the boys are getting into something."

I hang up the phone and rest my chin in my hands as I watch Clay meticulously line up his cars.

Chapter 7

"Hello, Leeann? It's Karen," says the voice on the other line. It has been two weeks since her first visit.

"Oh. Hi," I say as if she is a phone solicitor interrupting dinner.

"Leeann…look…I want to invite you to our autism support group tomorrow night. We'll have childcare available, so you can bring Drew and Clay, if you'd like."

"Autism support group?" I question. It feels like someone is holding a lighter to my cheeks. "Why would I need something like that, Karen? We don't even know for sure if Clay is autistic."

There was a long pause followed by a deep sigh on the other end of the line.

"Leeann, I'm sure this is difficult for you to accept, but Clay shows all the classic symptoms of autism. And if we are going to help him, we have to treat the symptoms. I think it would be good for you to go to this support group. You need to know there are other parents just like you whose kids have similar issues. You also might get some ideas on how to handle Clay's aggressive behavior."

Fine, I'll humor her.

"Okay, Karen. I'll be there."

I'm stuck on the truth of her comment, "We need to treat the symptoms." I can accept he has symptoms that need to be treated. I've known this for several months now.

I hurry to the den and turn on the computer. The search engine pops up. I place my fingers on the keyboard and type

A-U-T-I-S-M. My pinky finger hangs over the enter key. My fear has a definition. I am afraid of what I might find.

I hear my finger click the enter key. Ten hours later, my face still fixated on the computer screen, I turn my head to the window and see the morning sun sprouting through the peaks of the Wasatch Mountains. I feel as if all my limbs have been yanked out of their sockets and shoved back in. I secretly wish someone would beat me unrecognizable, and then drag my body in the street. I'm certain it would feel better than what I'm feeling right now.

I walk through the entrance of Kids On The Move and follow the paper sign with a plain, black arrow pointing down the hall. Parents are gathered in a semicircle talking with each other when I arrive. There is a shabby, plaid pastel sofa in the corner. I stand behind it, somehow feeling protected.

A mother introduces herself to the group and talks about her nonverbal, eight-year-old autistic son. I watch him in the corner shrieking and flicking his fingers in the air. Frustration overcomes her as she describes how he frequently takes his diaper off and smears poop everywhere—on the walls, the carpet, and his toys. She ends with, "I'm just not sure what I'm going to do. He is getting too big for me to remove him from dangerous situations."

Another mom stands and describes how her autistic child is bullied in school. She pulled him out and placed him into an "autism school," but he has regressed significantly.

I observe from the sidelines. My arms are crossed, hugging my sides.

I look at the woman who spoke first, her son now standing beside her. My thoughts drift, replacing their images with those of Clay and me in the future. My head suddenly feels full and heavy, and the lights become intolerable. My heart seems to forget how to beat. I struggle for air. I have to get out of here. Ghostly images of the autistic boy grunting and flapping in the corner are branded in my mind.

The next morning I call the office of Dr. Sam Coates, a pediatric psychiatrist twenty miles south of us, and schedule an appointment for a diagnostic evaluation.

"The earliest you can see him is in six weeks," the secretary says unapologetically.

"We'll take it, but please call me if you have a cancellation."

A couple of weeks pass. I grow even more concerned with Clay's behavior. He stares off into space for minutes at a time. I call his name and snap by his face only to be completely unnoticed. His forearms flap lightly at his sides as if his elbows are attached to his ribs.

Then there are those extremely rare moments in which I catch a glimpse of the little boy who is hiding inside the furthest corner of a hollow shell: the look on his face when we hold hands and I spin him around, the way he briefly comes alive when we dance, or his exhilaration when I give him an underdog in the swing. My instinct as his mother tells me he's in there. But he's fading deeper into oblivion as time goes on—further from my grasp. The deep-set panic that he'll be beyond my reach is so severe it controls me. I focus all my time and energy on pulling out the boy I used to know—the boy who occasionally appears when we dance. I shadow his every move, hoping to stave off the monster that threatens to forever consume him.

That evening I go to bed possessed by autism. Unable to sleep, I go back downstairs. Out of the corner of my eye, I see the "Signs and Symptoms" worksheet Karen gave us on the floor. I still haven't looked at it. I force myself to pick it up. I unfold it and carefully read through each symptom.

- Inappropriate laughing and giggling. *Check.*
- No real fear of dangers. *Check.*
- Apparent insensitivity to pain. *Check.*
- May not want cuddling or act cuddly. *Check.*
- Little or no eye contact. *Check.*
- Difficulty expressing needs. *Check.*
- Not responsive to verbal cues. *Check.*
- Sustains odd play. *Check.*
- Inappropriate attachment to objects. *Check.*
- Insistence on sameness; resists changes in routine. *Check.*

My eyes fill with tears as I finish reading a complete description of my son.

I suppose grief is the catalyst to the extreme motivation I feel to help our son. Somehow a switch inside me has been flipped. I feel compelled to do whatever it takes to help Clay. Any piece of information I find that gives me hope is fuel enough to sustain me, driving me to continue searching. I stay up all hours of the night investigating everything related to autism. I'm overwhelmed and intimidated by the breadth and depth of information I find. Some of the research even contradicts other findings. Sifting through the masses of research could take years.

I discover that I don't even have months.

In sifting through autism information, I find a *Time* magazine article, "The Secrets of Autism," by Madeleine Nash. At the end of the article it says, "Paradoxically, the very thing that is so terrible about autistic disorders—that they affect the very young—also suggests reason for hope. Since the neural connections of a child's brain are established through experience, well-targeted mental exercises have the potential to make a difference."

I find something else that catches my attention, something that sends a zing up my spine so intense I almost rise out of my chair. It's a policy statement for the American Academy of Pediatrics titled, "The Pediatrician's Role in the Diagnosis and Management of Autistic Spectrum Disorder in Children." I focus on the conclusions: "Early diagnosis has become increasingly important as recent studies have shown improved outcomes with implementation of early, consistent, and appropriate intervention strategies that have been individually tailored to the needs of the child and parents."

We have to start right away, while he is still young.

Meanwhile, the laundry piles up until it eventually topples onto the floor. Drew becomes fascinated with figuring out how many dishes he can balance on one another in the sink before they crash on the countertop. We're running out of food. I've been holed up in the den for four days now, and Drew is clearly frustrated with the lack of attention.

"Mom, when are you coming out!" he finally shouts at me one day.

"Drew, sweetie," I say, "I really need this time to figure out how to help your brother. You know how Clay screams a lot and doesn't know how to talk? We're going to teach him how to tell us what he needs and how to play with toys so he won't cry so much."

"Can I help him too, Mom?"

I pull him into me and give him a hug.

"You bet, Bubba. You bet. You'll be my number one helper."

In my further research, I stumble upon a recent article in the *Wall Street Journal* titled "Parts of the Brain That Get Most Use

Literally Expand and Rewire on Demand," by Sharon Begley. It states, "Even the adult brain is 'plastic,' able to forge new connections among its neurons and thus rewire itself. Sensory input can change the brain, and the brain remodels itself in response to behavioral demands. Regions that get the most use literally expand."

I read on about an early study in 1993 by Alvaro Pascual-Leone that reiterated this finding. He studied blind people and the way in which they received regular, powerful tactile stimulation from their fingers. He wired them up so he could measure the part of their brains that registers and processes the sense of touch, the somatosensory cortex. He recorded which parts of that portion of the brain registered sensation. He then did the same with non-Braille readers whose fingers didn't get that kind of usage. The results were very clear. The somatosensory cortex devoted to the reading finger was much larger than the comparable area for fingers in both blind and sighted people who didn't have the same demands placed on them.

By this time I am so hopeful and excited I can hardly contain myself.

"Sean, come look at this." I thrust the creased newspaper in his face.

"If the human brain can, in a sense, be 'exercised' in certain areas that are deficient, it can rewire itself on demand," I tell him.

"Interesting," he says. I can't tell if he really is interested, or if he's not sure what else to say.

"Do you know what this means for Clay?" I say. "If we're able to teach him through repetition, targeting those parts of his brain that are deficient, then his brain might be able to remodel itself in those areas. This is huge! It makes sense. Especially considering that the younger someone is, the easier it is for the brain to change in response to the input it receives. The article basically points out that the more you use one portion of your brain, the more synapses are being made, and so the stronger that portion of the brain becomes."

I might as well be addicted to a drug. I can't sleep that evening. All I can think about are the endless possibilities. I want Clay to live a life of pleasure and fullness. I want him to get married someday. To have children of his own. To partake of the sweetness that only intimate relationships can bring. What is a life without love?

And I desperately want him to call me Mom, to *really* know who I am. I want him to need my nurturing. I need to know that my love and affection aren't lost in the air between us before they're able to touch his heart. It's unbearable to feel rejected by my own child.

In the following weeks, days blur into nights as I stay up until all hours researching and planning a course of action. I can't focus on or talk about anything else.

One afternoon, I stumble onto a website that catches my attention and gives me great hope. I read about a family in Maine with an autistic son who has made amazing progress through what his father calls an Applied Behavior Analysis program, or ABA. His father notes the following improvements in his child after a year in the program: a significant decrease in the frequency of tantrums, newfound words and spontaneous language, appropriate toy play, and sustained eye contact. I devour every word, hanging on the success of this boy thousands of miles across the country.

As I read on, I find that a study on ABA was conducted by Dr. Ivar Lovaas, a professor at UCLA at the time. I perform another search on ABA and Dr. Lovaas, and find that Applied Behavior Analysis (ABA) is a research-based, therapeutic program used to reinforce positive behaviors and ignore or discourage negative behaviors. ABA has been shown to be effective with autistic children, and there have been some studies that show it can completely eliminate autistic symptoms in up to 47 percent of the children who are put into an intensive program. An intensive program consists of structured instruction and therapy for twenty to forty hours per week. Trained college students are used in most of the programs around the country, and most of the programs are home-based. I find the full text of the study and verify the results.

Dr. Lovaas once described the process as "building a pyramid block by block." Every self-care behavior, social behavior, communication skill, etc., is taught through the use of specific drills and exercises called "discrete trials."

ABA can rewire Clay's brain—like the article I read in the *Wall Street Journal*. It will function as the exercise his brain needs to catch up to where he should be. This is our answer! We will teach him over and over and build up those areas of his brain that are lacking. This is it!

With all the unknowns out there regarding a treatment for autism, there is one thing I now know for certain: We need to get our in-home ABA program up and running as soon as possible.

I call Karen the next day.

"Karen, are you familiar with ABA?"

"Yes."

"Does Kids On The Move provide ABA services?"

"No, it's pretty intense and really expensive. We teach parents a basic technique called 'The Learning Box,' which is similar to ABA.

"Hmm," I say. "Thanks. I guess I'll see you next week."

Karen makes a home visit a week or so after our phone conversation. We sit down next to each other at the table to set goals for our IFSP for Clay:

• *What we want to happen: Clay will be able to communicate.*
• *Steps to make that happen: Family will encourage Clay to use signs and words to request. Family will work with Clay on joint referencing. Family will encourage Clay to say common names and objects. Clay will have interest in other people.*
• *What we want to happen: Clay will calm self appropriately.*
• *Steps to make it happen: Family will receive information on sensory integration to help Clay calm. Clay will adjust to situations outside of the home.*
• *What we want to happen: Clay will increase his play skills.*
• *Steps to make it happen: Family will play with cause and effect toys. Family will go to floor time at Kids On The Move. Clay will understand the functional use of toys.*

It seems so simple on paper. I am determined to meet the goals as quickly as possible. I know it will be a tremendous task, but I'm willing to do whatever it takes to accomplish it. I ask Karen about the services they can offer to help Clay, besides "The Learning Box" parent training she referred to on the phone. She mentions a playgroup that he can attend once per week. I ask about speech therapy, and she offers one hour of therapy per month. "Once a month, Karen? Do you really think once a month will help him that much?"

"I'm really sorry, Leeann. That's all we can offer you at this time. Clay's needs are greater than we have the funds or staff to adequately handle. But we can also give him one hour of occupational therapy per month. This will help his sensory integration issues."

My eyes drift to her notes as she reviews her calendar for our next visit. I read:

Clay, two years old, concerns: no imaginative play, does not play with other children, does not follow directions, screams and throws tantrums most of the day, puts parent's hands over item he wants, will only eat bland foods that are tan in color and/or round in shape, and will not eat foods smooth in texture. Schedule Play-Based Assessment, Health and Hearing Exam.

I need to figure out how to augment the minimal services at Kids On The Move with additional outside intervention.

Jay, the occupational therapist, looks like a slightly older rendition of the boy on the cover of *MAD* magazine, but with thick black-rimmed glasses that take up most of his freckled face. I'm surprised that Clay isn't afraid of him like he is of all the others who have come over to evaluate him. Maybe it's because Jay is more relaxed and easygoing around Clay, and lets him scribble all over his yellow notepad while we talk.

Jay asks me questions about Clay's sensory issues while quickly scratching notes.

Clay appears to be hyposensitive in the proprioceptive system. He will only eat tan and round foods. He falls down the stairs multiple times per day and seems to have trouble with his balance.

"He jumps around the house, outside, everywhere— constantly. He reminds me of Tigger, you know, from *Winnie the Pooh*," I tell him.

"Do you have a trampoline?"

I shake my head. "Do you think that would help?"

At this point, I'm ready to sell my home to finance an African elephant if research can prove it will help my son.

"I think a trampoline, even just one of those inexpensive mini tramps, will help him develop better balance and coordination. The jumping compresses his joints and gives his body the proprioceptive input, or sensory input and feedback, his body is seeking. It will hopefully help him to be more aware of the space around his body."

He reaches into his bag, takes out some toys, and places them in front of Clay. Clay looks at them, but doesn't reach for them or seem interested. The last toy he sets out is a plastic tube with a lever on the side. Jay grabs the toy, "Here, Clay, let me show you how this works." Jay shows him how to do it, narrating each step. "You put the ball in the top, then pull the crank to make it come out the bottom." Clay is not amused. Jay takes Clay's hand under his, then places the ball in the top of the tube and pulls the lever. Clay picks up the ball and puts it in his mouth.

"We'll have to work on that one." He clears his throat nervously.

He fishes around in his bag again. He pulls out a soft plastic brush and holds it in the air.

"You'll use this brush to do the Wilbarger Brushing Method. Do this at every diaper change and before taking Clay into public. Brush his arms all the way down to his hands, and then his palms. Next do his legs, top of his feet, then bottoms of his feet. This will help stimulate the touch receptors. After brushing, follow up with joint compressions. Let me show you." I instinctively spring into position, ready to hold Clay in case he starts to tantrum.

He unfolds Clay's small arm and brushes, starting at the

top of his arm by his shoulder, all the way down to the top of his hand with one pressure-filled stroke. He then holds Clay's wrist and upper arm and pushes together for the compressions. I'm shocked that Clay is letting Jay touch him. He sits quietly, captivated by Jay's movement.

Jay gives me some activities to do with Clay that will help give him the proprioceptive movement his body needs. "Try jumping with him, swinging him on his stomach, and wrestling lots with Dad. He may even benefit from a weighted blanket to help him sleep better at night. Hopefully, by giving him more proprioceptive input, it will give him more body awareness and lessen his sensory seeking. Because Clay craves vestibular stimulation like jumping and swinging, he will be more calm if you brush him and jump with him several times a day and before going out in public. This should help calm him so that his sensory system won't get overloaded."

I'm hopeful this brushing method might enable us to go out in public without a complete meltdown. I can't wait to get started.

Chapter 8

"Sean, how in the world are we going to afford this ABA program?" I anxiously ask him one evening after putting the kids to bed.

"We'll have to make it work somehow," he replies.

"Thirty thousand dollars a year is a huge amount of money! Neither of our parents is in a position to help us. We'll have to put everything on the credit card, except the instructor's wages. We may even have to sell our house."

"I don't know, Lee. We'll have to explore different options. Maybe we can take out a loan and use our credit cards. I just have my fixed salary. Any additional income will have to come through my client cases. We help all of our clients with taxes, but not all of them are going to need financial products that will give us a commission. And I'm not going to sell someone something just to make more money if they don't need the product. But I can try and push some client cases through faster. Let's think about this more."

As a child, making money stretch was a family necessity. I never saw the inside of a restaurant until I was invited to a friend's birthday party when I was twelve years old. As I bit into the six-inch, crispy chicken sandwich at Burger King, I savored each succulent bite so long it nearly dissolved in my mouth before I swallowed it. I didn't know how long it would be before I could eat out again.

Making ends meet operating a cattle ranch proved to be a difficult task, even for the savviest rancher. There were long summers picking the ripe apricots from the trees to make apricot jam, or picking cherries and peaches from local orchards. We bottled the fruit in the summer so that we would have enough to last through the winter. Bottling days were akin to spending the day in a sauna, so I would soak my shirt in the sink filled with cold water, wring it out, then put it back on. It was the only way I could stand being in the torrid house without getting nauseated.

My mom used to sew multiple jean patches on the knees of my four-generation hand-me-down pants to extend their life until I grew out of them. Since I am the youngest, my pants had often gone through my two sisters, and sometimes my two brothers, before getting to me. Oftentimes the whole leg was replaced with scraps from the parts of my dad's old pants that were salvageable. Some of my jeans looked like a patchwork quilt. I was too little to care much, until one Sunday, when I was eight years old. We went to church, as we always did on Sunday. I passed a girl who looked slightly older than me in the hall on the way to Sunday School. She stopped, looked me up and down, jammed her hands onto her hips and said, "Hey, that used to be my dress, but my mom dropped it off at the thrift store a couple weeks ago." She flipped her hair over her shoulder and spun on her heel, her curls bobbling as she disappeared around the corner.

Our three-room house provided shelter for seven members of our family. There was only one tiny bathroom. If you wanted the door shut, you would have to stand in the tub to make room for it to close all the way. The house came with the ranch and had formerly been used to bunk prisoners while they were working. My sister Kristine used to lie to her friends about where we lived. If they asked if they could pick her up, she would tell them she would just meet them at their house, or wherever they were going.

My mom took great pride in that little house. She painted the kitchen cabinets burnt orange and pasted brown, flowered wallpaper on the outside panels. She recovered the chairs with cheap matching flower-covered vinyl with tiny ridges all over it. She used to tell us, "We may not have the nicest house or the nicest things, but at least you are clean and fed."

I started working when I was four years old, picking up hay bale strings for my dad for one penny a piece. At age eight, I raised a pig and sold it at the auction for $200. When I was fourteen, I began swathing hay and driving a semi-truck in the hot summers. There wasn't a lot of work available for a girl in the small town of Malad, Idaho, but I was confident I could do just as good of a job as the boys, if not better. Besides, I knew it was the only way I would be able to afford college.

My parents' example of hard work was unparalleled. As I matured, I realized that working hard doesn't always guarantee a big payoff.

You just had to hope it would.

In my next meeting with Karen, I ask her about starting an ABA program. "I've done some research on ABA, and it sounds like it can really help kids. But I also found that it's really expensive, and it's not provided by public schools, nor is it covered by insurance. Will Kids On The Move help pay for ABA?"

She says no, but DPSD might.

I look into DSPD—Division of Services for People with Disabilities—but we don't meet the salary requirements, which are basically low enough that you would also qualify for Medicaid and welfare.

I rant to Sean once he gets home.

"I am so frustrated that there's a program like this available for parents, but only to those who are wealthy enough to afford it or poor enough to qualify for funding. The health and well-being of a child should not be a financial decision. If an autistic child is fortunate enough to be born into an upper-class family, then they can afford all the treatment they need. If not, well, tough, because you just don't have the money to afford normalcy. Doesn't the government realize that it's in their best interest to attack this problem early? After all, there must be a huge cost savings to society if these kids get better. How are they going to afford care for all of the autistic adults in the future, especially since autism is growing at epidemic proportions? I recently read that the AAP and the U.S. surgeon general all recommend ABA as a first-line treatment for autism. That should be endorsement enough, don't you think? Sean?"

Sean is already halfway down the stairs heading for the den.

"Where are you going?"

"I'm going to send an email to the Utah Autism group and ask them if anyone has ever successfully litigated their school district to get ABA paid for."

Later that evening we receive a reply. A woman writes that she has an excellent attorney and has been in litigation with her school district for years. They are exhausted and on the brink of bankruptcy. She writes, "There is a lot of red tape that has to be cut. The Utah Education Board has a 'no-hitter' record against parents. Many have sued, none have won, ever. You're better off spending your time and energy finding money to fund your own program, rather than wasting it in a futile effort that could take several years to complete."

I feel defeated.

"Well, that was only one opinion," I tell Sean. "Let's see what other responses we get."

No one else replies, and when we call other veteran parents, it seems she is correct in her reasoning. I realize I have to focus all my energy and strength on fighting autism, not the system. At least not right now.

A few weeks pass, and Karen makes another home visit.

"Karen, I think…I think I'm ready to accept that Clay could have autism." I say to her, talking through sudden tears. "I'm just…I'm not sure how we're going to do this, but we want to do whatever it takes to make sure he reaches his full potential. I've read the research that says early and more consistent intervention leads to a much better prognosis. So I'm working in ultra-high gear right now. Even though sometimes I feel like the wheels are spinning and nothing is moving. We have an appointment next week with Dr. Coates for a diagnostic evaluation."

It is so quiet I can hear a high-pitched static in my ears. I look up to see a tear roll down Karen's cheek and another drips off her nose.

More silence follows.

"Leeann, having a child with autism is a long, difficult battle. I have a daughter who is twenty years old with autism. I'm a divorced mother of seven children. It has taken a huge toll on my family. I can see the stress this is causing you and your family. I can see it in your eyes. You haven't had any rest in weeks, and it's causing a strain in your relationships. This ABA program you want to start…I just don't know, Leeann. It's really intense and extremely expensive. I know you want to do what is best for Clay, but you need to slow down and think about this and how it's going to impact your family, as well as you and your health. People seem to think ABA will solve all their problems, even recover their child. From my experience, most of the time, this is not the case. It leaves people divorced, bankrupt, and their lives in shambles. I just don't want to see you cling to false hopes."

"Karen, I need whatever hope I can get to pull myself through this. If the program only helps Clay five percent, it will have been worthwhile. Right now I feel like we're grasping at straws, and this is the most solid one I've found so far."

"Well, you're obviously going to do whatever you want. But please think about this some more. I'm going to write a letter to the DSPD and request respite care. You and Sean need time alone to talk and get away from the stress of it all. I'll send you a copy of the letter for your file."

"Thanks, Karen, I'm grateful for your concern. But, I never want to look back and wish I would have taken more action. I just feel that it's right. I guess…it's just that…my motherly intuition is screaming at me to go, go, go!"

"All right, Leeann," she half-smiles. "Whatever makes you feel better. Good luck."

I know she disagrees with my decision, but how could I deny my child something that could possibly help him? If we can scrape together the funds, I have to at least give it a try.

I dread the thought of taking Clay out into public, let alone a place with other children. It's exhausting and humiliating. This time, however, it's a little different. It's our first playgroup session at Kids On The Move. This is the first step in the marathon. I know it's necessary to help him improve.

I reach for the surgical brush and begin brushing Clay down. I follow up with joint compressions. I carry him outside, and we jump on our new trampoline together. A smile emerges as he plunges into the air, as if he is momentarily free. I grasp his hands and we jump together in synchrony. He plops down in the middle of the trampoline, lowering his head toward the black surface, fixated on the weave of the fibers.

"Clay? Clay."

He glides his fingers over the tightly woven, nylon webbing.

"It's time to get in the car. Clay, look at me. Please?" Anxiety crawls through me as I try to remember how long it has been since I've taken the boys out in public.

As I arrive at Kids On The Move, my palms are sweaty and easily slip off the steering wheel. I reach into the car to unbuckle the boys from their car seats. Clay darts out of the car and into the parking lot. I run after him and swoop him up and into my arms. After dropping off Drew at the sibling day care, I carry Clay toward the occupational therapy room.

Karen meets me in the hallway. She puts her arm around me and hugs me. "Glad you could make it," she says.

We walk down the hall together the rest of the way to the occupational therapy room. The room is alive with kids playing all around. I see kids on swings, bouncing on giant rubber balls, and crawling through tubes. Their parents are at their sides helping them each step of the way.

Karen looks at me. "Let's take Clay through the course. First he crawls through this tube," she taps the padded barrel-like structure with her fingers. "Then he rolls down the mats. She points to each station as she is talking. "Next he jumps on the mini trampoline, then swings in the swing. Last, we'll take him down the slide and into the ball pit."

My smile relaxes. I feel like I've just gone through the course in turbo speed. I try to put Clay down, but he's clinging so tightly to my shirt that he nearly rips off one of my buttons. I finally pry him free, but then he starts beating his head against my leg repeatedly.

"Karen, I'm not sure this is going to work. There is no way he's going to do this."

"Then we need to make him," she says.

I clench my teeth so hard I feel the muscles pop out of the sides of my jaw.

"Go on," Karen says. "I'll help you know what to do."

I push Clay through the tunnel. He screams and savagely thrashes about, eventually lodging himself inside the tube with his arms and legs braced up against the walls in locked position. I push, then shove, then pull on his body. He won't budge.

"Let me help," Karen says. I push on one end while Karen pulls on the other. We finally wedge him through the tube.

Next, I stuff him into a big, padded barrel and roll him down a raised mat. He's screaming and sobbing uncontrollably. His pleading glare sums it up, as if asking, *Why are you doing this to me?* I'm heartbroken by the look on his face. It's the first time since his regression that he's tried to enlist my help. My innate voice says, *Stop this. Save your baby.* But I'm reminded that in order to truly save him, I must go on.

Tears flood my eyes, and I can hardly see. The other parents in the room pretend not to notice, but I can feel the weight of their stares. No one else's kids are creating this kind of havoc. I force him into the swing, but he kicks and thrashes about, refusing to take part in anything. My nerves are short-circuited, and I'm ready to collapse. I grab Clay and bolt for the door. Karen comes after me.

"I can't do this, Karen," I say, picking up my pace. "This just isn't working." My voice trembles. Tears dribble down my cheeks. I cry so easily lately.

Karen puts her hand on the back of my shoulder. I stop and turn around.

"Leeann, it will get better. Promise me that you'll keep coming. It will get better each week you come. Give it at least a month. He'll get used to the routine of the course, and it will become easier. It's good for him. He's learning. Now, come on. Let's go back. Music time is next."

"Music? He loves music." I mutter. Besides, I know I can't give up. I'm frustrated with myself for having a weak moment. Maybe music will be our ticket into Kids On The Move each week.

One by one the kids file into the music room. Karen lays out carpet squares for each child to sit on. Clay and I sit down together. He begins to howl. He tries to get up and run, but I hold him close to me. Karen gives each child "bees," or tiny rubber Koosh balls. I give them to Clay. Still crying, he throws them. He slams his head into my chest in perfect rhythm, causing our bodies to rock back and forth. The music starts to play and Clay quiets down for a moment. Hand in hand, I prompt each motion to the music. I force myself to get animated and sing along to the song, "Baby Bumble Bee." He starts to wail, growing progressively louder as the song goes on. I look up at the clock and count the seconds until music time is over.

I feel like I just finished running a marathon, coming in dead last. With Clay on my hip, I walk downstairs to pick up Drew. I peek through the side window by the door and watch him shoot down a plastic slide into the ball pit, surfacing with an open-mouthed grin. At least one of us is having a good time. As we get into the car to leave, I remember that we have to do this once a week. Karen's words run through my mind, "It gets better each time you bring him. He'll start to get used to it."

The next week comes faster than usual, and I find myself dreading it as I brush down Clay. I force myself to imagine him completing the course perfectly. He is smiling and happy. I grab a Diet Coke and buckle the boys in the car.

Clay still cries through the course, but not as much as the first time. Music time is still torturous, but slightly better than the week before. The next rotation is called "The Learning Box." Karen explains this to me as "somewhat like ABA." She gives me a box with puzzles, cause-and-effect toys, and what they call "reinforcers" like M&Ms, whistles, and other gadgets. I tell Clay to perform a task while modeling it for him and saying, "Do this." If he does it correctly, I give him a reinforcement that he likes—candy, hugs, verbal praise, and so forth.

Karen sets out a yellow chair for Clay, in front of a small desk. She and another woman who works there sit adjacent to him, demonstrating how it should be done. I try to get Clay to sit in the chair, but he plays "stiff legs" and won't budge. I try to sit in the chair with him on my lap, causing a super-sized tantrum. He flings his body flat on the floor and shrieks.

I look at Karen with a *what do I do now* look.

"Force him into the chair," she says. She sees my hesitation and shoots me a stern look.

"Leeann, he has to sit in that chair or he will never learn."

I shake my head. Her all or nothing approach pisses me off. But I know she's right.

I'm afraid to do it. Afraid of being rejected by my own child again and again.

"How—how can I make him sit in that chair?" I ask frantically, as if a gun is being held to my head.

"However you want," she replies. "But if you can't make him 'attend,' then he'll never be able to learn."

I don't think I have it in me to pin him to the chair and watch him go through physical agony while big tears roll down his swollen cheeks. But I have to. I summon my ranch girl toughness and bear hug him from behind, holding his body in the chair for the first sitting. He throws his head back into my chest repeatedly and yanks my hair. I hold him as tight as I can without hurting him and put my hand over his as we place the shape in the sorter. Then I cheer for him and let him go.

Never did I imagine I would be wildly celebrating my child putting a shape in a shape sorter. My lofty goals for his life are broken down into simple tasks for which most parents don't even get out the camera.

Chapter 9

It is Wednesday, June 26. Clay just turned two years old.

I crack the window of the car. Clay squeals in a sing-song fashion in the backseat. Sean is unusually quiet.

"Penny for your thoughts," he asks.

"Oh, just anxious to get this figured out so we can have a game plan."

He smiles at me. I can tell he's putting on a façade.

"I'm almost sure it will confirm our worst fears. But, I'm ready to accept whatever it may be," I say, looking out the window.

We pull into the parking lot and securely buckle Clay in the stroller so he can't run away. Inside the doctor's office, we pace the hallway, hoping to keep Clay occupied so he won't fight to get out of the stroller. As we pass the rows of windows, I slip into a reverie of Dr. Coates bursting into a deep, roaring laughter as he proceeds to tell us we're all crazy for thinking something is wrong with Clay. "Take a deep breath, relax, and go home," I imagine him saying. I nervously snicker out loud.

"What's so funny?" Sean asks.

"Ah, nothing," I say, knowing the daydream will never match my living nightmare.

Eventually, a man emerges from the hallway. He walks flat-footed, deliberate in each step, with a half smile that seems forced. He studies me as if he is reading words from my face. His hand quickly juts out. "Hello, Mr. and Mrs. Whiffen, I'm Sam Coates." We take turns shaking his hand, and then follow him down the hall to his office. As he opens the door, my eyes routinely dart from wall to wall, scanning all items within Clay's reach. I'm relieved to see there is nothing that Clay can hurl—given his aggressive tantrums. We sit on the sofa, leaving Clay in the stroller.

"Okay, let's get started. Tell me your concerns about Clay," Dr. Coates says, still looking at his notepad. His pen flickers between his index finger and thumb, poised and ready to strike the paper the moment we begin speaking.

"Our son is extremely difficult, behaviorally. We can't take him out into public without multiple, lengthy tantrums. He used to say 'mama' and 'dada' and wave good-bye and night-night, but his words and gestures have been replaced with high-pitched screams and squeals. Oftentimes, he will laugh for no particular reason at all. He doesn't really play with toys, other than carrying around his two trains wherever he goes. He likes to swing outside for hours on end, if someone pushes him. Kids On The Move, the local early intervention agency through which he has services, thinks he displays autistic symptoms."

Clay squeals in the background, fighting to get out of his stroller. I quickly hand him some brightly colored Duplo blocks.

"Has he reached all of his developmental milestones? For example, did he walk and crawl on time?" asks Dr. Coates.

"Yes, he reached them all," I reply. "Then, somewhere between fourteen and eighteen months he stopped looking at us, began squealing, and acted like he didn't know who we were."

"Does he like to play with his older brother?"

"No, he really doesn't like being around anybody, but he's especially aloof with people outside our family. He hides when strangers come—"

"When did you feel like he started regressing?" he interrupts.

"I can't pinpoint an exact date, but we knew he was slipping when he was between fourteen and sixteen months old. He stopped calling me Mom—"

"Does he play with toys appropriately?"

"No, not really. For example—"

"Does he know how to play with toys? That's all I'm asking, no more, no less."

I look at Sean with one eyebrow cocked.

Dr. Coates asks many more questions, and obviously prefers short, concise, answers. If we deviate in any way from his original question, he abruptly cuts us off and restates the question. He is very particular and thorough, making sure he completely understands our answers. Not our feelings, but our observations.

Dr. Coates sets the file on his desk and wheels his chair in toward Clay, who is frustrated with the blocks we brought for him. Clay pushes them around on the table making screeching noises, unsure of what to do with them.

"Clay," Dr. Coates says.

Clay continues to stare at the blocks.

"Clay!" he shouts, loud enough that I jump.

No response.

Dr. Coates claps his hands behind Clay's head. Still nothing, no movement. Not a blink or a shrug—the reaction kids automatically have when they are avoiding someone. He models for Clay how he should play with the blocks. He stacks the blocks, one on top of the other. Clay is unfazed. After several minutes of Clay's unresponsiveness, Dr. Coates wheels his chair back around to his desk and starts scribbling notes all over in his yellow pad.

Minutes pass by with only the rhythmic sounds of Clay slamming the blocks down on the table. The clanking sharply echoes off the walls. Finally, Dr. Coates looks up at us from his notes and fully exhales.

"Mr. and Mrs. Whiffen, I think your son has PDD-NOS… Pervasive Developmental Disorder, a form of autism."

In a strange sort of way I am relieved that we finally have a name for it, yet disappointed at the same time because burrowed inside I had hoped somehow we had it all wrong. I hoped it would be simpler.

I uncross my legs. I recross them. I lock my hands in my lap listening intently to what he will say next.

Dr. Coates continues, "A very young child like Clay may not yet demonstrate all of the criteria. In such cases, a diagnosis of PDD-NOS is given. Within the next year or so, as his development progresses, new symptoms may emerge which may later revise the diagnosis to classic autism. So, it is important he receive intense intervention as early as possible. You are fortunate to have caught this at such a young age."

"What are your recommendations for treatment, Dr. Coates?" Sean asks.

"Well, as you are probably aware, there is no cure for autism. It is a lifelong condition. However, many who have used ABA methods, or Applied Behavior Analysis, seem to improve somewhat. And, there is some solid research behind it."

"We're already working on setting up an in-home ABA program," I say.

"Great. It sounds like you're on the right track. Are there any other questions?" he asks.

As if a buzzer has sounded, he springs from his chair and opens the door for us. "I'll mail you my complete evaluation in a few weeks," he says with his arm extended, directing us into the lobby.

As Sean asks him a final question, I glance down at his yellow notepad sitting on the corner of his desk. I read the last sentence.

Clay could not cooperate for me to analyze some of his early skills, thus a full formal mental status examination could not be completed in terms of assessing all of the developmental skills.

Sean breaks the silence in the car by asking me how I'm feeling.

"Fine."

"Really?" he asks.

"Yeah, I think so."

"How come?"

"Because I knew. And I've cried all the tears I have. Don't get me wrong, I'm still empty, and it doesn't make everything better. In fact, it makes it real, more serious. It's as if my cover has been blown. Like my clothes have been ripped right off me," I say.

"Huh?" He looks over at me.

"I feel vulnerable. Now it's real. There's no more hiding behind ignorance or denial. But at the same time, I feel like we have nothing more to lose, and everything to gain. How about you, tough guy?" I ask.

"I'm okay. Besides, don't worry about me. It's you I worry about."

"You always say that, Sean. Come on, when are you going to give a damn about your own feelings? You don't have to be a martyr, you know. I love you and care about you more than anything else. You know that."

He shrugs his shoulders.

"Sean, it's okay to mourn. You're his dad. I know you feel it too. Even if you aren't sharing it with me."

"You're right," he says. "It's harder for guys though, you know? We don't rant and rave, cry, or express our feelings as much."

"Is that what I'm doing? Ranting and raving?" I shoot him a smile and hold his hand.

"No, Lee, it's just hard to explain. I'm as devastated as you are. I just show it differently. And I want to be strong for you."

"Sean, you're my best friend—you know that. I would rather be with you than anyone else in the world, no matter what I'm doing. We're going to do this, together. Just like you said."

He bobs his head up and down.

"I'm strong for you like you're strong for me," I say. "We're a team."

I squeeze his hand.

As I walk into our home after the appointment, the smell of last night's dinner hangs in the air like dense smog. The coffee table is littered with papers from studies and information gathered daily. The blinds are still drawn together. Toys litter the family room floor. Dust fuzzes on the television screen in odd shapes. Dried, sticky juice spills speckle the kitchen floor, which hasn't been mopped in weeks. Crumbs, apple cores, and other remnants of breakfast are still out on the table. I have always taken pride in an organized, clean home. There was a time when I couldn't even sit down to read a book unless everything was clean around me. I even alphabetized our CD collection! I was there, and now I'm here. I marvel at how our circumstances change our actions and attitudes. Our priorities rearrange, perspectives shift.

I fall onto the couch and contemplate what has just occurred. A part of me withered away today as the formality of the diagnosis crushed my dreams for Clay and what he could become—the barometer from which all parents measure their own successes and failures. How did this happen? I search myself for any character flaw that could have caused this disaster. Maybe I was too focused on my projects. What if I didn't pay enough attention to him? I searched my mind for foods I ate during my pregnancy. I tried to eat healthy—I really did. But what if I had too much junk food or didn't get enough rest? What if this really is my fault? I give myself several more mental lashings, after which I finally realize I may never know what caused his autism, and I can't do anything about it.

Dwelling on the past will not change the future. But focusing on the present will.

My mind swarms with everything I need to do to get our ABA program up and running. The energy I feel from the urgency of starting immediate intervention is enough to sustain me through many more long days and late nights, preparing to launch a program that could rewrite our son's entire life.

We learn that we first need a consultant to train us and the instructors we will hire as full-time staff. A mother I met through Kids On The Move tells me of a fantastic consultant who recently left a local agency to work on her own. She gives me some names of her current clients. I start dialing numbers. The families I visit with rave about her unique abilities to assess the child and mold the program around their level.

"She just had the intuition we needed to help our son through certain programs," says one.

"Sarah has the ability to see the end goal in mind and work toward it in a determined fashion," says another.

"She molded the programs around my daughter, so they would work to her advantage."

I'm relieved to hear of her flexibility because of my concerns with an ABA program—how strict and rigid it seems to be, regardless of the different needs of the child. I pick up the phone to talk with Sarah. Her optimistic and upbeat personality is infectious. We set up an appointment for the next week so we can meet together in person. I want her to watch Clay so she can give us her opinion on where he would start. I'm interested in observing how she interacts with him.

Wasting no time, Sean creates a website complete with pictures of Clay and an explanation of the program and what is expected of a typical ABA instructor. Upon completion, he calls the nearby university's newspaper and places a "help wanted" ad that reads:

Fun, creative, & personable students needed to work with our 2 yr old PDD/autistic boy in an intensive home program. This structured program uses Applied Behavior Analysis (ABA experience desirable, but not critical). Training provided, flexible hours. 8–12 hours per week in American Fork, starts at $8.25/hr. Please read entirely the following website for complete details.

The enormity of what we are about to embark upon, this ABA program, presses on me as I read each word in the ad. I'm a twenty-six-year-old stay-at-home mom of two boys. I have no idea how to run a program like this. My thoughts flash to Karen. I don't want to end up divorced. I don't want to end up bankrupt. We're not even guaranteed Clay will get any better. Sean's job as a financial planner is largely based on commissions—his salary not much more than the annual cost of running an ABA program. We're mortgaging our lives and our savings on our son's future.

How are we going to afford it?

How can we *not* afford it?

Chapter 10

It's midnight, and I'm buried in paperwork from a typical, research-filled day. The warmth from the air seeping through the open window seduces me into a semihypnotic state.

My hand falls off the desk and onto my lap, jerking me awake. I look up at our clock on the wall and watch the second hand progress, staccato-like, around the entire perimeter. Time presses forward with or without us. I force myself to keep working.

Throwing myself into researching and implementing treatment options gives me control over something that makes me feel so powerless. It also acts as protection from the tremendous amount of grief that stalks me, like a rabid dog poised for attack.

The next day Sean, Clay, and I meet Sarah at the home of another family who has used her as their consultant. I'm nervous, but also anxious to hear what she will say. We sit down with her in the living room.

"Hello, Mr. and Mrs. Whiffen, I'm Sarah Overall," she says as she sticks out her hand. Her entire arm is covered in dark pink splotches. At first I think it might be from a burn. Later I realize it is a birthmark.

Sarah is an all-natural, tree-hugging sort of gal. Her freckles dot her sun-baked skin and accentuate her gangly frame. She tosses her hair over her shoulder as if the intrusiveness is interrupting her thoughts.

I immediately begin to feel more at ease.

"And this must be Clay." She looks down at him and crouches to his level.

"Hello, Clay," she says in a high-pitched voice. Clay turns away and runs squealing through the house with his trains, one in each hand. She doesn't flinch.

I already admire her calm, yet professional demeanor. I'm relieved I don't have to justify or excuse his disturbing behavior. She knows. She's seen it all, and probably more.

We tell Sarah about Clay—his strengths and weaknesses— and ask for her thoughts on implementing a program for his unique needs. She gives us very detailed, frank responses. She doesn't promise recovery, but she does vow to work tirelessly, drawing on her knowledge and experience to guide her decisions in helping him improve.

Excitement travels through her animated facial expressions, like a visible electric current, as she talks about her experiences witnessing "her kids" progress. There is even a certain passion and remorse in her honest revelations of "her kids" that haven't done so well. The "tough nuts" she says, that she'll never give up on. She treats her job more as a calling rather than a way to make a living or even a hobby.

It feels similar to the first time I met Sean; I just sort of know and have a feeling inside that says this is the right person. I know she's the one. I want to jump up and say, "All right then, when do you want to start?" I'm relieved that, despite all the other struggles, at least we've found a highly recommended ABA consultant and someone I feel will be a good fit for our family. But I want to talk to Sean about his thoughts as well. We shake hands again with Sarah on our way out the door. Sean winks at me with a half smile. As for his thoughts…I already know.

Later that afternoon, Karen phones me to let me know that

Kids On The Move is offering a presentation on Floortime, an autism intervention method developed by Stanley Greenspan. Although I'm moving forward with our ABA program, I want to learn as much as I can about other interventions like Floortime so I can be better equipped to help Clay. But I don't want to go back to Kids On The Move. Just the thought makes me nauseous—like remembering something I ate during the morning sickness days of pregnancy. But I have to do it. I need to shed all my personal feelings, my privacy and inhibitions, my concern about what people think. None of that matters anymore.

As I walk into the lobby of Kids On The Move, I see the same worn, pastel plaid couch sitting off to the side. I take my place on the edge of the couch and take out my notebook and pen. The presenter introduces herself as Heather. "Follow their lead" seems to be her key phrase in talking about Floortime. She talks about joining in play with your child, letting the child be the guide. By doing this, you're finding a way into your child's world so that you can build upon his strengths, helping him to relate in meaningful ways.

I take copious notes and plan to use some of the techniques I learn to help Clay before we get our ABA program up and running. Floortime seems like it might facilitate our relationship and understanding of one another, something I can work on in conjunction with our ABA program.

I'm open to many treatment modalities, but I am attracted to the behavioral component of the ABA program. ABA starts with basic steps that, in our case, require a child to sit in a chair and perform a simple task like dropping a block in a bucket. Clay can't do this yet. Without mastering this, how will he ever learn anything? My nagging instinct tells me that Clay won't be reachable until we get his behavior under control.

After the presentation, I want to stand up and sprint to the podium to ask Heather a few questions. Instead, I anxiously approach her, timid yet exhilarated, like a child waiting for an autograph. I talk to her about Floortime and ask how she became involved with autism.

"I have a son with autism," she says.

I'm surprised at her candor. Even though I am beginning to accept it, I'm still not able to say that phrase out loud. I'm instantly drawn to her. I want to know everything she's doing to help him—how she overcame the initial grief, how he is doing…

"Ms…um…," my voice croaks. I clear my throat.

"Call me Heather," she says with kind eyes.

"How's your son doing?" I squeeze out, too quickly.

"While he is still autistic, he is doing quite well…he…"

"Is he able to speak?" I clumsily interrupt.

"Yes…yes, he can talk." She chuckles. "He talks about rockets 24/7, but at least he can communicate."

I am comforted as I imagine what Clay might sound like while telling me all about rockets.

"What therapies have helped him the most?" I ask.

"Oh, we've tried so many it's…"

"What do you think helped him the most," I interrupt again, instantly wanting to cover my mouth with my hand.

"We're currently running an ABA program, and I do Floortime with him on the side. We see Dr. Bryan Jepson for biomedical treatment as well. He's an ER physician who has a son with autism. Two days a week he works out of a small office treating kids with autism."

"Biomedical treatments? Bryan Jepson? Do you have his phone number?"

I continue to question Heather, taking notes on everything she says.

"I would love to talk with you more about this. I'm sure you're incredibly busy, but is there a time I can meet with you?"

"Let me double check with my supervisor, but I think I can make a home visit during work hours. I would love to visit with you more and meet your son."

"I'd love that. I better get going," I say. "Thanks so much for your help."

I run into the door, my nose pushing up against the glass, before pushing on the handle. I look around to make sure no one saw. I walk out to my car groping in my purse for my keys. I check all pockets. Nothing. I go back inside and Heather is the only one there. "Forgot my keys," I say nervously with a half grin. *She must think I'm such a dork.* I search the couch, the floor, retracing every step. Gone. I pull out my cell phone to call Sean. Heather approaches me.

"Where do you live?"

"American Fork."

"Oh, that's not too far from where I live. I'll just give you a ride."

"Are you sure?"

"Sure, it's no problem."

We spend the next twenty minutes deep in conversation, hardly taking a breath.

"I know your heartache," Heather says. "It brings back memories of my own feelings in dealing with Seth's diagnosis. Even though I've had time to let the feelings settle, I remember when the initial sting was almost too much to bear." She looks back and forth at me, then the road. She continues, "Not a week after my son was diagnosed with autism, I was driving down the road with him in the backseat. I looked in my rearview mirror and saw him do something strange with his fingers, something I had never seen him do before. I called to him to stop doing that. Stop that. My heart started to race, and I felt that I couldn't breathe. I later learned I was having a panic attack. I continued to have these attacks for a few weeks until I finally had to see a doctor to get them under control.

"Leeann, I'm so sorry you have to go through this. This is a really tough period. But the grief of the diagnosis will ease up as time goes on. You are a sharp, capable, young woman. I have no doubt that you'll know what direction to take in treating your son. You're really fortunate he's only two years old."

We share the same fears, hopes, and dreams for our sons. It feels so good to be validated…for someone to understand, someone who has walked the same path.

"Heather, how have you been able to afford ABA?"

"Well," she sucks in a deep breath, "It hasn't been easy. I've had to start working again, which is difficult while trying to run a program, but it's the only way we can barely afford it. My sisters are two of his instructors, so I don't have to pay them as much. I graduated in psychology and contacted a former professor at the university I attended and asked if there were any students who needed internships. I was able to get one student on an internship basis, which has helped a lot. I don't know, Leeann, there's really no easy answer to that question. I wish there was. I really wish there was." Her voice drifts off.

I'm disappointed to hear her struggles to keep her ABA program running. Doubt slices through my optimism about setting up our own program. But it's incredibly refreshing to swap stories with someone who has experience. Like a child rubbing a small hole in a frosted window, my isolated world is slowly opening up.

Heather pulls her minivan into my driveway, but I don't want to get out. I don't want to stop talking. We connect on a tangible level that engages my mind and opens my heart. I share things with her that would otherwise take years of friend-ship to reveal.

I manage to get out of the car and hop up the steps to the front door of our house. I wave as she pulls out of the driveway. I watch her drive to the end of the street, turn left, and disappear. I feel lighter and more energized than ever. Hope swells in my chest.

For the first time, I realize I have become a member of a new club. Whether or not I want to join this group is beside the point. I'm a member regardless. Heather, Karen, and many others I don't even know are members. I feel an instant closeness to them. They know my pain; I know theirs. They are walking this lonely path, suffering through sleepless nights, and shedding many tears in grieving for their child. Are we related? By blood, no. By circumstance, yes. There's a tacit bond unlike any other.

It's a sisterhood.

As I watch Clay scream and slam his head against the floor repeatedly, I have to do something. I have no idea what he wants, and he needs me to figure it out. I remember Karen once telling me that other kids have been able to pick up signing as a basic way of communicating.

I learn simple sign language from tutorials I find on the Internet, and we purchase videos in an attempt to teach it to Clay. We watch *Signing Time* together and sing along with the characters, Alex and Leah, while they teach us signs. I find myself singing the silly pizza theme song at least a dozen times throughout the day. Clay loves the music, but he still won't try to do the signs. I so wish he would—I'm convinced once he can communicate simple words, his frustration level will go down.

As I hold Clay on my lap while practicing the sign for "more," I notice his cheeks and the tips of his ears are red. I remember what Heather said about seeing Dr. Jepson. I want to find out more about his autism clinic, which happens to be located just a thirty-minute drive away. What I've heard about biomedical treatment so far makes me think this could be a way to address some of Clay's physical symptoms, those red cheeks and ears, his severe constipation alternating with diarrhea, and his food aversions, which seem to aggravate his behavior and other autistic symptoms. What's more, I want to know what is at the root of Clay's autism.

I head for the computer and immerse myself in research once again. I google Dr. Jepson's name and find his website—The Children's Biomedical Center of Utah. I find a link to several papers he has written, one of which is titled "Coming to Terms with Autism." I read his story, and I'm inspired by his desire to help others along the autism treatment path. Dr. Jepson and his wife began researching autism treatment options when his son was diagnosed, and they discovered there were other parents who were finding success with various biomedical treatments. Dr. Jepson, an ER doctor, was skeptical about some of the treatments, since they were considered "alternative" and he was a traditionally trained allopathic physician. He began looking into literature and studies validating the biomedical treatment options and quickly realized it was good science that had plausibility. My heart skips ahead as I read more. Maybe he can help Clay. I call his office and schedule an appointment for July 11, in two weeks.

The next morning, Sarah calls to talk about the instructors we're hiring and to schedule the two-day ABA workshop we're going to hold to kick off our program. The only time she has available for the next two months is in two weeks, the same week as our appointment with Dr. Jepson. We agree to hold the first day on Wednesday and the second day on Friday, with the Dr. Jepson appointment sandwiched in between.

"Listen, Leeann," she says, "if you decide to hire instructors without prior ABA experience, which sometimes works out best because they aren't so rigid in their ways, I would suggest you hire a 'head instructor' who does have experience to train and shadow the other three for two to three months until they are trained. This fosters consistency, which is a huge key to the success of any ABA program. I have someone in mind that might be interested. Her name is Nicole. She has worked with several families and has around four years' experience. I'll send you her contact information with the contract."

"Great! I can't wait."

"Me neither. I'll talk to you in a few weeks."

The thought of launching this small business, along with hiring and training staff, is paralyzing. But the gut-wrenching drive that comes from the realization that our son could disappear indefinitely kicks us into high-energy action. We're not just starting some business.

We're sketching our child's entire future.

Our newspaper ad delivers a much better response than we expect. There are over twenty students who call to inquire—even after reading all the information on our website. By the next week, we have it narrowed down to ten. The first two interviewees are definite nos. The third interviewee is almost twenty minutes late, which, according to my stringent personality, is enough to cross her off the list right away. Strike one.

"Hiiiieeeyyy, Sean and Leeann," she says loudly when she

finally arrives, all open-mouthed grin and tall frame bouncing up and down with personality.

"Hi, Anndalyn," I somehow manage to force out. I look down to see a large cow-print purse at her side.

"You can call me Andy. Is Clay here?" she asks boldly.

"Yes," I say. "I'll bring him in after our interview."

"Good, because I would love to meet him. Oh, by the way, can I get a ride to my friend's house after the interview?"

I remain expressionless despite the colorful monologue I'm having in my head.

Excuse me! She wants a ride home? She must have missed the part on the website where it says, "must have own transportation." Strike two. But it might as well be strike three—the inning is over. But Anndalyn isn't even fazed. She is either unaware of her faux pas, or simply doesn't care.

"What are your unique abilities?" I ask, after clearing my head. I glance over at Sean. He's grinning.

"I love working with people, especially kids. I also like to paint. I earned enough money to attend college by painting murals in kids' bedrooms. I loved it. Oh, and I really like to surf." She puts her hand up and makes a wave motion in front of her face. "I used to live only fifteen minutes away from the beach in California."

"When we call your references, what do you think they'll say about you?"

"Oh, wow. Um. Hmm. I think they'll say that…I'm a lot of fun, and I make people laugh. She slaps her hands down on her knees. "In the office where I worked most of last year, we played practical jokes on each other relentlessly. You have to laugh, you know, like totally have fun in life. That's what it's all about, right?" She continues talking in animated explosions and gestures, an obvious visual on how to live life to the fullest.

Like a roaring waterfall, she cascades with fun and enthusiasm. She is excited and passionate about children. I can't help but watch and listen in amazement of her free spirit, floating effortlessly in describing the fun escapades of her youth—a modern-day flower child *sans* the drugs, sex, and civil disobedience.

I find myself smiling and laughing throughout the rest of the interview, something I haven't done in months. I'm swept into her world of no reservations. Her cackling laugh is as fun to watch as it is to hear.

Clay walks into the room while we're lost in laughter.

"Hi, Clay," she says excitedly, and scoops him up into her lap. She plays a silly finger game with him, immediately captivating his attention. He's hooked. Within moments she has Clay interested in everything she's doing. I see it, but I still can't believe it. I haven't seen him like that with anyone since he began to disappear. Sean and I exchange looks of shock. We thank her for coming and tell her we'll call her in a few days and let her know our decision. She reminds us that she really does need a ride to a friend's house. After twenty minutes of aimless driving, something that happens when you have no address for your destination, Anndalyn finally remembers where the house is.

Home again after dropping her off, I begin talking with Sean as if I had held my breath the entire drive. This is someone with whom we are entrusting our child. To make a mistake would cost us a lot of time and money in training, but, more importantly, a loss of opportunity to help our fading son. We have to hire the right people. We must be sure that we're making an intelligent, educated decision. To hire Anndalyn would be going against all logical thinking. We battle our strong tendency toward the conservative, dependable, and somewhat predictable. Reason says, "No way," but my emotions say, "She's perfect!"

Sean and I review her résumé together. I search her job experience. My eyes grow wide as I chortle. "She worked at a law firm?" Her cow purse and cackling laugh flicker through my thoughts as I wonder if she had any professionalism to go along with all the fun. Later that evening, Sean calls her references. The first one is the law firm. He asks them what her follow-through was like, her dependability.

"You will love her," says the woman on the other end of the phone. "She'll quickly become your favorite employee. You'd be crazy not to hire her." Sean goes back to the dependability question, but the woman becomes frustrated and says, "Trust me when I say this—hire her! You won't regret it!"

As I mull it over in my mind, I try to prioritize the most important qualities in an ABA instructor, a mental list that includes, number one, great with Clay; and number two, responsible. I know that above all, we need someone who will be able to get Clay to respond. She can be an intelligent, dependable person, but if she can't unlock our son's potential, then none of the other traits matter. I keep coming back to Anndalyn and the way she played with Clay.

We have to hire her. I'm convinced she will reach Clay in ways that no one else can. We call her the next day and offer her the job. "I'm so excited!" she squeaks so loud I have to hold the phone a few inches from my ear.

Natalie is a very somber and serious person, even by my standards. She is hardworking and book smart, excelling in all her extracurricular pursuits while maintaining a 4.0 GPA. She is every employer's dream. Her résumé is near perfect. She is beginning work on her master's degree in public health. She loves children, and has spent time doing humanitarian service abroad, helping children from third-world countries. I like her tenacity. She doesn't settle for mediocrity. She hungers to learn and improve herself, setting goals she is determined to attain. I want someone like this on our team. We need someone like her to keep the programs running smoothly and consistently. I suppose I have a soft spot for her because, like me, she is from a small town. I can easily relate to her. We can see that Natalie and Anndalyn are so different that they would complement each other perfectly.

We interview a male prospect who also seems perfect in every way and extend the offer to hire him. He accepts our offer. We're thrilled to be done and to have such a great team. Two days later, he calls and says he's taken a job elsewhere. The settled and relaxed feeling quickly turns into a question of whether or not we can find another really good person to work with us before the two-day initial workshop with Sarah in one week.

We had already withdrawn our ad from the paper, since we thought we had the slots filled. So we either need to run the ad longer or find another candidate among those we've already met. Then, about an hour later, a young woman by the name of Trisha calls. She's very interested in the position. A friend of hers had given her a copy of the ad, and she had held onto it for a week, wondering if the job would be right for her. We ask if she can come to interview the next day.

Trisha is a breath of fresh air. Her cheery smile and upbeat personality are contagious. She's very genuine, with no fluff or cheesiness about her—just real, down-to-earth, and very caring. Her brown short curls bounce as she laughs. She is warm, friendly, and being from North Carolina, full of Southern hospitality. We bring Clay in the room to see how well they interact. She is very patient with him, and pursues him even when he seems uninterested. She flops down on the floor in her skirt and plays with him like he is her little brother. He half-smiles while still looking at the floor, and starts responding to her persistent gestures. She hasn't even left our home when Sean and I look at each other with that look of, "Yep, it's her."

She will fit in great with Andy and Natalie.

Sean calls Nicole and hires her to temporarily shadow the other three since none of them have ABA experience.

We're optimistic about our well-rounded team: Andy—fun, creative, energized; Natalie—intellectual, organized, and sincere; and Trisha—caring, genuine, and patient. They each commit to working with us for at least one year. I really feel they will become just like our own family.

I think about this as I pick up the mail and find a letter from Kids On The Move. I rip open the envelope, and then slow down to carefully read the words.

To Whom It May Concern:

Clay Whiffen is a two-year-old child, born June 20, 2000, who accesses services here at Kids On The Move. I have had the privilege of working with Clay as his primary service provider since May of 2002, when he entered our early intervention program. Clay has the diagnosis of PDD, within the autism spectrum. He has significant delays in the areas of communication, problem solving, reasoning, creative thinking, and social interactions. His cognitive skills are scattered and not appropriate for his age level. He does not yet play without direction or appropriately with a variety of relational play activities. Clay is gaining language; however, it is quite delayed and not altogether functional. His ability to communicate spontaneously to get his needs met or to engage people for social interaction is limited, as is other joint referencing activities, such as eye contact, showing an object, pointing to an object for shared attention. He has difficulty getting out of his home, into other environments. He does not engage well with his brother, other children, or adults. I believe this will be a lifelong disability needing significant services over time. As the family service provider, I also see the additional physical and emotional demands placed on the family because of the unique and challenging behavior children with autism spectrum disorders, and Clay, exhibits. It is my hope that Clay's family will receive services offered through DSPD, and that those services be put in place as quickly as possible. If you have any questions or concerns that I could address, please feel free to contact me.

Sincerely,
Karen Morris, M.Ed.
Early Childhood Special Educator

It's a copy of the letter Karen sent to DSPD. I feel as if I may as well be reading Clay's obituary. My eyes trip over specific phrases like, "significant delays in communication," "cognitive levels scattered," "doesn't engage well with others." But the catch-all phrase that I read and reread is, "I believe this will be a lifelong disability." Discouragement grows through my stomach and into my face.

As I climb the steps back into the house, I feel the heaviness of what is transpiring all around me set in once again. It seems to come in waves. For a fleeting moment I let the weight of the Goliath-sized task crush me. The responsibility seems too great. But I'm his mother. No one else knows my son as I know him. I have to do the absolute best I can, and be prepared to accept the results—whatever they may be. I give myself pep talks, focusing my energy to avoid the desperation that creeps into my mind.

I ache with the desire to have my son act normal. I question again why this is happening to us. I look all around me. I see our friends and neighbors with typical, healthy children. While they talk about the luxury car they want to purchase, or complain their child didn't hit a home run in last week's little league championship game, we're left wondering how we are going to pay the staggering $30,000 per year in program costs, or, even worse, whether our son will ever know who we are.

Other times I feel the swell of hope and determination overcome me. "I will never give up on him," I fervently say out loud, tossing the letter aside.

Glimmers of the Clay I used to know shine through. And it's those times when I know he's still in there—somewhere—shrouded in seemingly endless layers. I have to believe we will find him. He is there. I know he is. I press forward in sheer faith that what we do will help him, striving to keep my head up against all odds. My eyes are fixated solely on the goal.

We've only begun to untangle this Gordian knot known as autism.

Chapter 11

My attempts to get Clay to sit in the chair are futile. I'm determined. He's stubborn. Yet, I force myself to work with him daily. One day, after a black eye from a sippy cup being hurled at my head, a clump of hair missing, and still no unprompted block in the bucket, I dial Heather from Kids On The Move.

I try to hide my frustration, but it seethes beneath the surface.

"Heather, look, I'm doing everything. I have been doing everything they said to do at Kids On The Move, but I still can't get him to drop the damn block in the bucket." I take a deep breath. "Can you...can you just come over? Maybe he'll do it for you."

I loathe having to depend on someone else. It isn't in my personality to ask for help.

"Sure, Leeann. Let me look at my schedule." Pause. "How about Saturday?"

"Fantastic."

"How's Clay doing?" she asks as she comes inside.

"Oh, a little better. He finally learned how to sign "more."" He uses it even if it isn't appropriate for what he is requesting. We're working on him being able to use it functionally. I taught him to say "go" to release him when I push him on the swing. It doesn't really sound like the word "go," but it sounds similar. He only uses it when he's in his swing. I'm really looking forward to starting our ABA program. Our Initial Workshop is on schedule for Wednesday and Friday of next week."

"Wow, Leeann, you're really moving quickly. That's good. How long has it been since his diagnosis?"

"Four weeks. I don't know how we're going to afford this program though. I'll go door-to-door if I have to. I don't have the time or the energy to fight the state for funding. It would take all my time, resources, and energy away from doing what's needed immediately. We're getting ready to sign on a second mortgage and see how far that will take us."

I pick up Clay and we start up the stairs, Heather right behind, into our former office, now the "schoolroom," as we recently named it.

"I've set aside a room that we'll be using for Clay's program," I tell her. "I have some chairs and a table in there already, so we can get started." Heather follows me into the new school-room. It is bare except for a couple of shelves with a few toys on them. Heather brings out a plastic container full of puzzles, toys, and other reinforcers. She sets them on the table. Clay starts screaming, hitting my face, and kicking me. He claws at my neck. Through Clay's flailing arms I see the surprise in Heather's face. She comes closer, grabs his hands, and places them down at his sides. "Clay, don't hit your mommy. We don't hit."

I sit in the preschool-size chair and hold him in my lap. Heather turns to him and says, "Do this," as she drops a shape in the shape sorter. Clay grunts and struggles frantically to get free. I hold him tight. She reaches over the table and takes his hand in hers to help him complete the task. "Hooray!" we both shout as she pops an M&M into his mouth. Clay is surprised, yet pleased with himself.

An hour passes as we work on a few more activities—each of them greeted with Clay's extreme resistance.

As we stop and Heather packs up her things, it gets quiet.

She says, "It'll get easier as you're consistent. I wish all the best for you."

As she turns the knob on the front door to leave, I blurt out, "Does your son call you Mom?"

Leaning against the door with a thoughtful, somewhat concerned look on her face she says, "Yes…yes he does. Sometimes, it sounds a little robotic, but he does call me Mom."

"Sometimes when it's quiet and the boys are in bed, I try to imagine what that might sound like."

I hesitate to ask her my next question because I'm not sure I can take an honest answer.

"Heather, do you think Clay will ever call me Mom?"

She pauses, thoughtfully.

"I want to be able to tell you yes, definitely, he will and he'll mean it too!" She sighs. "I believe he will, Leeann. It's so hard to tell how far these kids will come. But I believe he will." She chuckles. "I don't think you'll let him do otherwise."

I scramble to make sure everything is ready for our initial ABA workshop, purchasing everything on the checklist Sarah included in the paperwork. I have the large three-ring binder for the instructors to log their notes, the spiral-bound notebooks for each specific program or skill that we'll be teaching him, dividers, plastic pages, the works. I also put a few of Clay's favorite toys and books in bins that line the wall. Our former office is officially transformed into an ABA schoolroom, although it really looks more like a cross between a Staples and FAO Schwarz.

Sean draws up employee contracts, including their hourly wage, commitment time period, no tax withholdings, etc. We are employers.

On the morning of the first day of the workshop, I drop off Drew and Clay at my sister Kristine's house. As I pull into the driveway, I see Sarah getting out of her car.

She is thirty minutes early to allow herself preparation time. We walk to the front door together. She senses my nervousness and tries to ease my tensions by telling me this is an exciting day—we're embarking on a journey to help Clay reach his fullest potential.

Soon Andy, Natalie, and Trisha arrive in succession. This is all new to them too, as none of them have any prior ABA experience. We wanted it this way so we can start out fresh together. Our conversation is laced with nervous undertones. After their training over this two-day period, they'll be expected to implement what they have learned, and it's no simple job. They'll be behavioral engineers, connecting the faulty wiring in a young boy's brain.

Nicole arrives last. She walks into the room like she is the queen of England. I smile as I watch her glide to her chair. She was highly recommended by former and current ABA employers, and she exudes energy and confidence.

We sit close to each other on the couch and chairs in the family room. Sarah stands up front and begins giving an in-depth overview of the ABA program. She is very articulate and professional. "Throughout this day we'll be talking about autism, including some of the research that has been done, after which we'll begin working with Clay. Initially when we work, I'll work with him. We'll do what you call a sitting, where I'll call him over to the table and we'll work for a couple of minutes, depending on his behavior. Either way, we'll keep him there until he is not crying. We will continue to work with him until the crying stops. Then we'll let him go."

I feel queasy as I begin visualizing the ensuing battle. Images of Clay red-faced, with tears running down his cheeks, thrashing about, fill my mind. She continues, "This will be an important rule that we follow from this day forward. We will never let him leave the chair when he is crying. We want him to learn that tantrumming will not get him out of doing the task. If he tantrums a lot during the sitting, I'll do multiple sittings to try to get through the resistant behavior."

I hope she wears football pads.

"Then we'll work on several basic programs, one of which will be Verbal and Non-Verbal Imitation. Imitation is one of the most basic skills we learn as babies, so we'll start by teaching him this method first. We want to start with a task that is simple, like this, so he'll be able to be successful. Then we'll build on what he has mastered or been successful with. Then I'll have each of you do a sitting. After that, we'll take turns doing a sitting. We'll talk about what you did well and what things we need to work on and answer any questions you may have. Friday we'll talk about maintenance, logging notes, and programs. By then I want to make sure you're totally comfortable with everything before starting out on your own. You have a huge advantage having Nicole shadow you for the first few months because she has a lot of experience as an instructor, and she is a great teacher. Okay, any questions?"

I look at their scared faces. They have no questions because they're still not sure where to begin. "Let's get started," Sarah says.

Sarah begins by telling us the origins of the ABA program for autistic children. She describes how up until the late 1960s, when a family found out their child had autism, professionals would recommend they put their child in an institution. They would tell them their child would not make any gains or even be able to learn anything. There's nothing that can be done, they said. The families were counseled to move on with their lives, have more children, and accept this tragic news.

Dr. Lovaas, a professor at UCLA, began researching children with autism in the 1960s. Most of his experiments were trial and error as not much was known about autism during this time. In 1973, he did a research study with children between the ages of four and nine years old who were all institutionalized. The instructors worked with these children eight hours a day, seven days per week. It was the first time that children with autism were taught complex language. Most children with autism have echolalia, where they just repeat what is being said rather than using it functionally in a conversation. Before this research, it was believed that children with autism could never have complex language skills, so it was a very important finding.

As I listen to Sarah's presentation, I am aware of how strange this is. I am sitting in a workshop learning how to teach my son small, simple tasks that most children half his age already know. I still can't bring myself to say the word "autism" out loud. In fact, I go to great lengths to avoid it altogether. I find myself dodging neighbors and friends, not answering the telephone. Even though I'm able to acknowledge Clay has autism, it's as if saying it out loud makes it permanent. Maybe it's my mind's way of sheltering my vulnerable feelings. I need more time for my susceptible emotions to become stronger. Time to heal my wounds.

Then Sarah describes how Lovaas did another study in 1981. By this time his methods were a lot more formalized and had evolved and improved. Nineteen children between the ages of three and five received forty hours per week of one-on-one ABA instruction while the control group of nineteen only received ten hours per week of ABA instruction. Everything was the same about the two programs except the hours. In a second group of twenty-one children not treated by UCLA, the parents chose whatever treatment they wanted, excluding ABA. Some chose speech therapy or special education classrooms. The study went on for two years. At the end of two years, they were placed in different categories. "Best outcome" included children who were indistinguishable from their peers. This meant if a professional were to come into the child's classroom, he/she would not be able to pick out the child who had gone through treatment. These children were successful in a typical classroom with no support or aide. "Middle outcome" children were those who made significant gains, but still showed some residual signs of autism. A lot of children in this category made language gains, but still had social or behavioral issues. "Low outcome" children did not show significant gains from their treatment. At the end of the two-year study, of the group that received forty hours of one-on-one instruction, nine out of the nineteen children were placed in the best outcome, eight of those children were placed in the middle outcome, and two were placed in the low outcome group.

I can almost hear the choir burst into singing "Hallelujah." Energy surges through my veins. I want to jump out of my chair, run around the couch, and proclaim to the entire room that we will work our hearts out so that Clay can be part of the best outcome group.

Sarah continues to tell us about the results. In the first control group, those who received ten hours of instruction per week, none of those children made the best outcome group. In this first control group, eight were placed in the middle outcome and eleven remained in lower outcome. In the second control group, not treated by UCLA, two of the children were placed in the best outcome group, ten of those were in the middle outcome, and ten were in the lower outcome.

Sarah flips her hair over her shoulder as she starts to describe the results of a follow-up study that Lovaas did in 1987 on the children who were in the best outcome group to see how they had maintained their gains in the initial study. The children were between nine and thirteen years old. He looked at the group of children from the forty-hour group. Eight out of nine had maintained the best outcome. One of the nine children had later been placed in a special education classroom. He also found that one of the children placed in the middle outcome category moved up into the best outcome. Sarah says this finding was really significant because it showed that even after five years of age, a child still has the potential to make gains. However, Sarah stresses, it is important to note the younger the child, the more pliable the brain.

"Because Clay is so young," Sarah says, "we'll start with twenty hours, then work up to thirty, and eventually forty hours per week. We are going to teach Clay basic skills using the principle of operant conditioning. Operant conditioning uses stimuli in the environment to evoke a response, and the consequence following that response either decreases or increases the likelihood that that response will occur again.

"So really what this means is that if I see a soda machine and I want a soda, I put my quarters in and push the button. The stimuli is the soda machine. My behavior was putting money in and pushing the button. The consequence I'm hoping for was the soda to fall out and for me to get my drink. The next time I see a soda machine and I want a soda, I'm likely to put my money in. On the other hand, if I'm at a soda machine and put my money in and nothing happens, I might shake or kick the machine. I might even try to put in some money again and try even harder. Eventually, I will realize I'm not getting the soda, the reaction I'm looking for. So the next time I see that soda machine, I'm going to keep walking. Those are the principles of operant conditioning."

I am writing fast…so fast that I'm wondering if it will make sense when I read it later. I try to capture each word, every statistic, and especially, each glimmer of hope on paper. I want to be able to refer to this often, even tape it to my wall if necessary to help keep me motivated on those days when discouragement may set in. My notebook is filled with my barely legible handwriting. My hand aches from clenching the pen in a death grip. I put my pen down and shake my hand. I chastise myself for not taking the optional shorthand course in college.

Sarah keeps teaching, with seemingly no end to her knowledge and focus. "What we're doing is called behavior modification. We manipulate the stimuli and the consequence to Clay's response to evoke certain behaviors. Basically, if Clay gives us the response we're looking for, we give him the appropriate consequence. We're not going to yell or do aversives. What we will do if Clay doesn't give us the response we're looking for is we will withhold the reinforcement. Whereas if he gives us the behavior we would like, he gets the positive reinforcement that will motivate him to give us that same behavior. For example if I say to Clay "do this" and I put the block in the bucket and he takes his block and throws it, I will just tell him "no," then give him the same instruction again. So he doesn't get the reaction he may be looking for, like making you angry or frustrated. If I ask him again and he does put the block in the bucket, then I will praise him and give him something he likes. Use a reinforcement that will motivate him to want to do what you ask. I cannot emphasize the reinforcement enough. The reinforcement is the gas that makes the car go.

"Almost everything we will do in a sitting will be in discrete trial format. We start with giving the instruction, or the "SD," discriminative stimulus, Clay will then give a response, "R." Then you will give the "SR," reinforcing stimulus, which is the reinforcement based upon Clay's response."

"Shouldn't it be 'DS' and 'RS'?" Sean asks.

"One would think so, but it's not. And I'm not sure why." Sarah replies.

New words are being flung at me in every direction, words that will eventually become a language that is required to live and communicate in the foreign country in which we've been forced to relocate. Little do I know we'll be fluent within a matter of months.

Sean leaves to get Clay from Kristine's house and to pick up pizza for lunch. We all gather around the table, chattering between bites about what we have learned. But I can't force myself to eat. I'm too anxious about what will happen in round two. I eye Clay laying across the three steps that go into the family room. He carefully stands his Buzz Lightyear action figure on the stair. It falls over. He screams. He tries again. It falls over. He takes Buzz and beats him against the carpet. His face turns bright red, striped with tears. "Let's go outside, bud." I say as I lift him from the stairs and give him a piggyback to the swing. As I push Clay in the swing, he is quiet. My mind runs through terminology and Lovaas studies.

Sean pokes his head out the back door. "Lee, we're ready. Bring Clay." I lift Clay out of the swing. He screeches and kicks to get down as I force him inside. We take our original places on the couch and chairs lining the family room and stare at Sarah in anticipation.

"Okay. I'm going to bring him to the chair now," Sarah says. I look up from my notes.

I feel like I need to warn her. "Are you sure you know what you're getting into, Sarah? Clay is so feisty and hell-bent determined."

"Believe me when I say I'm used to it."

"You haven't seen Clay at his worst."

"I used to work in a group home for adolescents and adults with autism. One day I was driving a van filled with individuals with autism, and a man around eighteen years old got out of his seat belt and attacked me. I pulled over to the side of the road so that we wouldn't crash. Then he threw me out of the van and started punching me in the face. I finally was able to get him to the ground and hold him down until someone came to help me. So when I tell you I can handle whatever is coming, trust me."

I visualize Sarah, who looks to be 115 pounds, holding down an angry autistic man probably twice her size.

"Wow," is all I manage to squeeze out.

"Holy crap! I would have been so scared," says Andy.

Sarah smiles with one side of her mouth as she flips her hair methodically over each shoulder. She sits in one of the two toddler-sized chairs by the table in the family room. On the table is a square block next to a shallow bucket. Clay is already screaming, uncomfortable with the strangers in the house. "Come here," she calls to him, in a dry monotone voice. No emotion or inflection whatsoever. Clay continues screaming. She gets up from her chair, picks him up, and carries him to the other chair. His body is writhing frantically in her arms. His arms and legs are thrashing. She places him in the chair, not releasing her grip, holding him as firmly as possible without hurting him. She sits down in her chair facing him, not once taking her hands off his arms. I can see that his strength takes her by surprise—he's barely two years old. Tears drown my eyes as I watch him continue to struggle. I scan the room. Everyone else is completely silent, watching bug-eyed with wonder and sadness. It pains us all to see a beautiful little child struggling as if his life is at stake. Yet we know Sarah has a job to do, and we wonder how she will do it, if at all. I know Clay's determination and endurance well enough to know that there will be a long battle of wills, and that he won't go down without a major fight.

His screams of anguish sear my soul. Sarah is unruffled. She's slow and deliberate in her motions, taking great care in making sure he doesn't hurt himself on the chair or table by gently moving his arms down. He's all over her, pulling her hair and slapping her face. She remains gentle, yet firm and consistent. She moves his hands down to his side, placing him in his chair over and over again so that he knows what is required of him. I cannot detect even a flicker of impatience or frustration in Sarah. He tries everything from playing limp as a noodle, to throwing his head and body backward repeatedly, hoping to wear her down. His head thumps into her chest, then pops her in the chin.

I've never been torn in so many different directions at once. I yearn to cradle him in my arms, saving him from all his distress. My motherly instinct is screaming at me to help him. He catches a glimpse of me watching him struggle. I look into his fear-stricken eyes. They seem to plead with me to save him. My grip tightens on the sides of my chair. It's all I can do to hold myself back.

I know with conviction this is the right thing for Clay. It has been well researched, and I feel it is the only program that will sufficiently tame Clay's severe behavior so that he can focus and learn. But I also know that if we can break his behavior without breaking his spirit, we will have accomplished a Herculean task.

I remind myself repeatedly that this won't last forever. After we get past this most difficult part, he'll be able to learn. We can't give in and deny him this potentially life-changing opportunity. Either he remains lost, or through this program he is found and will be able to make something out of his life.

I see Andy with a sober expression, at odds with her usual chipper personality. Her face is pale and she's intensely focused. Next to Andy is Trisha. She's wildly chewing her gum, her mouth still closed, but her eyelids frozen open, anxious to take in what will happen next. Natalie seems calm, but I notice her leg nervously bouncing up and down. Nicole is sitting by herself on the other side of the room, expressionless. I watch for any sudden movements, hoping that none of them will bolt for the front door.

I can't stand it any longer. I get up from my chair and go into the living room, where I sit on the sofa, prop my elbows on my knees and cover my ears. Sean comes in after me.

"Are you alright, Lee?"

"No, I'm not. How am I supposed to sit here and watch him struggle like this?" Tears leak onto my cheeks. I turn and look out the window to hide my face.

He takes my hand and puts it in his.

"I know it's hard, Lee, but we have to do this if we want him to learn."

"I know…I know," I say softly. I can see his reflection in the window next to mine. He is crying too. This is the first time I can recall ever seeing him cry. We wrap our arms around each other. Clay's sobs cloud our thoughts. Reluctantly, we eventually trudge back into the family room.

"Do this," Sarah says, as she places the block into the bucket. She immediately follows by putting her hand over Clay's, prompting him to place the block in the bucket. Clay, still screaming at an ear-piercing tone, swings his leg into the table, kicking it over on its side. Andy reaches over from the couch and tips the table back up, placing the bucket back on top. Sarah tries again. "Do this," she says, putting the block in the bucket. Still screaming, his limbs swimming through the air, he reaches over, grabs the bucket, and throws it to the floor. Clay stops screaming to catch his breath and in doing so becomes quiet for a millisecond.

Sarah yells, "Great job being quiet!"

She throws him up into the air and catches him.

"Let's go play!"

Sarah grabs the Buzz Lightyear toy, his favorite action figure, and flies him around the room with Clay continuing to scream the entire time.

"Come here." Clay runs to the corner. She walks over to him and carries him crying back to the chair. I groan, but I'm not sure if it's out loud or just in my head.

Two hours go by, and Clay is still screaming. I imagined he would give Sarah a challenging wrangle, but I thought he would have exhausted himself by now. My optimism begins to fade, and uncertainty takes its place. How long is it going to take for him to learn to sit in the chair? What if all the instructors quit because they really had no idea what they were getting themselves into? Is Sarah wishing she had never taken us on as clients? Just then Clay pauses again, and Sarah tells him he can play.

A minute or so goes by and she calls him to the chair again.

He screams.

And then it happens.

He pauses.

The room is quiet. We're all afraid to breathe.

"You did it, Clay!" Sarah shouts, as she hands him Buzz Lightyear. He sits quiet for a few moments playing with Buzz. The instructors all lean forward in their seats to glean the magic of the moment. We embrace the silence as it rescues our ears and nerves from Clay's strident sounds.

"You're being so quiet. Thank you for being so still," Sarah says in a childlike voice. "Let's go see Mom. You're being so quiet."

Clay lets out a small whimper. He walks toward me, and then collapses into my arms. His eyes are bloodshot and his head twitches against my chest as he inhales—remnants of his endless crying.

"Okay, well, any questions?" Sarah asks, turning around to move the chair behind her. The back of her shirt is saturated with sweat. "It looks like we'll be working on 'nonverbal imitation' and 'quiet sitting' for a while."

The instructors let out a nervous chuckle.

"Let's give him a break, then we'll call him back to the chair in a little bit and try several more sittings with him.

"I am definitely seeing some defiance," Sarah says, as if we didn't witness the toddler tornado before us. "I am happy to see that, because defiance is a good sign that cognitively he comprehends some of what is going on. I prefer a fighter over a child that's impartial. He has willpower. We want that."

Like a balloon with a small hole, I exhale slowly until I deflate. The muscles in my abdomen begin to relax. Defiance is good, I remind myself. He's a fighter.

Sean jabs me in the side. "See!" he says.

I roll my eyes. He loves to be right.

Still sitting on my lap, Clay shrieks intermittently as Sarah begins teaching the instructors how to implement the new programs. About a half an hour later, Sarah calls Clay back to the chair. It's a sense of déjà vu all over again, although toned down a notch.

By the end of this first day of training, I wonder how I'm going to remember everything I learned. I go to bed that evening dreaming of "SDs," "Rs," and "SRs," operant conditioning, Clay screaming, and a child that is free from the bonds of autism.

Chapter 12

It's Thursday. Time for our appointment with Dr. Jepson.

"How's this going to work having Clay with us in the appointment for an hour and a half? Clay usually doesn't last more than two minutes in situations like this," I say to Sean.

"Well, we'll just have to tag team him," Sean replies. "Dr. Jepson is used to kids like Clay. He'll understand."

We pull up to the brown brick building, which was clearly built sometime in the 1970s, or about the same time orange, green, and yellow Tupperware were the rage. Once inside I open the door and walk into the tiny waiting room with three chairs. Sherlyn, the office manager, greets us with a smile. She has a one-sided conversation with Clay for a moment, then hands us some paperwork to fill out. The waiting room is complete with Clay's two favorite objects—Buzz Light-year and a television/DVD player. We play with Clay in the waiting room until the nurse calls us back. As we walk into Dr. Jepson's office, I suddenly feel like we're in Toys "R" Us. In one corner is a TV/VCR. In another, an overflowing toy box. Next to us are play sets, books, and games. Dr. Jepson stands up to shake our hands and says hi to Clay as he pats him on the back.

I'm taken back by how young he looks. We all paint mental images of people we haven't met, and he doesn't fit my image in any way. His lanky yet healthy physique towers over Sean and me. He doesn't smile very often, but radiates calmness and humility. His triangular Adam's apple bobs in his long, narrow neck even when he isn't talking. Wasting no time, he sits down at his desk and invites us to sit in the chairs adjacent to him.

He begins by walking us through the biomedical approach to autism using a PowerPoint presentation on his laptop. The first slide contains four circles intersecting one another. The circles are labeled gastrointestinal, neurological, toxicological, and immunological. There are arrows pointing to a genetic susceptibility, with another arrow pointing to an environmental insult. He explains to us that autism is a complex metabolic disorder that involves multiple body systems, and that it begins with a genetic susceptibility coupled with an environmental insult of one kind or another setting off a chain of events resulting in the dysfunction of the four organ systems. He emphasizes that to treat autism biomedically, you have to correct the body's underlying metabolic abnormalities, the thought being that this will alleviate many of the physical and neurological symptoms. Treatments often include diet, nutritional supplementation, and detoxification. This is meant to fix the root problem, not just mask it.

I am instantly intrigued. Finally, someone can tell me what is happening in his body in a way that makes sense to me. I've been certain that Clay has immunological and gastrointestinal problems. His ears and cheeks, even the tip of his nose, are constantly red, most likely indicative of an allergy or intolerance to something.

Dr. Jepson continues talking. Clay's noises gradually escalate, and he starts throwing large toys around the room. But Dr. Jepson doesn't flinch or even seem to notice. I quickly intervene and try to redirect Clay.

I hear Dr. Jepson say, "The latest research shows that there seems to be a problem in the interaction of several biochemical pathways involved in the detoxification cycle of the body. In

2000, Sallie Bernard, a parent of an autistic child, along with several others, began investigating autism as a form of mercury poisoning." *Mercury poisoning.* I remember a website I had come across in my research recently, which mentioned heavy metal toxicity and chelation, which is the removal of heavy metals from the body through the urine and/or stools using the prescription DMSA or another type of chelating agent.

Dr. Jepson continues, "As you look at this paper by Bernard et al., you see that the symptoms of mercury poisoning are very similar to those of autism." I glance over and look at the comparison chart labeled "Table 2 Summary Comparison of Biological Abnormalities in Autism and Mercury Exposure." Under the heading of "Immune System," the mercury poisoning column points out that sensitive individuals were more likely to have allergies, autoimmune-like symptoms, and asthma. I look at the heading "Neurophysiology." I read "Causes abnormal vestibular nystagmus responses; loss of sense of position in space." My mind replays one of the many times Clay has tumbled down the stairs, and the many times he had acted "drunk" while walking, falling down multiple times.

"So how are kids poisoned by mercury?" I ask.

"Well," Dr. Jepson begins, "mercury, in small amounts, is everywhere in our environment. It's in our air, soil, and water. It's even in our dental amalgams that are in our teeth. The biggest source of mercury exposure to infants, however, is in vaccinations."

"Vaccinations?" I interrupt.

He goes on. "Thimerosal, a preservative used in vaccines, contains approximately 50 percent ethylmercury. In one day, some infants receive up to 100 times the EPA-recommended safe level of oral exposure of mercury based on weight for an adult. Obviously not all children are autistic, so most infants can handle that toxic load just fine. However, those with the right genetic mix, or predisposition, are adversely affected."

I glance over at the mercury comparison paper, my mouth hanging open. The words on the page begin to blur as tears fill my eyes. I blink repeatedly so that I can see. I'm not sure if I'm angry or deeply disturbed, or both. Why was I not made aware of this before vaccinating Clay? I scold myself for letting this happen.

But at least I'm finally getting some potential answers to the question of why I had a typically developing toddler lose words, begin having behavioral problems, lose gestures and social skills, and eventually become someone I didn't know or recognize anymore. Out of the corner of my eye, I see Clay start to push the television off the stand. I jump up and catch it just as it's falling.

Dr. Jepson proceeds, "Mercury can induce autoimmunity and inhibit the DPPIV enzyme, which is required to digest gluten and casein."

"Hmm," I say, nodding my head thoughtfully.

Dr. Jepson nods and continues. "The effect of mercury on the central nervous system can cause impaired motor planning, decreased facial recognition, blurred vision and constricted visual fields, insomnia, irritability, excitability, tantrums, social withdrawal, anxiety, difficulty verbalizing, altered taste, impaired short-term memory, and attention difficulties."

I sit back in my chair, stunned. He could have been reading the list of symptoms right from Clay's chart. I look over at Sean. He looks bewildered.

Dr. Jepson tells us about possible triggers other than mercury. He mentions how Dr. Andrew Wakefield from the UK has researched enterocolitis, an inflammatory bowel disorder, in autistic individuals. In doing colonoscopies on autistic children with bowel disorders, he found lymph node enlargement in the mucosa of the ileum, the last portion of the small bowel. Upon biopsy, he discovered the nodules were full of vaccine-strain measles virus. He hypothesized that the virus overloads their immune system. The children were unable to effectively clear the virus, resulting in chronic subclinical infection.

Dr. Wakefield's research is what I told my pediatrician about right before he rebuked me like a little girl.

"Dr. Vijendra Singh from Utah State University documented an elevated measles antibody response in the autistic group compared to controls. He also noted that the majority of those with elevated measles antibodies also had antibodies to the myelin basic protein," Dr. Jepson says. I later learn that protein is the fatty sheath around the nerve in the brain. "Dr. Singh had even found antibodies to the vaccine-strain measles virus in the cerebrospinal fluid of autistic children."

I hear a crash and look over to see that Clay had knocked over a stack of VHS tapes. Sean hops out of his chair to pick them up.

Dr. Jepson goes on to explain there are many variables involved, so studies like these are open to criticism. It's unlikely that autism is a direct result of the MMR vaccination, he says, but rather a combination of insults on the already fragile immune system.

Dr. Jepson pauses, but I'm completely unaware of any activity in the room. My head starts pounding like a bass drum. I'm spinning in information trying to sort out what I think might pertain to Clay. It seems to make sense. But I'm concerned that there is still a lot of research that needs to be done. While continuing to listen to Dr. Jepson, my emotions vacillate from angry to confused to "let's start treatment today."

"Antibiotics overuse," Dr. Jepson states, my ears instantly perking up, "has been a recent problem."

Yes! I want to shout. Clay had multiple rounds of oral anti-biotics. We learn that many of the bacteria that antibiotics are prescribed to treat are becoming resistant and difficult to eradicate. When an antibiotic is taken, it clears the body of both the bad and the good bacteria. This leaves room for pathogens to grow and take over, which is called intestinal dysbiosis. Because autistic children's bodies are shifted toward the Th2 immune response (responsible for antibody formation and allergies) rather than the Th1 immune response (responsible for viral and fungal infections), they have less ability to clear the harmful bacteria and restore normal gut flora. This intestinal dysbiosis, or yeast and bacteria overgrowth, can interfere with normal digestion and emit harmful metabolites that can exacerbate autistic behavior.

Dr. Jepson concludes, "Because of their diminished immune system function, many of the children are more prone to ear infections, eczema, and sinusitis. Most of the time antibiotics again are prescribed to treat these illnesses, further exacerbating the problem."

I look at Dr. Jepson in disbelief. "Are you telling me Clay's autism could have been a result of any or a combination of his vaccines, multiple rounds of antibiotics, extreme constipation alternating with diarrhea, ear infections, red cheeks, ears, and nose?

"Yes," he says. "The evidence suggests that this could be a piece to the puzzle."

"So what can we do about this?" I ask, now ready to take action.

Dr. Jepson skips to a slide on his laptop that shows a chart titled "Biomedical Treatment Options." There are four text boxes with arrows pointing from "Heal the Gut" to "Detoxification" to "Address the Immune System" to "Neurological Interventions."

"You may want to consider attending the Defeat Autism Now! (DAN!) conferences. DAN! is a group that advocates and supports biomedical treatments. Experts from all over the world come and share their research and clinical experience with professionals and parents."

Dr. Jepson recommends some lab tests, including a hair analysis, urine organics acids test, complete blood count (CBC), RBC minerals, liver panel, and a thyroid function test. He also recommends placing Clay on a strict gluten- (wheat) and casein- (milk) free diet. But I'm so overwhelmed with information, that I have to tuck this one away until I have more time to research. We do purchase the supplements he recommends for Clay to start—Nu-Thera without vitamins A and D, cod liver oil 2500 IU, zinc 20 mg, magnesium (1 cup epsom salt in bathwater).

I'm unusually quiet on the drive home. The bounty of information rolls like an overflowing surge in my mind. I can hear Clay in the back saying "Doh" in his sing-song voice, over and over again.

"Sean," I say, "one of my biggest concerns is that there haven't been any 'gold standard' studies proving the triggers he mentioned are the culprits. It would kill me to lose so much time and money chasing our tails around and around the biomedical arena. On the other hand, the evidence is pretty convincing. And it gives us some answers to Clay's medical issues that no one else seems to want to acknowledge. What if they're right? How can we risk not treating Clay biomedically? What if in ten or even twenty years down the road it's proven that these toxins played some part in the recent autism epidemic? Are we prepared to accept the fact that we could have done something to help Clay, but decided not to because there wasn't clear proof? Why are there always so many damn questions and no answers?" I say, slamming my head against the headrest.

Sean is quiet for a moment. "I agree with you. I think we need to do everything we can to help Clay and have no regrets. It's like this—our son has been kidnapped. Taken from us by this…autism. The kidnappers are asking for a hefty ransom. And there are no guarantees we'll get him back. Do we pay the ransom money? You bet we do. We don't even give it a second's thought. We will do anything to save our son. Anything."

"If we're ever able to get Clay back, I promise, I will be on the front lines helping parents navigate their way around treatment options. I will make this easier for them. All of the research and trying to locate various resources takes precious time. Time that could be used in getting treatment started sooner."

Being a typical middle-class family, we never go on luxury vacations or retreats. We eat out maybe once a week. Our house isn't fancy and our cars are simple. Even with that lifestyle, we are forced to pay for everything with credit cards so that we can afford to pay the ABA team wages with checks. I try to focus on the present so that we can get through each day. I can't worry about our financial future right now because our child is so much more important.

Friday, Day 2 of the ABA Initial Workshop, begins with our jittery conversation about what we learned on Wednesday, and what might happen today. And then it begins.

Sarah calls Clay to the chair. Clay screams and pounds his hands on his knees in desperation. Sarah walks toward him, but Clay turns and runs down the hallway. She catches up to him and wraps her arms around his small, stiff body and carries him to the chair. His screeches evolve into hysterical fits, and his flailing arm catches her in the face. All eyes are focused on Sarah's reaction. She remains soldierlike in her poise. Her calm, careful movements almost soothe my frayed nerves, as she remains focused on her goal of placing him in the chair in front of her. She cradles him in her arms as she readjusts her grip. Clay becomes quiet for two seconds.

"Clay, that's great," she says as she strokes his head. Then he starts screaming again. After thirty minutes of this, Clay seems to tire, and he stays quiet long enough that Sarah lifts him up in his chair and zooms him around the room. Then she hands him his blanket and sends him off to play.

Without taking a breath, she picks up the large, white notebook from the table and inserts worksheets for each program: Matching, Puzzles, Shape Sorter, Come Here, and Verbal Imitation. Using role-play, she teaches the programs to the instructors. She tells them how to log their notes using percentages for rate of acquisition and how to use specific codes for behaviors.

"Let's work through his behavior," Sarah says. "Then when we meet in two weeks, I want to see how you're doing in your sittings with him."

I begin to wonder if she is too optimistic when he can't even drop a block in a bucket.

"I like his tenacity." I hear her say through my discouragement. "I think he'll go places, Leeann. I really do."

A moment of reassurance sweeps over me, as I know that Nicole will shadow Andy, Natalie, and Trisha to ensure our program gets started correctly. I'm confident in Nicole's abilities. She comes highly recommended as a trainer not only by Sarah, but others as well. She's assertive and animated. She can turn on her energy with a switch, and she has a definite can-do attitude. She's bossy, somewhat sarcastic, and commands attention. Screaming and yelling don't faze her, but rather deliver the challenge she seeks. She has a task to do, and she's bent on doing it right. It's Nicole's way or no way. She's an absolute perfectionist.

But while I know her experience and personality is beneficial in training our instructors, she still rubs me like a rough seam on the inside of my pants. I'm grateful she will only be our secret weapon for three months, because I'm not sure I can stand her for any longer.

As the workshop ends, I reassure the instructors that we appreciate them, we're counting on them, and we are really looking forward to working with them—just short of falling on my knees and praying to the good Lord they'll come back tomorrow.

Andy says, "Leeann, you watch, we're going to get him sitting in that chair in no time. Don't worry. You'll see."

I smile at her, warmed by her conviction. I believe in her. I believe she can do it. I believe in all of them, with their different strengths and approach.

Later that evening, I read the boys a book of nursery rhymes while they're in the bath. I look at Clay. The tips of his ears, cheeks, and nose are bright red. I feel the water to make sure it isn't too hot. It's cool to the touch. "We better hurry boys; this water is getting cold already," I say. I read and sing "Blackbirds in a Pie," "Baa, Baa Black Sheep," then "Mary, Mary, Quite Contrary." I turn the page. "Humpty Dumpty sat on a wall, Humpty Dumpty had a great fall, all the kings horses and all the kings men couldn't put Humpty together again."

I stop reading. I compare it to the small army of people working hard to help "put Clay back together again."

Chapter 13

I mix the new supplements Dr. Jepson recommended for Clay into a bottle with a small amount of pear juice. It's Saturday, two days after our initial appointment, and I may as well be a compounding pharmacist—opening capsules here, adding liquid there, and shaking it all up. I plunge the rubber stopper into the mouth of the bottle and suck the orange liquid into the syringe. I snap on my latex gloves like I'm ready for surgery. I ask Sean if he's ready.

"Let's do it," he says, winking.

Sean lays Clay down on the floor, and before Clay knows what is happening, I quickly squirt the bright orange, gritty concoction into the side of his mouth. His eyebrows squeeze together. His mouth twists around in uncanny positions. His lips pucker in disgust. Still leaning over Clay, I look at Sean and he looks at me. Just as I turn my face back to Clay, it all comes shooting straight up, like a geyser. My face is spattered and dripping with the potion. I look down at the yellowish orange–colored droplets that speckle my shirt.

"Whoa," says Sean, trying not to laugh. He points to his cheek, "Uh, you have a little right there…"

I scream and wipe my face. "I hope this gets better," I say, my voice muffled by the apron.

The next morning, Nicole blasts through our front door at nine sharp, chattering nonstop.

"Oh, hi, Nicole," I say, shocked at her sudden entrance. She carries on for a few more minutes until she is interrupted by a knock at the door. I'm glad for the interruption, but even more grateful that it's someone who knocks. Hopefully, Nicole will take a hint.

"Hi, Andy! It's the big day. Are you nervous?" I say.

"Oh, maybe. Okay, not really. Hi, Clay!" She grabs him and twirls him around in the air. "Come with me. We're going to play!" she says as she tosses him up on her hip and bounds up the stairs to the newly designated schoolroom. Just like that, they're gone. No tantrum. No fighting.

Sean recently set up a video camera in the room and wired it to the TV in our bedroom so that we can watch and record every session—something we made sure the instructors were aware of—to help us keep a watchful eye on Clay's progress. I take a seat on our bed, anxious to see how his very first session will unfold. Natalie comes in and joins Andy—a strategy recommended to accelerate them through the learning curve. Clay does amazingly well. He has several tantrums, but not as severe as during the workshop. But it's obvious that he's uncomfortable and wants to get out desperately. He heads to the door many times, wanting the session to finish. He becomes obsessed with his Buzz Lightyear, which leads to screaming and crying because he wants to hold it and play with it instead of doing what he is asked.

Natalie and Andy sit four feet apart from each other, while Nicole sits in the window seat. Clay is standing by Natalie. I notice his tiny yet solid body. "He's just a baby," I whisper aloud as I watch his stubby little legs carry him clumsily over to Andy. An hour comes and goes. I'm still stuck to the TV, analyzing everything, watching for any sparkle of hope to shine through. It's so quiet in the house.

I glance out the window and see Drew playing in the sandbox. He scoops the sand with his digger, then empties it into the dump truck; his four-year-old imagination at work. I watch him find his way to the swing. His short legs pump in and out as he throws his head back to enjoy the wind rushing by his face.

I follow my routine of checking on the boys after they've gone to sleep. I love to watch them sleep, partly because I know it's one of the only times to see them perfectly still, and quiet. It's a serene, peaceful moment where I can reflect upon their goodness, regardless of the day's events.

I whisper the "secret" into Drew's ear—the one I say to him every night before bed. The same one my dad used to say to me when I was young.

"I love you, bushel and a peck, bet'cher pretty neck I do," I whisper as I brush his damp hair to the side and caress his cheek. "Hang in there with me, bubba."

I go into Clay's room. He's asleep with his legs tucked underneath his body, with his rear end sticking up toward the ceiling. I giggle softly, then lean over and kiss his red cheek. I savor the warmth and softness of his cheek, since he won't let me do it when he's awake. I whisper in his ear, "Keep fighting, buddy. We can do this." This soon becomes a nightly ritual.

Over the weekend, Trisha volunteers to stay home with the boys, so Sean and I go out for a long overdue date-night. We sit and talk in the movie theater, waiting for the show to start. I watch as people file into their seats, laughing and carrying on. But autism is on my mind constantly, leaving room for nothing else. Sean says something to me.

"Huh?" I say.

"Are you doing alright?"

"Yeah. I'm fine."

"No, you're not. You're not gonna let it go, are you?"

"It's just that…well, I look around at all these people in the theater. Most of them probably have children that are happy and healthy. That's all I ever wanted—happy, healthy kids. I want to run up to that…see that lady over there just laughing and talking to her friends."

"Yeah," Sean says.

"Her. I want to just run up and shake her and say, 'Don't you know? Don't you know that we just found out our son has autism?' How could this happen to us? He was a typical child… developing normally. How could he just lose all of his skills? I want answers."

Sean is quiet. I want him to tell me it will be fine, like he always does.

The lights go dim and the movie starts. I'm still uneasy. As I watch the movie, I wriggle in my seat, unable to focus or get comfortable. Once I'm finally able to let go enough to get into the story, I get this nagging feeling like something is terribly wrong. Then I remember.

Our son has autism.

Two days later, the speech therapist from Kids On The Move comes to our home for her monthly visit with Clay.

"How is his language coming, Leeann?" she asks.

"Slow," I reply. "But we're working on it. We're hitting it hard in his Verbal Imitation ABA program. He's still signing more and says "go" whenever he wants something. Actually, it sounds more like "Hiya" in a sing-songy style. The problem is, I'm just never sure what it is that he wants."

As she moves closer to Clay, he moves farther away. It

reminds me of the way magnets repel each other if like poles are placed together. She sits next to me at the kitchen table and takes a tool from her bag that looks like a rubber toothbrush with nubs instead of bristles at the head.

"There are some things you can do, Leeann, to stimulate his oral motor skills. Take his toothbrush, like this, and stroke down his tongue and inside his mouth. It will, in a sense, wake up his mouth, encouraging him to make more sounds."

She makes "Baa Baa Baa, Maa Maa Maa" sounds with him to see if she can stimulate any type of babbling. Clay looks out the window, expressionless. I notice his cheeks and ears are red again. She watches him thoughtfully.

"Narrate your day," She continues. "Talk about whatever you are doing at the moment in as few words as possible. If Clay attempts to make any sound during that moment, reinforce him by imitating the sound he makes, then saying the word you think he is attempting. When he wants something, tell him the word. Pause. Give him the opportunity to request what it is he wants. Then respond to his request."

So I try. I try it all.

I find that by pausing to let Clay respond, he tries harder to make a sound, even if the sound doesn't resemble the correct word I'm seeking. I brush his mouth before taking him on the trampoline periodically throughout the day. We interlock hands. Then I jump one jump and stop. I won't move until he attempts to make a sound. Though I'm looking for the word "up" when he wants to jump, he says "dah" for down.

I'll take what I can get.

Two weeks pass since our initial workshop with Sarah. It's our first team meeting, and I'm not sure what to expect. I'm anxious to get Sarah's opinion on how she feels Clay is progressing and her thoughts on how the instructors are coming along.

One by one each instructor arrives. Nicole arrives last, flanked by a toddler that looks at least six months younger than Clay. Fury sizzles up my esophagus and settles in my throat.

Why did she bring her? Why didn't she ask first? My stress level is especially high today, and my emotions are running close to the surface. I shoot a look of anger and frustration at Sean, shake my head, throw my hands up, and walk away.

He comes to my side. I grumble, "Why didn't she just bring all the neighbor kids to watch? It would have made for a great field trip, don't you think!"

"Lee, relax, come on. We can't do anything about it now. I'll talk to her about it afterwards."

The instructors discuss their sessions, comparing notes with one another, eager to learn more. They're still working together, but are now pairing with Nicole for each session. We begin the meeting with Andy and Sean doing "Come Here" between two people. Clay is squealing in the background as Andy says, "Come here." There's a pause, then I hear the pitter patter of his feet on the wood floor as he rounds the corner. His stubby legs barely leave the ground as he runs and falls into Andy's arms. "YYYEeeeahhh!" Andy shrieks in delight as she flies him around like an airplane. When she puts him down, Clay picks up Buzz Lightyear, his favorite stim toy—something from which he receives stimulation, either from obsessing about it or playing with it inappropriately—off the floor. (I've recently added "stim" to my ever-growing autism vocabulary.)

Then Sean says, "Come here." Clay looks at Buzz, then toward Sean's voice, then back at Buzz. After some thought, he puts Buzz on the floor, turns around and runs around the corner and into his dad's arms.

"All right!" Sean yells as he blows raspberries on Clay's belly.

"Come here," Andy says, interrupting their fun. Clay hesitates. He's slower this time as he makes his way around the corner. Halfway to Andy, he notices the light switch on the wall and flips it on and off, on and off. He eventually makes his way back to Andy.

"Pretty good," she says, giving him a lower reinforcement for his distracted response.

I'm thrilled he's starting to respond, even though it's in a small way, and it may not be perfect every time. I try to see each small success as a stepping-stone for greater things. Small successes act as rungs on the ladder of hope, the reward of course, being at the top. Without hope, I have nothing.

After the sample "Come Here" program, Andy goes back and sits on the couch. Then Sarah explains how to place programs on maintenance once Clay has mastered them. Her voice is steady, calm. So calm, I'm almost falling asleep. The late nights are finally catching up with me. I watch Nicole's eighteen-month-old daughter plop down, pick up a Buzz Lightyear book, and start looking at the pictures. She turns the pages with her tiny fingers as she looks intently at the bright shapes and colors. She sets the book down, then grabs the shape sorter and turns it upside down and shakes out the shapes. She places the square in the correct hole, then the triangle, and then the circle. It stings as I watch how advanced she is compared to Clay. I feel a pang of discouragement as I'm lost in awe of her developmental skills.

"Hi, Mama!" she squeals as she runs into Nicole's arms.

The pain burrows further inside and allows unbridled jealousy to seep in. I wonder again if Clay will ever call me by name. She walks over to Clay, who has been running around the house squealing. He doesn't notice her. Then, for no apparent reason, he screams and stomps his feet. Nicole's frightened daughter flees back into the safety of her mother's arms. Nicole picks up her child, and puts her on her lap facing her. As she talks to her mother, she cups her chubby hands on Nicole's cheeks. I watch with deep-seated envy as she wraps her dimpled arms tightly around her mother's neck. "Mama, Mama, wuv you," she says as she nestles her head on Nicole's shoulder.

Clay's screaming becomes louder, pulling me out of my intense observation. He whimpers through the next couple of sittings, but still makes an attempt to do what he is asked. He knows now that if he doesn't follow directions, he won't get out of doing the task. Sarah sits down to model how the nonverbal imitation sitting should be done. "Come here," she says, as Clay follows her to the table. She takes the wand out of a jar of bubbles and gently blows into the air toward him. For a moment he seems like a typical two-year-old batting at the bubbles flying through the air with his stubby arms and a wide-open smile. He giggles as a bubble pops on his face. He seems to have a certain fondness for Sarah, despite the rough days together in the initial workshop—or maybe because of their rough days together. I watch him move his tongue back and forth in his mouth, making his favorite happy sound.

Next Sarah places a fork and two identical baby bottle caps side by side on the table.

"Match," she commands.

Clay looks disinterested and starts to climb out of the chair.

"Nope," she says, matter-of-factly, and places him back into his chair, straightening him square to the table again.

"Match," she says again. This time he grabs the bottle cap and starts playing with it, putting it in his mouth.

"Nope," she says. I'm uneasy, wondering if he'll be able to complete this simple task that has been modeled for him several times already. She takes the cap out of his hand and places it back where it was on the table.

"Match," she says again. This time she places her hand on top of his, takes the cap, and puts it on top of the other cap.

"There it is, you got it!" she says in a playful, childlike voice, while patting his belly.

"Match," she says again. This time he takes the cap, looks at it, glances at the cap on the table, and places the cap on top of it. A flicker of happiness spreads across his face.

"There it is," Sarah says, picking up a pinwheel and blowing it near his face. "Nice one," she says, ruffling her hand through his hair.

Sarah runs through the sitting a few more times. Clay's answers aren't perfect, and he gets a couple more "nopes." But, overall, he seems to be grasping the concept. Sarah seems tireless in her efforts to help our son.

As Sarah begins talking about the sitting, Nicole's little girl starts talking loudly. It's hard to hear over her constant jabbering. I look over at Clay, who is playing with his Thomas the Tank Engine toy at the table. He tries to place the train on top of the hat they were using during the sitting. It falls off, clanking loudly on the table. Clay starts screaming. I look around, wondering if anyone else is getting anything out of this team meeting with all the distractions. Sean takes Clay out of the room and gets a different toy for him to play with.

I hear Sarah say, "Let's go through the five steps of acquisition with nonverbal communication."

Meanwhile, Clay begins opening and closing every door in sight. He comes to the bathroom door, which has a childproof handle. He tries it, and then screams when he can't get the door open. He grabs my hand and leads me to the door. He places my hand on the doorknob. I try distracting him with something else. He immediately goes back to opening and closing the doors. I look around. All eyes are on me. My inadequacies bristle as my life and my parenting skills are under a microscope. I grab *Goodnight Moon* from the toy bin and start to read. Clay hops off my lap and goes for the light switch. I hoist him up on my hip and take him into the kitchen for a snack.

When we get back from the kitchen, Sarah brings Clay back for another sitting. As he comes to the chair she flies a stuffed bear through the air like an airplane. He's staring at something to the side of his chair, not even aware of what she's doing. He's repeating "Doh, doh" in his sing-song voice. He begins to babble and whimper.

As Sarah begins telling us what she wants to do with the Verbal Imitation Program, she mentions sounds that Clay knows how to make, like "go" and something similar to "wow." She also mentions that she wants to start teaching him how to say "Mama" and "Drew." I haven't told her how badly I want him to call me Mom. I wonder how she knows. Nicole's daughter mimics Sarah, saying "go," "wow," and "mama" perfectly, looking very proud of herself. Sean is sitting on the stairs across the room. I shoot him an icy look. He grimaces and nods.

Evening comes quickly, and we're all tired from the events of the day. I put Clay into the bath and sit down near the edge of the tub to think about it all. I glance over at Clay, who is mesmerized by the lights above the bathroom mirror.

"Clay," I call out, waving my hand in front of his face. He doesn't flinch, flicker, blink…nothing.

"Clay, please stop. Look at me." I place my hand on his chin trying to turn his head toward my face. He resists. He's fixated on the light. Finally, on his own time, he loses interest and turns his head back as he splashes in the water. In his mind, he submerged deeper into his world. Then he came back just like that—just not all the way back.

I stare at the bathwater, imagining that he snaps out of it, that he wakes up one morning, jumps on our bed, plopping right next to my pillow, and says, "Hi, Mama!" He wraps his arms around my neck, his full cheek presses against mine. Then he pulls back and stares at my face and into my eyes. His finger traces around my face. He leans in and whispers in my ear "I wuv you." He pulls out his Thomas the Tank Engine trains and says, "Mama, play with me" as he races them up and down my arms.

I glance at the clock. It's 8:00 p.m. I anxiously put the kids into bed and get on the Internet to continue my research. I join several Yahoo! email groups dedicated to biomedical treatment in autistic children, hoping to learn the basics of biomedical treatment. But tonight, I'm specifically studying the gluten- and casein-free diet Dr. Jepson mentioned in our initial consultation. I learn many parents are having great success by removing casein, the milk protein, and gluten, the wheat protein, from their children's diets. *What food is left in a diet free of gluten and casein?* It seems extreme. How can foods from essential groups cause the body such problems? Besides, if a child has a true allergy, it would be evident with proper medical testing. I read on…after a trial of a gluten- and casein-free diet, parents were reporting gastrointestinal issues were resolving themselves, the guts of their children are healing, and their children are more alert and aware. My eyes widen as I read the last sentence of the latest article posted. "Some parents heard their child talk for the very first time." My forehead wrinkles and I put my hand over my mouth.

"I want him to talk to me," I whisper.

I'm led to a website dedicated to helping parents get started on this special diet. I feel slightly gullible for investigating this further, but if it helps Clay even just a little bit, it'll be worth it. I find a study that has been submitted for, titled "Innate Immunity Associated with Inflammatory Responses and Cytokine Production against Common Dietary Proteins in Patients with Autism Spectrum Disorders," by Jyonouchi. The study compares inflammatory cytokines, signaling molecules secreted in an immune response, in children with autism, nonautistic children with dietary protein intolerance, siblings of autistic children, and normal, healthy, unrelated children. It found a significant inflammatory response in autistic children to milk, wheat, and soy proteins. This response was made worse with the presence of abnormal bowel bacteria. Fifty-six out of sixty-one autistic patients showed positive response to a gluten-/casein-/soy-free diet. This is enough for me.

We have to give the diet a whirl. Maybe he'll even have better results because of his young age. But, how am I going to do this? He's limited himself to only two or three foods. Just thinking about having to learn how to make everything special for him makes me want to run away and never come back. I already hate cooking, but having to learn to cook without wheat and milk will be hell.

But I will do it. I have to do it. And I'll make it work, somehow. If I don't, I will always wonder whether it would have helped Clay.

I begin by making a list of the few items that Clay is currently eating: French toast, pancakes, chicken nuggets, hamburgers, fish crackers, French fries.

Sean walks into the room.

"Whatcha doing?" he asks.

"I'm making a list of the foods Clay is eating."

"What for?"

"I'm taking wheat and milk out of Clay's diet." I string it

together so quickly it sounds as if it is one word. I bite my lip nervously.

"What?" Sean replies.

"Remember when Dr. Jepson told us he thought it would help Clay's gut problems? When I researched it further, I came across a study that found it helped fifty out of the sixty kids who participated. Some of them even started to talk!"

Sean looks at me blankly. "Hmm."

"Believe me. I really don't want to do this. It will be a major change in our lifestyle. I don't know how in the world I'm going to get Clay to eat different foods when he only has a few things he'll eat anyway." See, Clay is adamant about eating only those foods, and limited versions of them. He'll eat McDonald's chicken nuggets, but not the ones from Wendy's or Burger King. "I know it won't be easy, but I have to try. Besides, we have nothing to lose."

"All right, Lee, whatever you think is best."

I'm grateful that he lets me fly. He has always been this way. He has confidence in me, and it gives me courage.

"Are we good?" I ask.

"We're good," he says, clicking the side of his mouth with his tongue.

I purchase Lisa Lewis's book *Special Kids, Special Diets.* I compile a list of acceptable and unacceptable ingredients and tuck it inside my purse. I also have a short list I found online that contains prepackaged foods that are currently GFCF (gluten free, casein free). I take great comfort in knowing I can buy mixes in a box, at least to get us started. I know I don't have time or patience to spend all day in the kitchen baking special foods that Clay may never eat.

As I scour the narrow aisles of the store, however, I notice there are very few pre-packaged foods and mixes, and they cost twice as much as basic ingredients. I cave in and buy several staple ingredients that I remember seeing listed in some of the recipes in the cookbook.

Soon I look in my cart and it's full of food and ingredients that are completely foreign to me, like tapioca and rice flour, guar gum, xantham powder, and Kinnikinnick bread mix. I remind myself that following recipes is like following any set of directions. If you can read, you can cook, right? My plan is to try to make the GFCF equivalent of what Clay is currently eating. This won't be so bad. French toast will be easy. I'll just make the bread from the GFCF mix, and he'll never know the difference. As for the chicken nuggets, I have a recipe that uses crushed potato chips for the outside coating. My confidence is waxing strong. This is doable. I gather, organize, and pray really hard. I'm finally ready to deploy.

I wait until Saturday morning to start this radical diet so that I can enlist Sean's help. He's the master at getting the boys to eat. I slice off a piece of GFCF bread from the freshly baked loaf. The knife sticks to the bread and squashes it down toward the breadboard. Luckily, it bounces back up to its former shape. I examine the front and back. It looks like a sea sponge straight from the Pacific Ocean. I hope Clay won't notice. Although it looks different than wheat bread, it's edible and smells delicious. I make French toast out of it, and the egg drains through the marble-size holes. Placing it on Clay's plate, hot from the frying pan, I pour 100 percent pure maple syrup on top, cut it into squares, walk behind the counter, and then turn around and close my eyes. "Nnnneeeeerrrrrroo," Sean says while flying around the room like an airplane with a bite of Clay's food on the fork. I hear the airplane stop, eventually landing in Clay's mouth. "Hiya," I hear him whine. "He tasted it," I whisper. "At least he…" Clay starts spitting. I turn around and spot the entire chewed up piece sitting on his plate. He starts to wail. It gets progressively louder. He kicks his chair and pounds his fists on his tray.

"There is no going back now," I shout over the noise. "If he thinks I'm giving up because he spit it out, he's nuts."

Sean looks at me, his eyebrows raised. "Good luck, sweetie."

I throw a piece of French toast at him, hitting his chest. "Try this and see if it's really that bad."

He takes a bite. "It's not the best, but you really can't taste a huge difference."

"Did you hear that, Clay? This is just the beginning, bud," I say as if he can understand.

The battle of wills goes on for two weeks. Clay is surviving mostly on fruits and vegetables. He needs more protein in his diet, but he won't touch any of the chicken tenders that I prepare.

I go to McDonald's and ask for an empty chicken nuggets box. I secretly place my newly baked GFCF chicken nuggets inside and hand them to Clay. He opens the box, takes one look at them, and screams. Then one by one, he throws them onto the floor and, for the grand finale, gives the entire box a swift swipe with his right hand. I watch as it lands on the floor upside down. "Well, then, little man," I say. "I guess you didn't like those." Damn. Now what? I thought my tricks were clever, but I guess they weren't clever enough to outsmart him. I have to admit this is a lot harder than I thought, and I thought it would be pretty hard.

I vow to persist.

Four weeks later, something incredible happens. I make him the GFCF French toast for breakfast that I have made him every morning for the last month. I'm not holding my breath this time. But I watch bug-eyed as he picks up a piece, puts it in his mouth, and starts chewing.

Keep it down, keep it down, I coach him silently in my head.

I watch him take a drink and see his tiny Adam's apple bob up and down.

"You swallowed it! You swallowed it! You did it! Wahoo!" I'm running around the room spinning in circles. I unbuckle him from his highchair and toss him into the air shouting, "Clay, you did it! You did it! You ate your French toast!" I turn on the music and we celebrate by dancing around the room. I blow raspberries on his belly as he giggles incessantly. Clay absorbs all the attention with a pleased expression. I put him back in his chair and he takes another bite, watching me the entire time to see what I'm going to do. He knows it's out of my element to go crazy, and I think he likes it. He looks at me as if to say, "Do it again." So I do it again. And again. And again. His tray is soon empty. I'm glad because I'm not sure how much longer I can carry on like a lunatic. I collapse on the couch and hug him tightly. "I'm so proud of you, honey. I know it was hard for you. But you did it."

It is a triumphant victory—the first of many to come. One meal down, lots to go.

I call my neighbor the next day to tell her the news. Her son, Cody, is Clay's age.

"It's a great day, Jackie. Sometimes it's the small things that mean the most, you know? This morning…"

"Did you hear that?" she interrupts.

"Hear what?"

"Can you hear Cody?"

"No. What's he saying?"

"He's saying his ABC's."

"What?" I ask. "Really?"

"He's been walking around the house saying all of his ABC's. And…get this…he started peeing in the toilet! Can you believe it?"

"Oh, wow. You must be so happy," I say, flatly. My excitement over the French toast episode melts into a kaleidoscope of stewing emotions as she continues to talk about her walking encyclopedia.

The chicken nuggets and pancakes are a harder sell, but over the course of another month, Clay is eating those as well.

Eight weeks into the special diet, I wake up one morning and look over at the clock—6:30 a.m. My heart starts to race, thumping in my throat.

I lean over and whisper, "Sean, did you hear Clay wake up last night?"

"No, did you?"

"No," I say, almost out of breath. Moving faster than I ever have this early in the morning, I get tangled in the sheets, tripping out of bed. I race to Clay's room. I lightly press my face against the small crack in his door. I can see him sleeping on his stomach, his back slightly rising and falling as he breathes. His legs are crossed and his rear end is in the air. This is the first time Clay has ever slept through the night. *Ever!* Maybe it's a fluke. I try to protect myself by not getting too giddy, in case it's just a coincidence. The next morning the same thing happens…and the next morning…and the next.

Sean and I haven't slept this well since before Clay was born.

Chapter 14

It's September, two months since we started the ABA program. A routine has been established. The instructor arrives at 9:00 a.m. and works with Clay until 11:00 a.m. I put Clay down for his nap around noon, and he starts his next session at 3:00 p.m. and ends at 5:00 p.m.

Sometimes it's bothersome having people in our home constantly. I think of our home as a sanctuary from the outside world, a place where I can be myself. But I've become an expert at putting on a façade—acting happy, being talkative and friendly around the instructors, even when much of the time I'm really feeling overloaded and pressed for time. Each day, as soon as the front door closes after the last session, I breathe a heavy sigh of relief. I can finally be me.

In a way, I really miss Clay when he's in sessions. He's with the instructors for four hours a day. I wonder if he'll eventually grow more attached to them than to me. After all, what I want most is for him to really connect with me as his mom, and not some mechanism to satisfy all of his wants and needs. At the same time, I feel relieved that I am free to run an errand at a moment's notice or go see a friend without worrying about Clay's behavior. Though I spend enormous amounts of time reviewing tape and managing our program, it's somehow more rewarding than holding a crying, needy toddler day after day, and finding constant failure in my inability to soothe him. At last I feel productive, even empowered. I finally seem to have a small amount of control over our lives.

"Come here," says Andy one day. Clay runs and sits down on the chair. Andy touches her index fingers together at the tips, pointing at one another. "Cut the pickle. Tickle, tickle!" she shouts as she tickles him all over. It pleases me to see him obey a simple command. Andy logs her notes at the end of the session. I notice Clay has lined up all the shapes from the shape sorter according to shape—four triangles, next to four squares, next to four circles.

Clay is excited to see me during the break, then cries and tantrums when it's time to go back to work. Trisha peels his limbs from my body, eventually wedging him free. His hands grab frantically in the air as he disappears into the room. It takes all my strength and willpower to hold myself back and not intervene. I reassure myself—someday he'll be old enough to know that this is an act of love.

Andy arrives in the morning with a bag of new reinforcers. She bounces in the kitchen to show me her new stash. She pulls out paper plates in the shape and appearance of animal puppets, and a flute. I laugh as she demonstrates her prowess at playing the small plastic instrument. I'm pleased at her creative efforts to motivate him.

"Clay will love them. Thanks for always thinking of ways to make the sessions more exciting, Andy. You're perfect for this job," I comment, remembering the day she came to interview with us. I shake my head, thinking about the comment her reference made to Sean on the telephone. "You won't regret hiring Andy." How right she was.

Later that day, a package arrives on our doorstep. It's the cod-liver oil that I ordered a week or so ago. It's one of the supplements Dr. Jepson recommended we give to Clay. I decide to add it to Clay's supplement cocktail. As evening approaches, so does the sick feeling in my stomach. Evening means supplements, and over two months later it's still a fight to get Clay to take them. I put on my apron and latex gloves, feeling like a soldier preparing for battle, and march the syringe filled with orange, grainy liquid up to Clay's bedroom where he and Sean are waiting. We lay Clay down and he starts to scream. I'm just about to squirt the vitamins into his mouth when he shouts what sounds like, "Buzz!" Sean and I look at each other, cautiously enthusiastic.

"Did you hear that? Did he just say 'Buzz'?" I say to Sean.

I wonder if I imagined it because I want it so bad. Besides, "Doh" is the only word he ever says!

"That's what I heard!" Sean says.

"Wow, Clay, you just said 'Buzz'!" I follow his eyes to where he is looking, and there I see his Buzz Lightyear toy. I instantly give it to him to hold as I tickle him and wrestle with him on the floor. "You did it!" Our eyes lock together, happiness spilling from both of us.

The next morning, I brush Clay's body in preparation for our last day at the Kids On The Move playgroup. Clay's inter-action with other kids has become limited because Kids On The Move has increased the amount of time we spend doing "The Learning Box," their version of ABA. It significantly cuts into the playgroup time, so I decide our hours are better spent with our ABA program.

Karen greets me as I round the corner and walk into the room.

"Leeann, come with me for a minute."

Clay and I follow her down the hall and into a different room. There are kids playing with toys, and some are even talking.

"What's this?" I ask.

"This is where the speech therapy class meets. I think Clay is ready to join this group."

"Really?" I say, trying not to let too much excitement escape.

"He's able to attend now, and even say several words. Being with these children will help push him further in the right direction." Karen says. The light glistens in her eyes.

"Great. Okay."

I hear someone say, "Time for snacks." The children rush to line up at the long white table and sit in the blue plastic chairs. The woman who works at Kids On The Move sets a muffin on a napkin in front of each child. I take from my purse Clay's gluten- and casein-free pretzels and set them on the table in front of him. The mom at the end of the table stares at Clay's food. At the end of snack time, she approaches me.

"I noticed that you brought snacks from home for your son," she says.

"Yes. He's intolerant to wheat and milk products."

"Does he have celiac disease?"

"No. My son was diagnosed with autism several months ago, and the diet has really helped him."

"My son, Jacob," she points to a stringy-haired child, his bangs almost covering his eyes, "is speech delayed. My husband has celiac disease. So most everything I cook for him is gluten free. Look, if you ever need some help...you know...cooking for your son, call me. I've been doing it a lot of years." She fishes in her purse and pulls out a pen and an old receipt. She flips it over, and scribbles her name and phone number, then slides it across the table. "Leslie. My name is Leslie."

"I really appreciate that, Leslie," I say, ripping off the bottom part of the receipt, then jotting my contact information. "I'm Leeann." I slide my paper to her and smile.

Drew is in the family room playing with his construction vehicles. There's a tiny knock at the front door. The door opens slightly and Trisha peeks in and says "Hello?"

"Oh, hey, Trish. Come on in."

Drew watches thoughtfully as she walks up the stairs and into the schoolroom.

"Mom," he says, "Why does Clay go up into that room with those girls?"

I'm not sure how to answer his question in a way his four-year-old mind can understand.

"Drew, you know how Clay cries and screams a lot, and can't talk?"

"Yep," Drew nods, looking at me, his eyelashes are long and full. His round cheeks slightly jiggle, as he totters back and forth.

"Clay needs help learning. Those girls that spend time with him in that room are teaching him how to talk and learn so that he can be a big boy like you some day."

"Oh," he says, resuming play with his trucks again. "Can I go up there and play with them?"

My heart aches.

"Not this time, Drew. When he is a little older you can. Hey, betcha can't get me!" I scream and run outside as he chases me out the door.

Later that afternoon, I go up into our bedroom to watch the session through the video feed. Trisha is doing a Verbal Imitation sitting with him. "Say 'Baah,'" says Trisha. "Bayaah," Clay responds in his high-pitched, sing-song voice. He's beginning to imitate sounds, and is starting to learn how to chain those sounds into words. It's thrilling to watch, yet excruciating at the same time. It's been such a slow, tedious process. I continually remind myself that we can't build a house without first pouring the foundation.

Shortly after Clay's session ends, I hear the pitter-patter of his bare feet on the kitchen floor. I run to him and twirl him in the air.

"There's my boy!" I say happily. I put him down and he immediately runs to the pantry door.

"Kayaan, kayaan," he says in his slurred, whiny voice. He places his hand on the door and looks up at me briefly. My heart does a somersault. He wants something. I've never heard that word before. I frantically try to decipher what he is saying.

"Great talking, Clay," I shout, buying myself more time.

"Kayaan," I say back to him. I quickly open the pantry door and let him choose whatever he is asking for. He instantly grabs a handful of gluten-free pretzels. I'm puzzled. "Kayaan" doesn't even remotely sound like the word "pretzels." As I sit down to help him put his puzzle together, I remember something. Yesterday, when we were standing by the pantry I asked him if he wanted his crayons. "Crayons" sounds just like "kayaan." His crayons are kept in the schoolroom. Obviously he didn't really want his crayons. He must have just related that particular word to the pantry where we were having our conversation. Smart. Or maybe—normal. While other parents dote over their little "geniuses," I'll take normal any day. There's a little boy in there who is paying attention to every detail, trying to make associations with words. My spirits are lifted. He's making progress.

Drew and Clay have so much energy, getting them to sit on my lap to read a book feels equal to taming a wild bronco. So, I settle for reading to them in the bath each night before bed, where at least they're contained for a short period of time. They have no choice but to sit and listen. That evening I read them the book *Where the Wild Things Are*. I glance at Clay as I read about the terrible monsters gnashing their teeth. He looks at me with his silky-smooth cherubic face, bright blue eyes, and tow head. His cheeks haven't been red for over a month, I remind myself. His complexion is normal. My shoulders loosen. A wave of satisfaction comes over me. The diet, supplements… all of this is helping him! His body looks healthier. After he gets out of the bath I look at his profile. His belly isn't bloated, and he is no longer alternating constipation and diarrhea. His behavior is so much better and he seems to feel better.

It's Sunday, and I'm making lunch in the kitchen while chatting with Sean. For a moment, it seems like we're somewhat of a typical family. I absorb the goodness. No sessions, nobody coming in and out of our home. The boys are coloring at the counter.

"Sean, do you hear that?" I say.

"Hear what?" he replies.

"Exactly. There's no squealing or screeching right now. It's getting a little better, I think."

There's a lull in our conversation. I look over at Clay. There he is. His shining eyes are fixed on my face, not in a staring "I'm in my own little world" way, but really looking at me. I look at him carefully, afraid he might look away. I cautiously move in closer.

"Hi, Clay…sweetie…you're looking at me," I say, my voice quivering. I cover my mouth with my shaking hand. He continues to look me right in the eyes with a look that I have never seen before. His eyebrows crease as he studies my face. It's as if he's seeing me for the very first time. A tear spills down my cheek as we continue to look deep into each other's eyes. I want to capture this moment forever. I cup my hands around his face and kiss him on the forehead. I close my eyes and press my forehead to his.

Later that evening when it's time to give Clay his vitamins, I complete my mixing routine and go up the stairs and into his room. I'm much more confident this evening. He's gaining weight now, and he seems to feel better. His tantrums are tapering off. We're going in the right direction—I can see it! I lay Clay down and hold his arms down. I bring the syringe down by his face. His hand pops up unexpectedly and grabs the syringe out of my fingers. He then shoves it in his mouth, his lips pucker around it like a sucker. I quickly squirt it in. I sit there looking at him in shock and disbelief at what just happened. There is no fight, no battle, not even slight resistance. In fact, he helped me give it to him. I start to laugh.

"Wow, Clay!" I shout. "You did it, buddy!" I whoop and holler, moving his arms up and down to a fake beat. "You did it, you're da man, you rock," I sing.

We giggle together.

Chapter 15

It has been three months since Clay's diagnosis. We go to church this morning, and as I leave the nursery after dropping off Clay, I look up and see a woman walking down the hall. It looks like Brandie. I follow her for several steps until I catch up. She glances over her shoulder.

"Brandie? Hi!" I wonder if she still thinks I'm a jerk. I stand there trying to figure out what to say.

Finally, I start. "I, um, I owe you an apology, and a deep-felt thank you. That day you came and talked to me…"

"Look, I'm sorry I butted in that day…I shouldn't—"

"No. Please." I put my hand up. "You saved me a lot of time, and you were right on. I appreciate you having the courage to approach me. I know I was abrupt, and I'm sorry. You didn't deserve that. You were just trying to help. I couldn't stop thinking about what you said to me that day. I didn't want to accept it, but I finally took Clay to get a diagnosis. We have been able to get an early start on his treatment because of you. You saved us so much time. I'm not sure how to thank you."

"What treatment are you doing?"

"Well, we started an ABA program, and I put Clay on a special diet. We have an appointment tomorrow with Dr. Jepson who will help us treat him biomedically. He's on a bunch of supplements—"

"We tried ABA. Just couldn't get him to respond," she says, slightly defensive.

"Who was your consultant?" I ask.

"We didn't use one. We just did it ourselves." She says. "Also, I don't believe much in the diet stuff. We tried that too. Didn't see much difference."

"How long was he on the diet?" I ask.

"Oh, a week or so. I really just think he was born this way. There's nothing we can do about it."

"Brandie, I just hope you know how grateful I am for you talking to me that day, and I hope we can be friends," I say, before I head for the door.

She smiles.

Later that week Clay struggles when it's time to go into the schoolroom with the instructor. He tantrums at least half of the session. The other half he's controlled by his obsession with lining up objects. I watch as he arranges everything: the cow puzzle piece next to the horse puzzle piece, next to other plastic animals he found somewhere…it never ends. When Natalie moves an object that is part of a "lineup," he falls apart. She redirects him. But, eventually he finds his way back to "the lineup." The redirecting cycle starts once again.

My heart crashes to the bottom of my stomach. What is happening? I haven't added or taken anything away. Nothing. I'm left with an unsettling feeling. The afternoon session seems to go better, but I'm still concerned with the intensity of his morning tantrum. But this becomes my normal pattern. Wherever I am, whatever I'm doing, I overanalyze his behavior. I observe every movement, gesture, or expression. No action of Clay's goes unnoticed. It's persistent and nagging, like I must scrutinize everything he does. If there's any sort of abnormality, I must know what it is so I can try to find some solution for it. I notice other parents who have a child with autism doing the same thing. We can't simply smile and watch our kids—we need to hover over them, watching and waiting for those inappropriate behaviors. We're constant gardeners just waiting for the weed to sprout in our fertile ground so we can hurry and try our newest spray to get rid of it. Every behavior must stem from something, and I must find its solution.

It's Saturday afternoon, and I take a break by going shopping and out to lunch with my mom and two sisters. It feels so nice to get out and socialize. There's no talk of autism, instructors, programs, Clay's future…nothing. In fact, I notice that almost an hour passes where I haven't thought once about anything related to autism.

My mom stops by the house to see the boys before embarking on the long drive home. Drew is thrilled to see her. He jumps right in her lap and starts talking nonstop about every construction vehicle ever made. Whenever she tries to talk, he interrupts with another big story. She looks over at Clay, who is quietly playing with his matchbox cars in the family room. She walks toward him. He doesn't seem to really notice she is there.

"Hi, Clay. It's Nana," she says. "Nana loves you." She kisses his cheek.

He looks her in the eyes for a brief moment. Her eyes float in her tears. They spill over onto her cheeks as she gives him a hug.

"Oh, you're doing so well, kiddo. Keep it up," she whispers.

I suddenly realize how focused I've been on my own grief and so busy trying to figure out ways to help Clay. I haven't spent much time thinking that my mom may also be grieving for her grandson. I see the tenderness in her touch and the softness in her eyes.

Defeat Autism Now! (DAN!) is preparing for their fall conference in San Diego, California. Several of my email groups are abuzz with the latest developments and list of presenters. The moderator compiles a list of attendees from the group. I feel a dire need to attend so that I can hear about the latest biomedical treatments, and also so that I can gain support from others and hopefully get in on some thought-provoking discussions. I need to be there, but I know we can't afford it. Every penny earned goes toward paying for our ABA program, supplements, and special diet ingredients. I wonder how we can make this happen. Over the next few days I brainstorm various ideas. I explore the logistics of holding a fund-raiser.

That evening after the kids are in bed, Sean says, "Lee, I know how bad you want to go to the DAN! conference. It would take so much time and stress to put together a fund-raiser. It would also take time away from helping Clay."

"Sean, I just don't know what else to do. I really want to go."

"Lee, I know. Just listen. Remember the Harrison case? They signed off on it today. We'll be getting at least $500 in up-front commissions."

The prospect of going billows inside of me. But we really need to use the money to pay for Clay's treatment. Our budget is so tight, it doesn't allow for any additional expenses.

"I can't," I say, shaking my head. "We need that money to pay the instructors."

"Lee, either way you look at it, we're using the money to help Clay. Let's worry about paying the instructors when the time comes. Right now, I really think it's important for you to go."

I wrap my arms around him and hold him close. "I couldn't do any of this without your support," I whisper. My lips brush his ear.

I recall our short courtship, then marriage—two very different people from contrasting backgrounds coming together, yet there was something inside each of us that drew us together and pulled us deeply in love. That something continues to burn.

He still teases me relentlessly about when he asked me to marry him. My answer… "I'm scared."

"This isn't exactly the reply I anticipated," he told me while still down on one knee.

"Also," I continued, "I need private time—at least one hour, every day."

He still married me.

Making sure Sean is equipped and briefed on all the supplements, session schedules, and strict gluten and casein meals is akin to writing a build-it-yourself missile guide. I nervously hand him his agenda, totaling five pages in tiny 10-point font.

"Are you sure you're going to be okay?"

"I'll be fine," he says, waving me off.

"Oh, and make sure you don't use the same knife to cut Clay's bread that you use to butter the bread for you and Drew. Also, do you want me to show you how I mix the supplements one more time?"

"Lee, I'll be fine. Just go!"

My palm is sweaty from clutching my small but heavy bag. I walk out of the airport and into the sticky, humid Friday morning in sunny San Diego, California. Leaves from the palm trees reach out and cast a sheltering façade. A passerby brushes my shoulder, leaving me in the wake of the aroma of freshly cut onions. I look down at the blackened curb. I need to get to the resort, but how or where to get a taxi? I grew up in an Idaho town with a population of three thousand. There was one grocery store, one gas station, one four-way stop, and no traffic light. I wait by the curb and observe. Twenty yards away I see a woman with her hand in the air. A yellow taxi whizzes by and screeches to a stop next to her. The driver gets out, takes her luggage, and puts it in his trunk. They drive off. A minute or so goes by before I see another taxi. I put my hand in the air. A gush of oil-laced wind blows into my face and whips through my hair as the taxi barrels past me and down the road. The man standing next to me says, "Like this, ma'am. They've gotta be able to see you." He thrusts his arm out in the air and leans into the road assertively, while yelling, "Taxi!" A yellow cab circles around and comes to a stop next to us. "Thanks," I mutter, avoiding his eyes.

The Town and Country Resort buzzes with parents, researchers, physicians, and hotel employees. The speakers listed in the conference program are from all over the country, many of whom I have read or heard about from books, email lists, research papers, and other parents.

It is a privilege to be here, and I want to soak up all the knowledge I can so that I am better equipped to help Clay. My anxiety level begins to drop as I look around the room at the thousands of people. I'm surrounded by parents just like me—members of the club they were forced to join. They have some of the same fears, concerns, and thoughts as I do. I may be here alone, but I am among friends who are fighting the same battle. Some of them are even laughing—letting loose and having a good time. I want to get to that point. I want to be able to let myself go in the moment, and not feel the pain afterward reminding me of the great tasks that lie ahead.

The lights dim as Dr. Sidney Baker walks up to the podium. He begins talking about the DAN! movement and how it originated. When the next speaker takes the podium, I begin to feel extremely light-headed. I close my eyes, and open them again. I'm spinning around in my chair. My cheeks feel clammy. The room becomes speckled with black splotches. Afraid I will pass out, I quickly exit and search for a restroom. The only one available has a line out the door and into the hallway. I quickly sit down and put my head between my legs.

"Are you all right?" I hear a woman's voice ask above me.

"Yes, fine, thanks," I fib.

I think it through. I have to get back to my hotel room. But, I'm not sure I can make it without passing out, despite the fact that it's not very far away. I walk briskly, taking intermittent breaks to hang my head between my legs. About halfway there, everything begins turning black, and I fall into a bench. I awaken several minutes later, disoriented as to where I am. I reach for my cell phone. I grapple with calling Sean because I don't want to worry him. But I'm afraid that I'll continue to feel faint, and I don't know anyone here at the conference.

"Sean, I just passed out in the hotel lobby. I'm not sure what's going on."

"What? Stay where you are, I'll call for help."

"I think I'm okay...hello?"

Dial tone.

Eventually, two armed security guards find me and escort me back to my room.

"I'll call for a taxi to take you to the ER, ma'am," the man says.

I quickly say, "No, no, really, I'll be fine."

I know we don't have enough money for me to go to the hospital. All of our money needs to go toward treatment.

"Uh, ma'am? Ma'am?" I faintly hear the man say.

The room around me fades in and out of blackness.

"You really ought to see a doctor," I hear someone else say. I do, days later, and it turns out I have severe iron deficiency anemia. He recommends blood transfusions, but I opt for the less expensive iron pills. Until then, though, I'm forced to struggle through on my own.

"Why? Why is this happening? I *need* to be here," I say as if someone were there with me. "I can't miss this…"

I wake up the next morning feeling groggy, but better. I look at the green numbers on the digital clock next to me. I have been asleep for over ten hours. I'm still weak and light-headed, but I feel well enough to attend the conference. As long as I remain sitting, I seem to feel fine.

I hang on every word of the presentations. I take frantic notes to ensure I don't miss anything, and so it makes sense when I review it again later. The gluten- and casein-free diet is spoken about in detail. I hear about glutathione (the body's main intracellular antioxidant), PANDAS (an autoimmune disorder triggered by a streptococcal infection), mitochondrial dysfunction, the role of omega-3s and mood disorders, chelation, proper nutrition and vitamin supplementation, gastrointestinal health, and much, much more. A couple of the speakers discuss case studies from some of their patients. Many sound like they have symptoms and behaviors very similar to Clay's. I listen intently to each treatment plan administered and the outcome of that child's situation.

By the end of the day, I'm exhausted and have an enormous headache. I go to the lobby of the conference center and sit down in a chair to review my notes. I'm halfway through the first page, when I get interrupted.

"Hello," a woman says. It startles me.

"Hello," I say smiling. I continue reading.

"Do you have a child with autism?" she asks. I'm not really feeling conversational after a long day and large headache, but I want to be polite.

"Yes, I do," I say, still looking down at my notes. I squeeze my pen. Ridiculous, but it's still difficult for me to say that out loud.

"I have two sons with autism," she replies.

I look up from my paper.

"Some days are tough, but we all make it through somehow. It's those small moments that mean the most…the look in my son's eyes when he briefly looks into mine and we connect. The days he takes my hand in his. The smile he has on his face when he discovers something new."

I look at her thoughtfully. I can see happiness in her eyes, which seems to shroud her pain.

"I draw on those moments to help me make it through the tougher days," she adds.

I nod thoughtfully.

"Sometimes I feel such a void. Like there's a faulty connection, or a short of some sort, and I'm scrambling to find which wires to connect so I can see that light again."

The light shines off the tears filling her eyes.

Trying to avoid any more emotion, I quickly say, "How are your sons doing?"

"Well, Rob is eight years old, and severely autistic. He is unable to communicate well and is aggressive. Keith is my ten-year-old. And he is doing amazingly well. He has an aide attend class with him, but is able to function mostly on his own. Ask him anything about space and space travel and you will not be able to get rid of him. Having both boys with autism—it's been difficult on our marriage. My husband left us after Rob was diagnosed. But we're okay. We just do the best we can."

I feel my own sorrow and pain become diluted as I listen to this woman talk about her life. I anguish for her struggles. I admire her determination and motivation despite her grim situation. Her courage and optimism are infectious. I realize that our situation could be much worse.

"What's your name?" I ask her.

"Laura," she replies. "I'm from Canada."

I feel like I have an instant connection with this woman— after only talking with her for a few minutes it feels like I've known her for years.

"I'm Leeann. I'm from Utah."

"Best wishes for you and your family," she says, getting up to leave.

"Wait," I say, motioning to her with my hand. "Thank you. Thank you for talking with me."

Dr. Sidney Baker's first slide reads, "The First Tack's Law: If you're sitting on a tack, it takes a lot of aspirin to make it feel good. Tack-sitting remedy is tack removal. Second Tack's Law: If you are sitting on two tacks…removing one does not result in a 50 percent improvement. Chronic illness is, or becomes, multifactorial."

Yes, we have to get at the root of autism if we are to have any type of positive response. And, yes, again, autism is very complex. It appears to involve so many factors and body systems. The metabolic systems of each individual are so unique. Kids respond to the same treatments differently, sometimes even opposite to one another. It's daunting, but I'm with people who understand, and who can help make a difference in the lives of our children. Suddenly my energy rushes back.

Now, it's time to put everything I learned into action. I feel like a colicky horse at the start of a race, ready to jump the gate once the shot is fired.

As I review my notes on the airplane, it's clear that the next treatment that I want to try is chelation, the extraction of heavy metals. Clay has been on the GFCF diet for a couple of months, we have treated him for gut dysbiosis by giving him Diflucan (antifungal) and Flagyl (antimicrobial), and he has been on a solid supplement regimen. I'm ready to do more. I want no regrets.

The chelation schedule Dr. Jepson suggests is three days on and eleven days off. We begin the next weekend. The chelation prescription DMSA, or brand name Chemet, comes in capsules with little tiny balls the size of a pinhead. I put the balls into the syringe and add a little pear juice. I shake it up, and squirt it into his mouth every eight hours. As the midnight dosage approaches, I take the liquid-filled syringe that smells of rotten eggs into Clay's dark room. I brush his damp hair from his forehead. I lean over the railing on his crib and kiss his warm cheek.

"Clay, we can do this. Keep fighting."

Chapter 16

I hear Drew's laughing fit through the open kitchen window as he wrestles with Sean outside on the trampoline. I peer through the aspen leaves on the branches that block a portion of my view. Clay is screaming from the ground, wanting to get up.

"Dow, dow," he yells. Then he pauses as if to remember the correct words.

"Uh, uh," he says.

Sean hoists Clay up onto his back and they bounce over and over, with Clay laughing in delight. I walk outside to join the fun. Clay gets off the trampoline, runs to the swing set, and climbs into his airplane swing. He pounds the front of the swing with his hand and squeals for someone to push him. Drew gets into his swing and mimics Clay. Sean stands in front of the boys' swings and lets them pretend to kick him over. He lets out a dramatic grunt and falls to the ground as their feet swing near his body. The boys laugh and squeal with delight. Sean lies on the grass; his body isn't moving. "Do it again, Dad!" screams Drew. His smile is so big his cheeks make his eyes squinty. Sean remains motionless on the grass.

Clay climbs out of his swing while it is still swinging. He falls to the ground, gets back up, and runs to Sean and pats his back. He tries to open his eyes with his fingers.

"Uh, uh," he says.

Did he come over to see if Sean was all right?

Sean looks over at me in disbelief. "Did you see that?" he asks.

"Wow, that's fantastic!" I shout. "He cared enough to see if you were okay."

Sean tries to re-create the situation. He lies on the ground again, and Drew runs over to him. "Wake up, Dad, wake up!" Drew calls. Clay's swing has stopped, and he is playing in the sandbox, totally unaware that Sean is lying on the ground again.

"Well, maybe we just got lucky for a minute," I say.

We see glimpses of progress—some big, some small. Sometimes we never see it again. Other times it becomes a permanent part of his progression. It is like a piece of gold in the water. When the sun is positioned just right, it catches the metallic color and glistens so that we can see it. Otherwise, it looks like just another rock on the bottom of the riverbed.

That afternoon Drew and I blow bubbles on the back porch. "Mom, why can't Clay talk?"

"Well, sweetie," I begin before I really even know what I'm going to say. I know autism is way too big for a four-year-old to fully grasp, and I don't want him running around telling everyone he knows, or doesn't know, that his brother has autism.

"You know how Trisha, Andy, and Natalie come every day?"

"Yeah," he says pursing his lips to blow another bubble.

"Tricia, Andy, and Natalie are helping Clay to learn how to talk and how to learn so that he will be happier."

"Oh," he says, squinting as he watches a bubble float upward, then pop before it disappears into the sky.

"Let's see who can blow the biggest bubble," I say.

Since Clay has been functioning at a nine- to twelve-month-old level even though he is two years old, we're slowly progressing chronologically through what a typical baby would do from the nine-month age forward. He is babbling, making sounds, and trying to form words for certain objects.

"Do this," Andy says one day as she places the block into the bucket, and then pats the top of her head with her hand. Clay places the block in the bucket, then pats his head with both hands. Andy prompts his other hand down.

"Do this," she says, again showing him what to do.

He was looking out the window when she gave the instruction.

"Nope. Do this," she says again.

This time he plunks down the block in the bucket, but forgets to pat his head.

"Pretty good," she says, flatly. Clay becomes frustrated and screeches as he lunges for the bucket. He grabs it with both hands. Andy pries the bucket away, and Clay's squeals grow louder.

"Do this," she says, bringing the tips of her two pointer fingers together for a compliance drill. Clay follows along. "Good job, Clay," she praises.

"Do this," she says, touching her nose. Clay touches his nose.

"Good, Clay!" she shouts. "That's much better! Give me ten," she requests while holding up her hands. Clay tries to give her ten, but she moves her hands. "Whoop!" she says, laughing and tickling his armpits.

"Give me ten," she says, moving her hands back as he tries to slap them. Clay squeals with delight. The next time she asks him to put the block in the bucket and then pat his head, he does it perfectly.

Searching for help for my son has become an obsession. Am I doing enough for him? What if there is something out there

I'm not familiar with that might really help him? My fears are driving me to find answers: fear of choosing the wrong treatment methods, fear that Clay may never call me Mom, fear that we may never really know our son, fear that I have somehow caused this to happen, fear of...failure.

Being busy helps to quell my fears. But it also burrows me further into isolation. The phone never rings anymore unless it's a physician's office or an instructor. My friends have stopped calling. I don't call them either. Don't they understand that this is what I must fully commit myself to do? I don't need anybody outside our family. *I can do this myself,* I argue—trying to feel better. But am I purposefully shutting myself off from the outside world so that I won't have to face the hurt...the hurt I feel from watching typical children interact with their mothers? Could it be that I truly can't relate well to others anymore?

The next Sunday at church, we sit in the very back row—to provide a quick exit if needed. We have recently started attending again as a family. Our attendance has been spotty since Clay's behaviors became so disruptive. It feels good to be here together, and it signifies Clay is making progress. The organ starts to hum. My mouth is moving to the words of the hymn we are singing. I look at Clay. My voice hangs on the last word in the verse.

"Shoe, shoe!" I hear him say. His mouth breaks into a smile as he grabs the toe of his brown loafer.

I grab him and put him on my lap.

"Clay, great talking! Yes, shoe," I say excitedly as I reach down and touch my shoe. "My shoe!"

"Cacar," he says. Smiling proudly, like a doting mother, I quickly reach into the diaper bag and pull out a gluten- and casein-free cracker and hand it to him. My smile doesn't disappear until it is wiped out completely by a tiny voice coming from the row in front of us. "Mama, I go potty."

As I look toward the voice, I recognize the two-year-old child as our neighbor, Jayce.

"Mama, go potty," he says again.

"Wait just a minute, Jayce!" she whispers loudly.

"Airpane," he says as he touches her face. He picks up his toy airplane and begins flying it in the air.

I'm immediately thrust back into the realization that our journey will be long, and this is just the beginning. I have to be grateful for every small step, I remind myself. No matter how much I wish it were true, Clay is not going to wake up one day and be cured.

Sean notices me staring at this child. He reaches over and puts his arm around me and pulls me in close to him. I miss him. We are both so busy going in our own directions—he's working long hours to provide for the enormous costs of Clay's treatment. My time is spent managing the program and trying to help Drew feel included. I hope he understands why I have to put so much time into doing all I can to help Clay, especially during this crucial window of time. Though our paths are headed toward the same destination, I wish we could spend more time traveling together.

The telephone rings.

"Hi, Nora! What's going on?" I say excitedly. I've never met Nora in person, but we have been in contact through the Utah Biomedical email group. She has a five-year-old son with autism.

"Hey listen, Leeann, I was able to schedule a meeting with Senator Orrin Hatch's top health and education aides regarding the upcoming legislation on IDEA (Individuals with Disabilities Education Act). Can you come to a planning meeting we are having Thursday night? I'd like you to share your story with them, if you don't mind. You know, about the program you're running and the progress Clay has made," she says.

Excitement swirls through my body. "Let me see what I can do. I would really like to be there. Whatever it takes to make a bold statement and to try and get more help for our children. What a fantastic opportunity. We need to make sure we are prepared for this."

On a Thursday night in November, at least a dozen of us parents gather in an empty conference room. As we begin brainstorming, a mom raises her hand. "I think we need to compile photos of our children in a three-ring binder and present it to them to personalize this meeting."

We all nod in agreement.

"Yes," I add, "we also need to share our individual stories and attach it to the back of the photos. We need to make this real to them and frankly share with them the devastation it causes. Make sure you include financial sacrifices, emotional turmoil, and anything else you feel would bring it closer to home. We can't let this opportunity get lost in the moment. We need to make a lasting impression."

Nora makes assignments to various participants. "Daniel, will you give an overview of autism, including diagnosis, treatment options, expenses, etc. Leeann, will you share your personal story with them? I think it will really make an impact, especially since Clay has made so much progress already. "Sure," I say, energy pumps through my body, "anything to spread awareness."

Four weeks later on a cold evening in December, I run up the hundreds of steps to the Capitol building, checking the contents of my bag for the third time to make sure I have all my presentation materials. The crisp air penetrates my white blouse. I wish I had worn a coat. I'm excited. I'm nervous. My stomach burns. I want them to understand. But can they really understand, without having walked in our shoes? Probably not, I tell myself. But at least we'll do our best to give them a snapshot into our lives.

We file into a small room with cubicle-style walls and a chalkboard. Padded folding chairs line the perimeter. Eventually, the two aides come in and take their seats behind a table. They seem eager and willing to listen. Nora stands. She introduces herself and those of us in attendance.

"We are here today on behalf of our children with autism," she begins. "We appreciate your willingness to meet with us and hear our concerns. In regards to the upcoming IDEA legislation, we would ask that you take into account what we are about to share with you. Having a child with autism presents unique challenges. Ensuring our autistic children get appropriate intervention is crucial to their success. We ask that this evening as you listen to our stories, our presentations, that you will gain an understanding of our needs and you will share what you've felt and learned with Senator Hatch. First, Daniel Clark will give an overview of autism."

Daniel clears his throat several times as he steps forward. Holding his paper out in front of him, he begins reading in a stern, baritone-rich voice.

"This is exactly what IDEA stipulates that the school district should provide—and I quote, 'special education and related services designed to meet their unique needs and prepare them for employment and independent living.' The process for us has been very expensive, time-consuming, stressful, occasionally discouraging, and sometimes lonely. But never once did we doubt that we were doing the right thing for our child. This was the 'appropriate' education that our child, and every other child with autism, should have the opportunity to receive."

He continues, "In 1987, the nation was captivated when an eighteen-month-old girl in Midland, Texas, whom we came to know as 'Baby Jessica,' fell into and was trapped near the bottom of a backyard well for fifty-eight hours. The community and nation rallied around the efforts to save this little girl. Her faint and tiny voice could barely be heard by parents and rescue workers, and it was difficult to guess how badly she'd been injured. As they formulated a plan to rescue her, she continued to slip farther down the narrow pipe. Heroic efforts were made to drill a twenty-nine-foot tunnel in order to ultimately rescue her. Many people across the United States wept openly with relief when she was finally pulled to safety.

"Our small children with autism are likewise stuck in a deep well of noncommunication and emotional distance, and many are slipping farther away from us. The disorder is frequently noticed at around eighteen to thirty months, and their faint and tiny voices grow more distant over the passing months when no action is taken. Their parents are crying out desperately for help—they know that many of these children can be saved with the right services. But their cries for help frequently go unheeded—nobody is heroically coming to their rescue. The school districts and insurance companies offer little assistance, while local, state, and even the federal governments look the other way."

I want to stand up and start cheering and clapping, maybe throwing in a couple cartwheels or a flip. I settle for doing the electric guitar in my head.

Daniel goes on, "The good news is that there are effective ways, both behaviorally and medically, to treat the disorder of autism. The solution lies in getting adequate federal funding for research and education, and ensuring minimum treatment standards at the state level."

Next, Laurie Jepson reads a statement from her husband, Dr. Jepson. It is powerful and to the point.

Nora looks at me. It's my turn. Strangely, my anxiety eases, as I walk to the middle of the room and put my VHS tape into the VCR.

"Ms. Shipp and Ms. Patt," I begin, addressing the aides, "our goal is not to cry on your busy shoulders because of our various predicaments, but rather to present the facts—financial, medical, and educational—that encompass autism spectrum disorders, and their impact on our state. But please understand that a significant amount of information is personal—even research from nationally respected organizations and government entities—because it is derived from the lives of individuals and families who face this daunting situation.

"To begin, I will show you one example of a two-year-old with an autism spectrum disorder. This was filmed in July— during a two-day initial kick-off as we began our in-home, intense behavioral therapy program. Please understand that the professional consultant is simply trying to get our son to obey a request to sit down in a chair. The response is identical to the response that we, as his parents, received whenever we tried to get our son to sit in his car seat, stroller, grocery cart, bench at church, and any other typical daily activity."

I press play on the VCR and turn up the volume. Clay is screaming as Sarah tries to get him to sit in the chair. I look away. It's hard for me to watch. As I scan the room, I see a familiar pain in each parent's eyes—some even nodding. I let it play for at least a minute, though it seems like an hour. I press pause.

"It doesn't matter if I rewind or fast-forward; the footage is the same—for two straight days, several hours each day. This persisted for the first week or so, to varying degrees.

Our son used to tantrum for approximately 60 percent of his waking hours, at times banging his head on the floor. When Kids On The Move, the state's early childhood intervention program, first came to our home to evaluate our son, prior to this footage, they were shocked at the duration and intensity of his screaming. After a few months, they confessed that they could not provide the level of help that our son needed.

"Now, let me show you a video we taped of some therapy sessions last week, approximately six months later, with our same child."

I press play. As I hear Clay's tiny voice over the television speakers, I'm overwhelmed with emotion. My throat closes off. I manage to compose myself enough to say, "This is after only six months of his behavioral intervention program. His tantrums have improved markedly. He went from almost no words to a vocabulary of nearly a dozen words. He constructs puzzles designed for kids twice his age. He is only two and a half years old. The other day, I watched him laugh with his older brother. It's been a long time since I've seen his smile. We feel like we're slowly getting our little boy back.

"Before, I never would have dreamed this to be achievable in years, let alone in several months. But, statistically, for children who are involved in this form of intense behavioral intervention, approximately 50 percent are eventually mainstreamed with children their age, and are indistinguishable from their peers. In other words, they are no longer diagnosed as autistic. This is the great news—substantiated treatments exist for children with autism-related disorders. The bad news—they are neither covered by insurance, nor by the state of Utah, and most families cannot afford the treatment. I plead with you to please help us get our children back. Thank you for your time." Clapping emerges from the room. I go to the other side of the room and sit in my chair, still breathing heavily, my chest moving like ocean waves from nervousness coupled with passion.

As I go toward the door on my way out, I feel a tap on my shoulder. I turn around, face-to-face with Hatch's aides.

"Do you have an extra copy of this video?" one of them asks, pointing to the video in my hand. "We would like to show it to Senator Hatch."

"Absolutely," I say. "Please take this one." I hand them the VHS tape and watch them silently walk out the door in their business suits and high heels, wondering if it will really make a difference.

The next week, my parents come to town for another visit. Drew jumps into Grandpa's arms, perching his small rear end on Grandpa's belly. We stand by the kitchen counter and visit while Grandpa tussles with the boys in the living room. My mother brings out her highly anticipated grocery sack full of fun games for Drew and Clay, and chocolate for Sean. The boys start running around in the living room, causing a lot of commotion. I start to tell them to be quiet when I see my dad hop up out of his chair, run across the room, and sit down in a different chair.

"We better go see what in the world is going on in there," I say to my mom. Just then, I hear Papa yell, "Trade chairs!" Immediately he, Drew, and Clay run around the room squealing, and giggling while scrambling for a chair. My mom and I look at each other, then back at them. I watch Clay throw his head back into the air and laugh as he runs around the room diving into the closest couch or chair. His grin is fixed through the entire game. Then, I hear Clay shout, "Trey char." He scrambles up and runs across the room, plopping down in a different chair.

"He gets it," I say. But I'm unsure if any sound escapes from my mouth.

Chapter 17

Clay beats me in our race to the front door. I reach for the knob, and he takes my hand and moves it away. In his squeaky high-pitched voice he says, "No, okay." His little hand reaches toward the doorknob and grasps it. He looks back at me, then back to the door, turns the knob, pushes the door open, and walks into the house. I hear the telephone ringing. I rush to answer it, the bag of groceries swinging wildly at my side.

"Oh, hi, Leslie." I am delighted it's someone other than a physician, consultant, or instructor. "How are you and Jacob doing?" I ask, remembering her kindness when we first met during snack time at Kids On The Move in September.

"We're all right," she replies. "He's started picking at his face, though. He does it so much it is leaving scabs all over."

"Oh, Leslie, I'm sorry."

"We recently had an appointment with a pediatric neuro-psychologist."

"Really? What did you find out?" I ask.

"She diagnosed him with PDD, pervasive development disorder."

"Oh, Leslie, I'm…"

"No, it will be fine. She said he'll need a little speech therapy, and to get my name on the waiting list for the autism preschool sponsored by the school district."

I can't believe what I'm hearing. *A little speech therapy? A waiting list? This isn't early, intensive treatment.*

"Leslie, look, if you need help setting up an ABA program,

I have everything you need. You can share all of our materials. I really think it will help him."

"We're okay. But thanks for the offer."

I start to say something, but stop, then start again. "Just think about it? Please?"

"Sure. Hey, listen, I'm going to be assembling some gluten- and casein-free mixes for Jacob. I decided to take out casein as well to see if it helps him to stop picking. Would you like to join me? You can take some home and try them out."

"That would be a huge help. I'm sure Clay is getting tired of the few bland selections of GFCF foods that I know how to make."

Just then, I catch a glimpse of Clay spinning around the living room, his eyes on the ceiling, his arms straight out. I immediately feel like I just ate something rotten.

"Gotta run, Leslie. I'll see you soon." I set the receiver on the counter.

"No," I say to Clay. But Clay keeps spinning until he falls down. He gets up and starts twirling around again.

I go to him and playfully tackle him onto the couch. "Whatcha doin,' kiddo? Ya tryin' to dance? Well, come on then!"

I turn on the music, and we glide across the family room. I hold him tight against me. "Stay with me now," I whisper in his ear.

Since Clay is in therapy for four hours each day, and Drew goes to preschool three days per week, I manage to find some time to give back a bit. I drive to Dr. Jepson's clinic and volunteer for a couple of hours, usually visiting with new patients, helping to provide support, and answering basic questions. After one particularly busy day, Dr. Jepson calls me into his office and asks if I will serve as the co-chair for the Education Committee of the Children's Biomedical Center, his nonprofit organization. I am thrilled, but hesitant, wondering what kind of time commitment it will require. I want to make sure I am dedicating most of my time to helping Clay first. Then, I'm instantly reminded of the commitment I made to help others when we started.

"I understand, Leeann. Just do what you feel like you can do."

"What responsibilities will I have?" I ask, hoping to get a bigger picture.

"You will be working with individuals and organizations in helping them to understand what biomedical treatment options are available to kids with autism."

"Sure, I'll do it," I tell him as my stomach leaps with the thought of helping others in the club.

Our committee starts holding support group meetings at the biomedical center, the local music store recital hall, and the neighborhood Wild Oats, a health food store. I also begin work on an ongoing project of compiling autism resources into one comprehensive manual. Sean joins the fund-raising committee of the nonprofit and is involved with helping to organize a fund-raiser. Through this we become acquainted with many wonderful folks in the autism community.

Drew and Clay sit on the barstools at the kitchen counter, drawing with their colored pencils. Their feet swing back and forth, thumping the board beneath the counter in perfect sync. I set out bread on the paper plates sitting next to them for the ham sandwiches we're having for lunch. I hum along to the violin in "Bach" by Vanessa Mae, one of Clay's favorite dance songs. I open the refrigerator and reach for the ham. "Mom," I hear a tiny, high-pitched voice say. My body is bent over with my head still in the fridge. I stop humming. I might have stopped breathing. I slowly rise, until my eyes are peering over the refrigerator door. I don't trust my ears.

"Mom," Clay says again, looking directly at me. He's holding out his cup.

The simple word I have strained to hear over years of unforgiving silence cleanses me of any pain I am feeling, replacing it with a triumphant joy so overcoming that I'm paralyzed, afraid if I move it won't be real. My eyes gape open with emotion, staring as if trying to take in every feeling my sensory system is experiencing. Time ceases to exist. I capture the song playing behind me, the light coming through the window, the look on his face, his sweet voice.

He called me Mom and meant it. As powerful as an electric shock, a jolt of energy surges through my entire being. I take his cup and walk backward to the sink. Still fixed on him, I fill it to the top and set it on the counter. He sips at it, slurping, his eyes peering over the top.

"Clay!" I finally say, holding my arms out. "You called me Mom!"

Drew echoes in the background. "Clay, you said Mom! You said Mom!"

I lift Clay up off the stool and put him on my hip. I reach out and take Drew's hand. I turn up the music and we dance around in the kitchen—free and uninhibited. Nothing else matters. I put Clay down and wipe the tears from my eyes. I see my reflection in the toaster and see that my mascara has bled onto my cheeks. I snatch Drew's and Clay's hands and pull them in for a quick huddle. Our heads bunch together and my arms are around them.

"Do you guys know how much I love you?" Drew nods his head. I pull them in close, hugging and kissing them at the same time. Our cheeks squeeze together. We dance some more. Clay bounces up and down on my hip smiling and giggling.

"Mom," he says again as he puts his hands up to his face.

February 2003. We visit Dr. Jepson to discuss further treatment options. To any bystander, our conversation must have sounded like we were talking in secret code.

"What do you think about TTFD or Allithiamine?" I ask. We just completed round seven of DMSA chelation. "Is it too much to chelate him with DMSA and boost his glutathione? Does it cross the blood-brain barrier?"

"We don't know exactly how it works—we do know that it has a sulfate and methyl group in there and thiamine, which is B-1, which does cross the BBB and can help heal the neurons. But where it actually goes across and chelates the metals, we just don't know yet. It does seem to either chelate or allow your body to chelate, because you do get metals out—for some, it chelates better than DMSA," Dr. Jepson answers.

"What about NAC?" I ask. "Is this too much to add at once?"

"I'm starting to think that NAC is the way to go because of my experience as an ER doctor giving it to patients who need to increase their glutathione. It actually boosts glutathione more than a glutathione supplement itself. The mercury paper says to be cautious with it when you still have a lot of the mercury on board. But, after you're chelating for a while you could probably introduce it. I don't think there is any reason to not do it."

As we continue the conversation, I'm surprised at how much I've learned. Since I was a little girl, I'd dreamed of being a doctor. I always had an intense interest in how the body works. In a small sense, I have another natural motivation to finding answers for Clay. I like working with mysteries, trying to find a way to solve a problem.

"What do you think about doing some immunity testing?" I ask.

"I think it's a good idea. I think the most important immunity testing is the myelin basic proteins antibodies so you know if he has autoimmunity. The only real reason to do some of the other tests like IgG subclasses and natural killer cell function is to see if he has general low immunity."

"How much are the tests you just mentioned?" I ask Dr. Jepson.

"The myelin basic protein test costs $180. The measles titer test runs about $130. Those are the two I would recommend. The combination of all the immunity tests would cost between $500 and $600," he replies.

The muscles in my gut tighten, knowing we are still scraping to even pay our instructors.

"We won't be able to do them all, but maybe we can do the most important ones," I reply.

"I recommend that you at least have a measles, mumps, and rubella antibodies test done through Dr. Singh's lab. He isn't able to do testing right now because of funding issues with the university. But I'll let you know when it is resolved. You can get them done in other labs, but I don't think they're as reputable as Dr. Singh's lab."

"Does folate make B12 work?" I ask, pressing on.

"Yes, they are commonly codeficient. You should try and get at least 800 mcg of folic acid if you're doing the methyl B12. You may even be there with what is in his multivitamin. You may just have to add 400 mcg. It's fine if you go over that," he replies.

As I visit with Dr. Jepson, I admire how approachable and sincere he is. It's something I haven't seen in a physician before. He is completely without arrogance or a know-it-all attitude. I respect him immensely and feel like we're walking together along this road, rather than that we have the parent-child relationship that some physicians create. He is trekking along his own journey and can empathize directly with us. And he's a member of the club.

I love to learn more about these complex medical issues. Not just for the primary benefit of helping Clay, and not even just because I like learning about how the body works, but also because I feel a sense of empowerment. I don't have to walk blindly, following whatever some doctor recommends, as if he were speaking a foreign language. I take responsibility for the treatment of my son, and it feels good. I can't do anything without Dr. Jepson, and others like him, or Sarah and our instructors. But I'm steering the ship, and they are my trusty crew. And the medical puzzle pieces are fitting together more. They make sense, and I crave more information.

It has been nine months since we started winding our way through the maze of various treatments. The twice-daily supplement regime is as routine as eating breakfast every morning. Our lives are as scheduled as that of an army cadet in training. I continue to marvel at Clay's progress, and for each small, sometimes painstaking, step in the right direction.

The compounding stress has had its way with my immune system, though. I've had strep throat five times in the last year, chest pains and heart palpitations, and severe anemia. I had a painful stomach ulcer that came back twice. I have always been really healthy until now.

"Mahm," Clay says in a whiny voice as he heads for the door. "Mahma." There it is. He's calling for me again. I'm watching the session from our bedroom television. Oh, how I want to gather him up in my arms and kiss his sweet face.

"We'll see your mom soon. Let's play catch," Trisha says, grabbing the black and red striped Nerf football. "Put your drink down, Clay, so you can catch the ball," she tells him. He puts it on the floor, and then holds his arms out with a grin.

I'm getting by on very few hours of sleep. I'm worn down and irritable. Yet I constantly remind myself that time is our enemy. We have to press forward, no breaks, no vacations, nothing. This window of opportunity is too precious to let slip away. I pray for strength. I pray my anxiety will diminish, and I pray to have a normal life.

I pray for a miracle.

I hear Sean walk into the room. I remain focused on the computer. He sits behind me and plays with my hair—my favorite thing to have him do. The room is quiet except for the sounds of my fingers clicking on the keyboard. I almost forget he's there until his voice breaks the silence.

"Hey, let's go out," he finally says.

"How are we going to do that?" I snap. "We don't even have enough money to pay the instructors."

"Well…then…we can rent a movie and watch it after the kids go to bed."

"Sorry. Can't. I have to review session footage and do more biomedical research."

He is never one to whine or protest, but I can sense strong disappointment and frustration. I swivel around in my chair and face him. I put my hands in his.

"I love you, and I want you to know that." I reach out and touch his arm. "But please understand that right now I have to do this. It won't always be this way."

The look on his face reminds me of the look my mother gave me when I did something to disappoint her. To disappoint means to fail. My fear of failure exceeds logic.

"Please hang in there with me. I need you too much. I know we haven't been able to spend much time together.

But please know how much I love you. I need your love and support."

I watch as he turns and walks out of the room.

As I continue to review tape and type notes, I can't stop thinking about how Sean and I met.

We were kids at a small college in Idaho. I was nineteen, and he was twenty-one. I worked part-time for seven professors in the Communication Department for nearly two years. He was a communication major. One day one of my favorite professors came to me and said, "Leeann, I have someone I want you to meet."

"Berg." Her real name is Robyn Bergstrom, but I called her Berg. "Seriously, I don't need a guy right now."

"Just humor me, okay," she sang with a crooked smile, flitting her fingers in the air.

"What are you up to? Berg? Come on," I pleaded as she headed out the door.

Ten minutes later, a handsome young man entered the room.

"Uh, hi," his lips parted into a smile.

It was quiet.

"Can I help you?" I said.

"Professor Bergstrom sent me up to get a video for her to show our class. She said you would have it?"

What? I looked all over and finally found a VHS tape on the top of my computer monitor with a yellow sticky note that read "Sean." I try to hide my grin.

"This must be it," I said as I handed it to him.

He asked me where I was from, and thirty minutes later we were still talking.

"Uh, I better get back to class," he said. "Professor Bergstrom might need this."

We both laughed nervously together.

He flashed me another grin before disappearing out the office door.

"Oh, hey, Sean."

He popped his head back in.

"Can I see that tape?"

"Uh, okay." He handed it to me.

I scrawled on the sticky note next to his name, "Muy bien, Berg."

Three months later, we were engaged. Six months after that, we were married—a spontaneous act uncharacteristic for both of us, and something I had vowed would never happen until I was at least thirty years old.

Sean explodes with energy and breathes determination. I have always been deeply attracted to his sense of well-being, his carefree demeanor, and his intelligence. He is motivated and strives for excellence in everything he does. He is a storyteller and can fully engage an audience, eloquently painting detailed pictures in everyone's minds until you're so caught up in what he is saying, you forget where you are.

He is also charming. Too charming. In college, there were times he was asked eight and nine times to a girl's-choice dance. Most women love this about men. To me, having to compete with other girls is a major turnoff and a game in which I have never and would never participate. So it's a good thing he actively pursued me, because otherwise it may never have happened.

He is an amazing husband and father—something that comes easily to him. When I'm ready to call for a time-out, he can play with the boys for hours and be perfectly content. They wrestle, eat junk food, play with Legos, and watch Bugs Bunny together. I love the strong bond they have, but secretly wish they would worship me the way they worship him. He is everything to them. It is one of his most attractive qualities, yet it leaves me feeling incompetent, reinforcing my deep insecurities as a mother.

I, on the other hand, have always been incredibly focused. I set goals and am hell-bent on achieving them. Most of this stems from insecurities I've had since my youth. I had an inferiority complex about not having name-brand clothes and other material things my friends had. It built a chip on my shoulder so big that no goal I accomplished was enough to knock it off. The chip has driven me all my life to prove myself and my worth. I have to do, and accomplish, to feel good about myself…to feel like I am as good as the next girl. This same focus and determination is a force that will drive me to unearth every clue that may contain the answer to helping Clay.

Together, Sean and I make a great team. We are each other's best friends, each serving as the other's underpinning. Our unique strengths and weaknesses complement one another, allowing us to create balance within our family. We'd rather be with each other, doing anything, than spend time away from one another with other friends.

But how can I help Sean know how important he is to me? I made a promise to myself, and to Clay, that I would fight this with everything I have. I have to persevere. We've always been a team, and I know I can't do it without him.

Autism is tugging on one arm, life is tugging on the other. I just hope these two battles don't tear us apart.

"Leeann?" I hear Andy call from upstairs. The session has just ended. "Can I talk with you?"

"Sure, what's up, Andy? Is everything okay?" I'm concerned by the serious tone of her voice. She's hardly ever serious.

"Hey listen, Leeann...I...well." She shoves her hands farther into her pockets and lifts her shoulders while shifting her weight. "I'm going to Madagascar to serve a church mission," she says excitedly. Then a concerned look flashes across her face as she bites her bottom lip. My heart skips a beat.

"Wow..." I say, with a half smile, trying to mask my extreme disappointment. "Madagascar. I'm not even sure where Madagascar is, but, well, it sounds like a great opportunity for you."

"Look, Leeann, I have a friend who..."

"No thanks, Andy." I raise my hand in the air. "I appreciate you being concerned, but I just need to let this sink in. I'm just not sure how we're ever going to replace you. Clay loves you so much, and you have such a way with him." I stop talking so that I can suck in the tears. I hug her. She has worked with Clay for a year now. He is doing so well, and a lot of that is because of her. I want to scream out, "I can't let you go!"

"Leeann, I love Clay, and I love your family." Now she is crying. "The experiences I've had here, and the knowledge I have gained are...invaluable. But this is something that I have to do. I know it's the right thing for me. I hope you understand."

"Andy, look, we're going to miss you. So much! You've helped Clay in ways that only you could have. But, ultimately, you have to do what you feel good about, not anyone else."

I look at the floor. Is this me talking? What am I saying?

I take Clay outside to get some fresh air before lunch. We jump on the trampoline, and then I push him in the swing. But it's all pseudo-play because of my intense focus on my conversation with Andy. We walk over to the apple tree together. Red and green swirled apples speckled with brown wormholes hang from the tree. A warm breeze blows the cotton from the neighboring trees swirling through the air all around us. It is so thick it gets stuck in our eyelashes and on our clothes.

The sound of an airplane catches my attention. I turn my head upward toward the sky and put my hand on my forehead in a salute, shielding my eyes from the sun. I point to the sky as I say softly, "Look Clay, it's an airplane." Clay looks upward, squinting and grimacing from the glaring sun. "Air-pane," he says, pointing up toward the sky. Together, we watch the airplane move slowly across the sky. "Fwy…lye…airpane." I stand there looking at him through the magical white fluff floating through the air. Time freezes. I count the words—one, two, three. Fly like airplane. He set a new record. And I know what he is saying. I know what he means. I'm taken back by his ability to express himself in this moment. This small child… he's come so far.

"Baby, we *are* going to fly," I say. "We're going to fly like that airplane. You'll see…you'll see…"

We go back into the house so I can feed Clay lunch and get ready for the afternoon session. I get on the phone and call everyone I know who is running an in-home ABA program to see if they know of an instructor who might be interested in working with Clay. I finally reach a friend who raves about a potential instructor.

"She is by far the best we have ever had, probably even the best in the state," she tells me. "We've been at this for a long time, Leeann, you know that. She is professional, yet personable, and she is my son's favorite instructor. Her name is Brooke." Yeah, I'm thinking, but you haven't met Andy.

I call her right away. She agrees to interview with us. We meet the next day, and she leaves a perfect first impression. Brooke is professional, but friendly, and seems very mature for her age, somewhere in her early twenties. She has had several years' experience working in an ABA program, and seems to be flexible and willing to learn. I watch her interact with Clay, and he seems drawn to her. She quickly grasps what reinforcers he likes and is able to quickly form a friendship with him. I am surprised because I never thought we would even come close to finding someone who could give us what Clay needs. Her leadership and wisdom will be a great asset to our team. I am so relieved to have found someone of her caliber.

At our next team meeting, we bring out the calendar to schedule regular sessions for the fall. Just as I'm marveling at how well Brooke fits into our team, Natalie looks up at me with those eyes.

Dammit. Not that face.

"Um, Leeann," Natalie says.

I force my eyes to answer her.

"I've been meaning to talk to you about this, but, well…I'm going to the Dominican Republic for a semester."

I blink long and hard. "Oh, no, Natalie! You can't! You guys are killing me," I say in a whiny, crooning voice. I smile to cover up my intense frustration.

She returns the smile, nervously. "I have to. It's for my major in Public Health. But I don't have to leave for four more months."

"Can't you…can't you use this for your major?" I say, putting my arms out to include everything in the room. "As an internship…or something?"

"I need to go, and it will be a great opportunity for me to learn more and to gain experience overseas."

"All right, Natalie. All right." I throw my hands up in the air and let them flop down to my sides. "I guess I'll let you go," I say facetiously.

Inside my guts are twisting all around, and suddenly I feel tired. As I absorb the news even more, I begin to feel saturated, like a full sponge. I turn and look out the window.

"We just did this," I muse, so quietly no one hears me. I point to Trisha.

"Don't even think about it," I say, jokingly.

"I'm good. I'm good. You don't need to worry about me."

Truly, we never have. She's been steady from the beginning, connecting with our family on a very personal level. She is, as far as we're concerned, another member of our family.

They all have become part of us, and a permanent part of Clay's future. Though I have managed to maintain an employer/employee distance, having someone working with me and my child, in our home, up to six hours per day, with the same goal in mind of turning his entire future around, it's tough not to become somewhat attached. Losing them means more than losing an instructor. It also means losing a friend and an important ally in the heat of the battle.

Chapter 18

Clay is going to preschool.

Well, we're trying to get him in, anyway. Preschools are filling up quickly for fall 2003. Sarah wants Clay enrolled in an in-home preschool with a maximum of ten students, one that will allow an instructor to accompany him. I know it might be difficult to find one that has all of these parameters, but I am optimistic. I call several friends and develop a good list of teachers who are highly recommended.

That afternoon, I start dialing.

"Hi, I'm interested in enrolling my son in your preschool. Are you full?"

"Not yet," the high-pitched soft voice on the other line replied.

"How many children do you allow in your classroom?"

"Only eight," she cheerfully replies. "I like my students to get to know one another. It's nice for me to keep the numbers small so that I can give them one-on-one attention."

Hmm. I like the sound of this, and she is only a mile or so from our home.

"I have a son with autism," I begin. "However, he is doing quite well since he began an intensive program we started almost a year ago. He would need to be accompanied by a shadow, one of his teachers..."

"Ma'am," the sweet voice turns stern and businesslike. "I'm afraid we can't help you."

There is silence on the line.

"Do you know of anyone else who might be more accommodating?" I jab back.

"Nope. Sorry."

Click.

I sit there, looking at the phone I'm still holding in my hand.

I begin dialing the next number.

"Yes, hello, my name is Leeann Whiffen, and I am looking for a preschool for my son. Your name came highly recommended. I would like to ask you a few questions."

"Sure, okay," the woman replies confidently.

"I have a son with autism…who…"

"You know Mrs., um—"

"Whiffen," I reply.

"Yes, Mrs. Whiffen, I really don't have the resources to help your son."

My spirits sink. "I understand. Thanks anyway," I say, letting the air escape through my lips until they vibrate.

I call six or seven more preschool teachers, all who give myriad excuses as to why they can't take Clay as a student. The earpiece on the telephone is hot from pressing against my ear for so long. But I refuse to stop until I get to the end of the list.

The next woman is very polite and understanding.

I tell her, "He will need an instructor to come with him each time. The instructor will only be there to take notes on his behavior and to help him and others in your class if needed," I say matter-of-factly.

"Okay, Mrs. Whiffen, I will send you an information packet. Let's get him all signed up," replies the twangy voice.

I hear kids screaming in the background.

"What do I need to do?" I say loudly enough she can hear me over the commotion.

"Just fill out the information I send you and mail it back to me."

"Okay, then. I would like to meet you in person, so I will drop it off at your home," I say.

"Sure, sure whatever," she says distracted by a child wailing into the phone.

"Take care," I shout as I hear the click on the other line. I am not at all comfortable with this woman. The visit should be interesting.

A couple of days pass and the woman with the twangy voice calls me back.

"Is this Mrs. Whiffen?"

"Yes, it is."

"This is A B C Preschool," she says, smacking her lips while eating something. "Mrs. Whiffen, I'm afraid there is a problem."

"What's that?" I ask.

"Well, I double-booked your son with another child. I just don't have room for your son."

"That figures," I mumble.

"What did you say, dear?"

"Oh nothing," I manage to squeeze out in a somewhat believable voice. "Have a nice day."

I hang up the phone. I'm quickly running out of options. I look down at my paper. Among the crossed out names and notes I notice one more preschool I still need to call.

I quickly dial the number.

"Yes, um, Mrs. Jackson?"

"Yes, that's me," a woman with a mature voice replies.

"Are you teaching preschool this fall?"

"I am," she replies.

Please let this be the one, I plead, crossing my fingers behind my back. If Sean were here, he would tease me about being superstitious.

"Mrs. Jackson, I would like my son to attend your preschool. I have heard that you only allow eight children, and many have commented on your hands-on curriculum and your tender way with the kids. Do you have room for my son?"

"Well, yes, I do. I actually have one more spot, which is quite rare. I had someone drop out at the last minute."

"Oh, good," I say, somewhat relieved. Now I have to drop the bomb.

"Mrs. Jackson, my son has autism…" I pause for a reaction…nothing…I continue, "He is doing quite well since we started his early intensive therapy about a year ago. He still, however, will need one of his instructors to accompany him to school. How do you feel about this?"

"Wwwell," she stammers. I squint my eyes and rub my forehead to prepare myself for her answer. "I don't know why it wouldn't work. I mean, well, I'll give it a try, Mrs. Whiffen. I've never experienced this before, but there is a first time for everything, isn't there?"

I want to drop the phone, jump on the bed, and run around the room several times.

"Well, then," I say. "When do we get started?"

The first time I meet Amy is at an Autism Biomedical Support Group held in the recital hall of a local music store. She approaches me afterward and asks if she can take me to lunch one day. She tells me she cuts hair, so it would need to be on a Saturday.

"You do hair?" I ask, examining the roots of my neglected mane. "Can we do hair instead of lunch?"

I arrive in her studio, situated just outside her home thirty miles south of where I live. I sit in the black vinyl chair and spin around slowly, looking at the hundreds of sepia photos of her four kids covering all four walls.

She tips my chair back, carefully places my head in the sink, and turns on the water. The spray hits the sink, creating a fine mist that settles onto my face.

"What would you like done today?" she asks.

"You know, Amy, if it were two years ago, I would have searched *People* magazine and found a photo with the exact haircut to bring. Now, I'm not sure it would bother me if you shaved me bald."

"Really?" She pulls out a drawer and grabs a Bic razor.

We giggle.

"Just make me look better than I do now. That should be easy. Tell me about your son," I say.

"I have two-year-old twin boys, Jack and Ryan. My husband and I had a difficult time getting pregnant after our first two girls were born. We tried everything. We finally resorted to in-vitro fertilization. That's when the twins were born. Since birth, Jack has suffered from chronic ear infections, diarrhea, and severe gastrointestinal reflux. His sleep is erratic, and his development is tragically behind his twin brother's. Ryan is a constant reminder of where Jack should be. Ja—."

She stops abruptly as if wondering whether to continue.

"Jack was jumping on our bed the other morning. You know what my husband said? He said, 'Do you think he'll still be doing this when he's forty?' We looked at each other for a minute in shock and horror. Then we busted up—a side-splitting, wicked laugh that left us exhilarated and breathless. Leeann, it's not funny, but there's sometimes…"

I shake my head. "I know, I know."

"Are you going to the autism conference in Salt Lake next weekend?" she asks.

"I'm planning on it," I reply

"Do you want to ride together?"

"Sure."

She finishes my hair and blows it dry and styles it for me. She swirls me around in the chair and I look in the mirror. "Now that's what I'm talking about. Perfect!"

The woman at the front desk of the Salt Lake City hotel welcomes Amy and me, and shows us to the room where the autism mini-conference is to take place. It's the first time I've been in an organized setting with parents of autistic children since the DAN! conference eight months ago. It's like getting together with family during the holidays to reminisce and talk about past times together. As I look around the room, I notice friends that I have met along the way. I feel safe among them… those who understand every frustration…every fear. Most of us have put our lives on hold to help our kids. Many successful careers have ended, friends have been lost, bankruptcy and other financial woes crept in, hearts were broken, and dreams shattered. But we know we have each other, the club, and we have hope. And our hope is made stronger when we hope together.

"We are thrilled to be here this morning and want to welcome all of you to this autism mini-conference," says Dr. Paul Hardy, who is conducting the conference. "Why don't we start by introducing yourselves and telling everyone why you are here?"

Amy sits down after introducing herself. It's my turn. My palms are sweaty, and I can almost feel the stomach acid sloshing around, burning my insides. Amy pokes me under the table to tell me to go. I take a deep breath and stand, "Hello, I'm Leeann

Whiffen, and I have a son with…" I pause for a moment. *Okay, don't stall now*, I tell myself silently. I look around the room and see everyone looking at me in anticipation. It's quiet except for the shuffling of papers on the table behind me. "With autism," I say, as I sit down. *Ugh,* I groan under my breath. I lean over to Amy. "What is wrong with me? It's been almost a full year since diagnosis! Why is it still so hard to say out loud? Did I really think he would be completely fine by this time?"

"Give yourself some slack. It's still hard for most of us here," Amy whispers back.

Dr. Bryan Jepson is the first speaker. His first slide says, "Follow those who seek the truth, but flee from those who have found it," by Vaclav Havel. I think back to Clay's former pediatrician who told us, with absolute certainty, "Your son is much more likely to get smallpox than autism." The sound of his nasally voice whines through my mind.

Dr. Jepson is deliberate and passionate. "Autism is the most common developmental abnormality." He shows a graph with autism incidence studies in California, the state thought to have the most reliable autism incidence data. The curve on the graph rises steadily over a period of ten-plus years. "Clearly, according to the data, autism is rising at epidemic proportions. But there is no such thing as a genetic epidemic. So, there is obviously an environmental factor at work, and finding what it is could take decades, especially with the lack of funding for quality unbiased research."

The last slide of his presentation shows a picture of a clock and the heading, "Do we have any more time to wait?" I can feel the energy pulse through me and into my limbs. *No, absolutely not,* I think to myself.

Dr. Paul Hardy is the next speaker. He covers neuropsychiatric disorders affecting children and adolescents. I can't help but think he looks like the typical psychiatrist portrayed by Hollywood. His black, thick-rimmed glasses and yellow polka-dot bow tie complete the ensemble. He talks about the co-morbidity of autism and various other psychiatric disorders. He draws fancy diagrams, one of which looks like a cluster of grapes, as he shows how autism can overlap with ADHD, bipolar disorder, and obsessive-compulsive disorder.

Dr. Vijendra Singh from Utah State University gives the next presentation, covering viral autoimmunity in autism. He stands only about 5 feet 4 inches tall. He is extremely intelligent, but I have to strain to understand what he is saying through his thick Indian accent. As he delves further into his presentation, he shows graphs from data gathered during his recent studies. "As you will see here," he says, pointing to a graph, "the individuals with autism are much more likely to have antibodies to measles virus and myelin basic protein. Our research suggests that autism is caused by a viral insult, coupled with a compromised immune system." I'm intrigued. More answers.

But at the same time, there are too many answers. One scientist says it is thimerosal in the vaccines poisoning our children. Here, another world-renowned scientist says his research shows it is the measles virus in the MMR vaccine wreaking havoc on their immune systems causing neurological damage. How do I decipher what is and isn't causing Clay's autistic behavior? Even then, how can I possibly address all of these abnormalities? There just isn't enough time, resources, or clear information. And even if I do learn exactly what caused his autism, the only thing that matters now is trying to reclaim him from it.

I rush up to Dr. Singh afterward, navigating my way through the crowd.

"Dr. Singh, I would really like to have my son's blood tested in your lab for measles antibodies and antibodies to his myelin basic protein. But Dr. Jepson told me you are no longer able to do this. Is this still the case?" I surprise myself with my uninhibited behavior—something contrary to my former personality. I marvel at what we are driven to do when the stakes are high.

"Well, yes," he says in his thick Indian accent. "My funding has nearly dried up at this point, and I am no longer able to analyze any samples."

"Dr. Singh," I plead, "I understand you have a highly reputable lab, and I will do whatever it takes to have my son tested. Is there any way at all?"

"Well," he chuckles, brushing the tip of his nose with the back of his hand as he briefly looks at the floor, then back at me. "If you are willing to have Dr. Jepson draw the blood in his office, and immediately drive up to Logan to my office, I will test it for you for a small fee."

I impulsively reach out and clasp his hand with both of my hands.

"Dr. Singh," I'm not sure what to say. "Thank you so much," I finish, bouncing his hand up and down.

We swap emails over the next several days, and he gives me directions to his state-of-the-art lab. I have Dr. Jepson's office painstakingly draw Clay's blood, then I manage to get away for the day while I drive the vial of blood 115 miles north to Logan, Utah. The dotted lines painted on the freeway whiz by the car, hypnotizing me into a relaxing meditation. It takes me a couple of hours before I'm finally on campus and pull up to the rectangular, red-brick building that houses Dr. Singh's office and lab. I park the car and look at my directions as I walk toward his office, securely clutching the padded box containing Clay's vial of blood as if it contained an irreplaceable, rare artifact. I replay the scene that took place earlier this morning. Five people hovering over Clay holding him down, while the nurse poked a butterfly IV into each arm, wrist, then hand. Poked nearly eight times, Dr. Jepson finally was called in. He successfully placed the needle in the top of Clay's foot—the last resort.

An intricate diagram of the brain is displayed along the hallway. I stop to look, fascinated by its complexities yet intimidated by the unknown. The human body is such an amazing creation. We've only begun to untangle the convoluted mysteries of the brain. I turn my head sideways toward the sound of footsteps coming down the short, narrow hallway.

"Mrs. Whiffen," an accented voice echoes through the hall, as a stubby man rounds the corner and comes into focus.

"Hello, Dr. Singh," I say, smiling. "Thanks again for meeting with me."

He shows me to his office and invites me to sit down. His office is typical of an old university—small, with painted cinderblock walls, a steel desk, and file cabinets. Shelves line the walls and are crammed full of neuroimmunology textbooks. Some of the shelves bow near the center from the weight of all the books. Most of the books are hardcover, at least as thick as the width of my shoe. I wonder how he removes one without the rest falling on him. "Give me a minute, please," he says as he taps away on his keyboard.

"Sure," I say. I feel a deep gratitude for him—for narrowing his scientific focus to autism, and for the genuine passion he has for finding answers to what seems to be one of the most misunderstood developmental disorders.

"Okay, Mrs. Whiffen, let me get some information on your son, and then I'll give you a tour of my lab." He verifies Clay's name and birthday, and then asks me several questions about his medical history as he types my answers into the computer.

His lab is complete with rows and rows of long tables, microscopes, and other instruments used in analyzing samples. I didn't imagine it would be so large. He shows me what they do with the samples and how they are tested. I get a crash course in neuroimmunology, and without taking a breath, Dr. Singh says, "Let's get something to eat." We go to a nearby restaurant on campus for lunch. I am already formulating more questions to ask him.

We order and the waitress takes our menus. She comes back with our drinks. I fidget in my seat while sipping at my water through the straw, the ice jingling in my glass.

"So, Dr. Singh, what made you decide to narrow your research efforts to autism?" I ask, knowing he had studied other neurodegenerative disorders in the past. He finishes chewing the bite of sandwich before answering.

"Early in my career, I began researching multiple sclerosis. Several years ago, I realized there was a dire need for more autism research. I put in a grant to the National Institutes of Health for an autism study, and it was approved."

I jump to the next question. "For those individuals who show high antibodies to the measles virus and myelin basic protein, what treatment options are available and most effective?"

"Well, I'm not a medical doctor, but many are doing IVIG, intravenous immunoglobulin, a plasma protein replacement therapy that helps regulate immune response by maintaining adequate antibodies and reduce infection. Also there is something called plasmapheresis, but it is quite invasive. This is where the plasma, containing the protein and antibodies, are removed from the blood, treated, and then returned for circulation. Then there's the sphingolin, bovine (cow) myelin basic protein, that some have used with success."

"Do you believe autism has a viral etiology?"

"Yes, I do," he says, wiping his eye behind his glasses. "That is clearly what my research is suggesting. Even in miniscule amounts, the measles virus could cause swelling in the brain that damages developing neural pathways in children with compromised immune systems."

He looks at his watch. "It has been my pleasure, but I need to get going," he says. I look at my plate and notice most of my salad is still there. I stand and shake his hand and thank him again. I sit back down and pick at the rest of my salad while I look out the window and watch his head bob forward as he walks away.

The next day, Clay's urine toxic metals test results arrive in the mail. I tear open the envelope and unfold the paper. As I look at the bars on the graph, my eyes are drawn to the longest horizontal bars, extended from aluminum and tin, which are in the elevated range. My eyes scan the page for mercury. The bar is the width of a pencil lead. It is in the normal range, barely detectable. I'm disappointed, hoping to see the mercury bar running off the page. That would make things much easier to understand.

I know that the tests aren't always accurate, and it's frustrating. I email Dr. Jepson and ask why we aren't seeing metals like lead and cadmium being excreted. If environmental toxins are part of Clay's problem, why aren't we seeing them?

He replies within an hour saying, "It's a random sample. It can give you an idea of what is being excreted, but is by no means a true measure of the toxic body burden."

I wish the tests were more definitive.

Chapter 19

Through the video feed in our bedroom, I watch Trisha carefully lay out object cards on the school table for Clay to sort.

"Give me all of the toys," she says, looking directly at Clay. I hear a hint of her Southern accent in the word "all."

Clay hands her three cards with toys on them. "Where's the rest of them?" she asks, with her hands out in the air.

Clay rocks back and forth on his knees. "Rest of them," he echoes.

She prompts his hand to the toy cards.

"More music," he says.

"If you get it right next time, we'll listen to music, okay? Come over and sit with me," she says, patting a chair. Clay plops into the small, blue plastic chair.

"Give me all the toys," she says.

He instantly gives her every card that has a picture of a toy on it.

"All right, Clay! Go play!" She presses play on the boombox and "Instanbul" by They Might Be Giants starts thumping through the speakers.

"Go pway," shouts Clay as he jumps around the room. "Go pway!"

It's the perfect time of the year to visit my mom and dad on the ranch in Idaho. The boys spend hours throwing rocks in the water flowing down the ditch, watching the water skippers—or "donkey devils," as my dad called them—scamp about, skimming the surface of the water. They play hopscotch on near-petrified cow pies and maneuver around the fresh ones, occasionally getting a shoe stuck. And if they're really lucky, Grandpa lets them ride his horse, Cisco, who is probably only twenty rides away from her last gallop.

I look forward to the two hour car-ride with Sean—necessary time for us to reconnect. We play a DVD and put head-phones on the boys. Then we talk…and we talk…without any interruption. I do most of the talking, and he listens. This trip I get to drive so that he can manage the kids on the way.

At one point I look over at him and say, "So, how do you think Clay is doing?"

He pauses and looks out the window, then turns and looks straight ahead.

"I can't believe how far he has come. He is talking now! He calls us Mom and Dad. We're so fortunate."

"We have…yes, we are," I say, nodding. "We still have a ways to go, though, don't we?" I say, sliding my fingers across the seam on the steering wheel.

"Yes, but we have to remember where we started. He hardly screams anymore, and he is able to express himself using words most of the time."

"You're right. Sometimes because I'm with him so much, I forget where we started. He has made amazing progress."

"Lee, imagine one day," he says, "that Clay is doing so well, he can go to school, fully integrated into a regular classroom."

"Sean," I interrupt. I put my hand on his knee and lightly squeeze. He knows I don't like to think so optimistically that far ahead for fear that talking about it out loud will jinx us.

"No. Lee, really. You're so superstitious! What if he gets to that point?"

"We'd move away and not tell anybody about his past and start a new life. Look, Sean, I don't want this to follow him around. Maybe it's my motherly nature, but I don't want him stigmatized."

Finally I pull into the long gravel driveway of my parents' home. They are waving to us from the front porch.

"Nana! Papa!" Drew shouts as he unbuckles himself, jumps out of the car and races up the steps to give them hugs. Clay is not far behind. His short, stalky legs carry him as fast as they can manage. My mom hugs Drew, "Hi, Drewby," she says in his ear. She turns to Clay and says, "I like Clay."

"I like Nana," Clay replies.

Hmm. Good dialogue. I can never let a moment with Clay escape without turning it inside out, analyzing it from every direction. As usual, greetings are quick and to the point. In my mom's typical fashion, she beckons us to come have some lunch. Right now. This means no taking your time, no dillydallying, not even a quick stop in the bathroom.

We quickly find our places at the table and close our eyes to say the prayer. "Oh," I say, getting up, "I forgot to unload the cooler." My mom shoots me the look.

"Lee, sit down," Sean says, putting his hand on my leg. "I'll get it."

Each time we travel, we bring a cooler stuffed full of Clay's special foods. Homemade chicken nuggets, GFCF pancake mix, plenty of fruits and veggies just in case, GFCF snacks, and filtered water. My parents drink water that comes from a well near their house. The well is so deep, apparently, that the water turns the insides of their tub and toilet a brownish-orange color. I've urged them to get it tested, but they wave me off as if I'm some crazy environmentalist.

"When I get the call someday that you two are rotting from

heavy metal poisoning, don't tell me I didn't warn you," I say with a half smile.

"Oh, Leeann, stop," my mom says. "You're paranoid."

Sean unloads the cooler onto the floor with a loud thump. "This is yummy," Clay says, holding out his fork. "That's yummy," he says again, with a cooked carrot hanging out his mouth. Then he looks at my mom and says, "Nana is yummy."

Sure it sounds strange, but he is engaging her. He has the desire to get her attention. We gaze at him as if he just correctly answered the final question on *Jeopardy*.

After lunch, I go outside to play with the boys. Clay instantly runs down to the end of the driveway. "Not again," I say to Drew. I was hoping he would have forgotten about them by now. At the end of their gravel lane, my parents have two round, red reflectors staked into the ground on either side. We're deep in the country, so the nearest road light is about a mile away. Without these, especially in the snow, they might never know where to turn onto their gravel driveway.

Clay has an odd fascination with them. They are the first things he plays with when coming to my parents' house. Part of the attraction is their shape. Round. I watch him flip one back and forth. He pulls it back as far as it will go, until it nearly touches the ground, then he releases it. He laughs as he watches it spring back and forth. I had hoped he would forget about them this visit, signifying a leap of improvement.

I walk to the reflector on the other side of Clay. I look around. I carefully pull it back and let it go. I watch it flip back and forth. "Clay, come on, let's run through the sprinkler," I say, picking him up and spinning him around. He comes willingly, which offsets my earlier disappointment. I press my lips to his ear and sing a song Andy used to sing to him from the movie *Mary Poppins*.

Let's go fly a kite
Up to the highest height...

Clay loves Cisco. Horses intrigue him. It's one of the few, core parts of his personality he didn't lose when he regressed into autism. She is a perfect horse for the boys—old, gentle, and steady. I have fond memories of being with our horses as a young girl, and I'm so glad we live close enough that the boys can experience some of those same feelings.

Clay walks out of the house in Grandpa's shadow, sloshing around in his two-sizes-too-big cowboy boots. Grandpa is wearing his cowboy boots and the same old straw hat that looks like it has been run over by his pickup truck one too many times. Grandpa grunts as he hoists Clay onto Cisco. His forehead buckles into seven or more creases, while he simultaneously twists and bites his tongue—as he always does when focusing intently on something. Clay grins as if he just won a lifetime supply of round bouncy balls.

"Do you like that, Clay?" I pat Cisco on the head. Her tail swishes back and forth. Her back foot stomps on the ground and her skin twitches, scaring the flies into a buzzing frenzy.

"Yes," he says, peering from under his hat.

"Yee Haw," I say.

"Yeeeeee Hawwww!" he shoots back as he throws his right arm forward.

Later that afternoon, we take the boys to a park several miles east of my folks' home to play. It's complete with a rickety swingset, a merry-go-round, and a slide. I've forgotten how relaxing it is to live among sprawling fields of alfalfa. In Utah, I'm used to seeing sprawling fields of newly built houses and big box stores, nuzzled against the backdrop of the Wasatch Mountains. I close my eyes and suck the air through my nostrils, trying to taste the experience through my nose. I open my eyes and see Clay planting himself by the stop sign not far from the play equipment. I watch him look at the stop sign from all different directions. I go to him, pick him up, and put him in the swing. No tantrum.

It's the end of Clay's first session, and Natalie opens the front door on her way out. She stops and turns around.

"Oh, Leeann, I almost forgot. My mom is in town. She would really like to meet you, Clay, and the rest of the family."

"I would love to meet her!"

"Is a couple hours too soon?" Natalie asks.

"I'll be here."

"I'll call you before we come," Natalie says.

"Great. See you in a bit."

I check my watch just as I hear the doorbell ring.

"Hello, Mrs. Gavin," I say, shaking her hand. "It's very nice to meet you. We adore your daughter and are so happy to have her on board."

No response. No expression.

She looks around the house as if she thinks it will tell her more about me than I can ever say in words.

"So," I say, uncomfortable with the silence, "you're from Montana? Do you live in the country, or—"

"We live in…hasn't Natalie told you?"

"Well, yes, I just…I guess I forgot exactly where in Montana…you know, the city that you live in." I clear my throat. *Okay, this is going well.* Her eyes are drilling holes through my head.

Drew starts tugging on my pants, as I painstakingly try to carry on the conversation. I ask her about her other children.

"Mom," Drew whines, "I need some paper to draw."

"Just a minute, bub." I don't want to be rude and interrupt her.

"Mom, I need some paper now," he whines louder.

"Hold on, honey," I say to him as I continue to listen to her.

"Right now!" he yells, and he swats my leg with his arm. The vein zigzagging the side of his neck is bulging.

I bend down and say in a low voice, "Drew, we don't act that way."

Drew starts yelling and crying. He throws a toy at me, narrowly missing my head. Mrs. Gavin's eyes narrow as she looks at me. The crease between her eyebrows deepens. Her lips are puckered in disgust.

"Don't you know why he is acting this way?" she says flippantly, jabbing her finger in the air toward him. "It is because you don't spend enough time with him. You are so involved with helping Clay, Drew gets left out. Look at him, he's crying for attention."

Her words ricochet off the walls and plunge into my chest. I stare at the floor to avoid her piercing eyes. As I begin to recover from the shock, extreme rage sets in. Heat flashes up my neck and into my face. I feel like my head might blow off.

"Actually," I say, through clenched teeth. I'm not sure whether I want to jump on her or claw her eyes out, "We are very aware of the enormous amount of time we spend helping Clay. For that reason, both my husband and I make sure we spend quality one-on-one time with Drew every day," I hear myself say. I'm drowning in my own thoughts of inadequacy. I look over at Natalie, who is bright red and staring at the floor. She finally looks up at me with a look of *I'm so sorry.*

Why do I feel like I have to explain myself to this poisonous woman? I just want her to get the hell out of my house.

"Wow, look at the time," I say, looking at the clock on the

wall just above Natalie's head. "We have a few places to go before Clay's session ends."

"Well, then, I guess we'll be going now," says Natalie's mom as she walks toward the door.

"Good…I mean…okay," I say as I slam the door behind her. I scream and slam my fist against the wall next to the door. There are a number of words that pop into my head that I want to yell, but Drew is at my side. I slide down the wall and crumple to the floor. I'm trembling with pain and anger.

Drew comes to me and sits in my lap.

"Mamma, you alright?"

"Yes, Drew, come here, buddy." I hold him in my lap for as long as he will let me. The top of his head becomes wet from my tears. Then he runs off to play.

We place an ad in the local university newspaper to fill Natalie's position. We receive so many calls that we have to pull the ad sooner than the time originally scheduled. We interview twenty students from the local university, again. I know it's over when Kimber, who recently moved from Las Vegas to attend Brigham Young University, walks through the door gushing with enthusiasm and ready to take on the world. She has three years' experience working in an ABA program and her references rave about her. "Lucky for you, sad for us," they say one right after the other. She engages Clay with unbridled energy and an inherent ability to capture his attention. She slides in seamlessly over the next two weeks.

It's a blistering Saturday in May, a record-breaking 90 degrees. We take the boys to an outdoor mall in Salt Lake City. There is a large, round, in-ground water fountain built into the sidewalk. It's made in the pattern of the Salt Lake City Winter Olympics logo, with round, strategically placed holes. About ten other kids are playing in the fountain. The water sporadically shoots out of the holes in the ground, timed with the playing of the Olympic theme song through outdoor speakers above. Drew and Clay look at us with those eyes that say, *Can we please?* "Go ahead guys, have fun." We take off their T-shirts and let them scatter. Sean and I sit on the bench to talk. Mid-conversation, I hear a lady cackling. "Look at that little boy," she says pointing. I immediately look all around and spot Clay. His shorts and underwear are pulled all the way down to his ankles. There he is, standing over a fountain that's blasting water in his rear end, gleefully happy, totally naked. Dodging blasts of water, I strategically hopscotch my way over to Clay. By the time I get to him, he is trying to kick off his shorts.

"Clay, no, honey, you can't go naked in the fountain. There are other people here who will see you. No, Clay, you have to keep them on."

I wrestle with his wet, slick body, trying to pull his shorts back on. People are pointing and chuckling. Clay starts to scream.

"No, okay!" he says over and over.

I yell to Sean, "Time to go!"

Drew reluctantly comes with us. "Moooommm, we hardly got any time to play," he says.

"I know, son, we'll come back some other time."

On the way home in the car, I vent to Sean.

"It's like whack-a-mole. You know, that game the kids love to play at Chuck E Cheese. You whack one down and three more pop up. You have to work three times as hard to win."

Chapter 20

Dr. Emily Benway, our new pediatrician since I switched from Dr. Keller earlier this spring, is running behind schedule. Luckily, we're late anyway, since traffic into Salt Lake City was backed up. The waiting room is full of mothers and kids. Kids circle the office chasing other kids. Mothers read to babies on their laps. The television is blaring in the corner. There aren't any seats available, so I stand and hold Clay. He puts his hands over his ears and buries his head in my shoulder.

A year ago, he never could have handled this "sensory hell." He would have been on the floor screaming in pain. I'm so grateful we don't have to deal with that as much anymore.

"Clay," I hear the nurse call from the doorway, over the chaos. "Right this way," she says. Clay kicks to get down. I set him down, and tell him to follow me, while holding out my hand. I follow the nurse a short distance down the hallway. I look behind me, but Clay isn't there. I go toward the waiting room entrance and pop my head around the corner. I don't see him anywhere. I hear the nurse say, "Did you forget something?"

"Um, hold on a minute."

"Sure," she says with a sigh, looking at her watch.

I start down the hallway in the opposite direction. I look in the rooms with open doors. "Clay," I call. "Honey? Mama's looking for you." The office seems much larger now than when we were packed into the waiting room. My heart starts to pound, the sound moves up and into my ears. Okay, don't panic. He was just with me. But what if he went out through the front door as someone was coming in? No, I would have seen him. What if he is in the elevator, or even worse, the road? My brisk walking turns into a jog as I make my way down the labyrinth of long, narrow halls, frantically looking in every direction. My eyes dart to the bathroom door. It's closed. I knock quickly, then push it open. It hits something. I peer around the door and see Clay's shoe. "Ahhhhh, Clay," I say, my chest heaving up and down. "There you are, son. Please don't run from Mommy. You need to stay close to me. I don't want to lose you." His big blue eyes look directly into mine. His eyebrows are raised. "Hi," he says in his high, squeaky voice. "Find him?" he says. Then I remember his instructors have been playing hide-and-seek with him as a reinforcer. I'm proud of him for generalizing that skill...*I think.* He's coming along. At least we haven't had a tantrum. Yet.

Dr. Benway's short black curls bounce as she walks into the room looking at Clay's chart. A pencil is tucked tidily behind her ear. She is wearing trouser jeans with pumps. No white overcoat or official name tag. She peers over the chart and smiles. She turns to Clay, "Hi, Clay." Clay's eyes brush her face, and then he looks away. I think back to our first appointment with her earlier this year and how understanding and supportive she was of the treatment decisions and therapy we were doing for Clay. It was such a different experience from the one with Dr. Keller.

Dr. Benway proceeds to give Clay his three-year-old well-child exam. I am nervous at how Clay will react to her intrusive poking and prodding. She holds out her otoscope as she prepares to look in his ears. She purses her lips and makes a chirping sound with her mouth. "Clay, can you hear the birdies? Let's see if we can find them in your ears." Clay cocks his head to the side.

She refers back to his chart. "His weight is up from the fifteenth percentile to the fiftieth percentile. That's great news," she says, perky. "I am amazed at the progress he has made, Leeann. Are you still seeing Dr. Jepson?" She went to medical school with Dr. Jepson and highly respects him.

"Yes. We still see him. Unfortunately our insurance won't cover any of our expenses. So, I'm not sure how much longer we'll be able to afford to have Clay go there."

"If there's any lab work I can do here in my clinic for you, let me know. Your insurance is more likely to pay for it that way. I would be glad to help. In fact, I can write a letter to your insurance company asking them to cover the costs you are incurring through Dr. Jepson's office. Would you like me to do this?"

"That would be really helpful, Dr. Benway. Thanks so much." I want to jump up from my chair and hug her.

The next day is the first day of swimming lessons for Drew. Through a wall of windows, I watch him bob up and down in the water. He smiles and waves at me through the glass. I do a cheesy smile and a little wave back.

I notice a young mother approaching the front doors with a baby stroller and a toddler on her hip. She struggles to fit her stroller through the doors. I hop up from my chair and open the doors for her. "Thanks so much," she says. I sit back down in my chair. Her little girl with tightly wound white curls runs around the room, flapping her arms and making screeching sounds. She looks about Clay's age. As I watch her circle the room squealing, she reminds me of how Clay used to be. She seems autistic. Just then the mother's baby bangs his head against the back of his stroller over and over and starts to cry. She unbuckles him and he runs around with his sister.

I lean over to the mom and ask, "So, do you have a child in swimming lessons?"

"Yes, I do," she says, eyeballing her young children while pushing up her glasses with her index finger.

"How old?" I ask, wondering if he and Drew are in the same class.

"He's almost five."

"Wow, you must have your hands full."

"I do," she says, brushing her bangs out of her eyes. "Sara, no, no," she says as the small girl runs into the men's dressing room. She turns to me, "I'll be right back." I can tell she is eager for an adult conversation. When she returns, Drew runs inside, dripping with water, teeth chattering.

"Mmom, wwhere's my towel?"

"Right here, babe." I put the towel over his head and dry him off.

I lean over to the mom I just met. "Maybe we can talk tomorrow," I say, noticing her son is in Drew's class.

"Sure, my name's Kristen."

"I'm Leeann. See you in the morning."

The next day, Kristen comes inside just as swimming lessons begin. She catches my attention and waves.

"Hi, Leeann," she says, sitting down on the chair next to mine.

"Hi there."

As she approaches, I notice her three-year-old is toting a baby's bottle. Her beautiful, blonde locks are shaped so perfectly they look like she is wearing a wig.

"What are your kids' names?" I ask.

The girl starts crying. Kristin ignores her. Then the boy starts crying.

"I'm sorry," she says, shaking her head as she sits down next to me again. "My daughter and my son have fragile X syndrome.

Most children with fragile X have autistic-like tendencies as well. It makes it extremely difficult to take them out in public. It's a 24/7 job. I'm sorry."

"Oh, please don't apologize! I actually have a son who is autistic, so I understand where you're coming from."

She looks at me for a few seconds before she says anything else. "Really?"

"I can't imagine what it must be like having two, though," I say. "What exactly is fragile X? I know it's genetic, but what is the scientific explanation?"

She starts talking as if I had just looked up the definition in the encyclopedia. "Fragile X is a genetic disorder caused by a mutation of the FMR1 gene on the X chromosome. We didn't know our daughter had it before we got pregnant with our son. Then we found out he has it as well. My five-year-old doesn't have it."

"I'll bet it's tough just managing things most days," I say.

"It is. It's really hard to go out in public. As you've seen, there's always someone crying or a problem that needs solving. My family is really supportive. Sometimes my mom will come over and watch the kids so that I can go to the grocery store or run errands. But frankly, there are some days where it's too much for me to get out of bed in the morning."

"How is your autistic son doing?" she asks.

"Well, he is progressing," I say, not letting on to how well he really is doing. I tell her about the ABA therapy we are doing with him.

"Have you taken him to Kids On The Move?" she asks.

"Yep, we've spent a lot of time there," I say, chuckling.

"My two go there. But they are short on funding, and don't offer much," she replies.

Her kids are running around out of control at this point. They have torn down two posters from the wall.

"I better run. It's been nice talking with you, Leeann. I'm going to go put the kids in the car."

"Take care, Kristen."

I watch her walk out the door with her two kids, one under each arm.

Birthday boy Clay, now three years old, sits at the head of the table with his cowboy hat on, and his gluten- and casein-free, white and orange striped fish-shaped Nemo cake in front of him. He is ready to blow out the candles. "Hold on," I say. "Let me get the camera." Kimber, Brooke, and Trisha are sitting around the table with us. I can hardly believe one year has passed.

We started in the bottom of a chasm so deep we thought we may never be able to emerge. Now, we have risen to places we weren't sure we would ever get to, where we're able to see the vast distance we have covered, and a place where we can look to the surface to give us more hope, and fuel our desire to overcome. The joys we have experienced are much sweeter since we have also tasted frustration and sorrow. The improvements are adding up and are finally beginning to outpace any regression or plateau.

Clay has flourished in ways that were only imaginable in my dreams.

Sarah adds a potty training program. The thought of Clay being out of diapers gives me enough energy to hike a small mountain. I tried many times before to teach him how to use the potty—peeing on the Cheerios as targets (I spent several days trying to get the urine smell off the floorboards for that one), the timer method, bribes, a token system, and on and on.

Sarah tells us to have Clay wear his diaper over his underwear. I try to envision this, my face twisting around as I finally get it right. Over, then under—Oh, over his underwear. "We will start by taking him to the potty every thirty minutes. Now is the time to think of your best reinforcements, because we are really going to need them," Sarah tells us.

Clay doesn't care that his diaper weighs close to that of a bowling ball and that he's soaked through his underwear. Day after day it is the same routine until three weeks later I decide to try no diaper, just underwear. The day the urine trickles down his leg and soaks his underwear is, amazingly, the last day Clay is in diapers.

In an effort to save money, my GFCF-diet friend Leslie and I purchase an entire cow from a local organic cattle rancher, and split the cost of the beef. Since I started Clay on the diet, I also transitioned our entire family to mostly organic foods. She phones and tells me she has it in her freezer ready to pick up.

The next afternoon, I put the kids in the car, and we go over to pick up the beef. She opens her front door and smiles when she sees me standing on her porch.

"Hi, Leeann, come on in," Leslie motions with a wave of her arm.

"Well, I have the kids in the car and we're…"

"Have them come in too," she says cheerfully. "My kids would love to play with them."

I glance down to see Jacob, only in his diaper, hiding behind her leg. He momentarily pops his head through her legs, and I can see the sores on his face that he's caused from picking at himself. He looks up at me, and then darts down the hallway. I feel my gut tense. I'm bothered again that the neuropsychologist told her that even though he had PDD, he would be fine with a little speech therapy.

I look at the car, and then back at her. I chew loose skin from my bottom lip. "Well, I'm kind of in a hurry, and…"

"Oh," she says, waving her hand in the air, "It will just be for a minute."

This is the third time in two months she has asked if our kids could get together to play. Each time I had an excuse. I don't want her to see how well Clay is doing because I don't want to make her feel bad. Each time we talk, she asks about his progress. I try to change the subject.

She steps in front of me and outside the door. She runs down the steps and begins walking toward the car.

"All right," I say, feeling trapped. "But only for a minute because we really need to get going." I send the boys to play with Jacob, hoping they can avoid any interaction with Leslie.

We discuss the website she is helping me create for the Children's Biomedical Center while we unload the meat out of her freezer and into the trunk of my car. As we walk back into the house and sit down, Clay knocks on the back door. I open the door a crack.

"What's up, bud?" I ask. His chest heaves up and down as he struggles to get enough air to talk because he's been playing so hard.

"Gotta go potty," he says, holding himself while tiptoeing in place.

I look behind me to find Leslie staring in surprise. Her eyebrows are perched, her hand on her hip. She mumbles something inaudible.

"Oh, it's, it's, um, down the hall, right there," she points, her eyes still fixed on Clay.

He brushes by her and runs down the hall and into the bathroom.

"He's...potty trained? He's talking so well...*really* well. Leeann, I can't believe this is the same kid I saw over a year ago. Why didn't you tell me?"

I look at her sincerely. "It took us a few months of intense ABA-program potty training to finally get it down," I say, downplaying the significance. "Besides, I didn't want to make you feel bad. We've traveled this road together, as moms trying to help our sons. I didn't want you to feel resentment toward me, and most importantly, I thought it might compromise our friendship. I have tremendous respect for you, your family, and all other families who are going through the same experiences. Please don't take it personally, I haven't told anybody yet in the autism community how well he is doing."

"No. No! I'm happy for you. And I don't have ill feelings toward you or your family," she says. "I want the best for you guys, and I'm thrilled for Clay."

I know she is sincere, but I can't erase the image of her whitened face.

My anger toward Dr. Keller has never entirely drained—the last of it festers in my subconscious. I find myself thinking about him as I learn more and interact with more doctors. I wonder how many other children there are who are suffering from developmental delays that he has somehow missed or ignored. I also wonder if he continues to freely give false information regarding autism and infectious disease rates. I don't want thoughts about him clouding my head...I want to call him, but we don't see him anymore. I decide to write him a letter.

I have always believed most people have good intentions. I know he believed what he told us, and wanted to help us make an educated decision. His opinions and rote answers directly reflected the stance of the academy to which he belongs. Just like any other medical academy, the American Academy of Pediatrics has a large influence on pediatricians and how they practice. Pediatricians depend on their organization to give them best practice parameters and up-to-date treatment information. Many pediatricians, especially those not affiliated with a teaching university, rarely have time to seriously study and consider new research, developments, and treatments. They're stuck in a revolving door of patients, forced to keep their consultation time down to a few minutes.

He didn't know the facts. He didn't know the signs. If I hadn't seen the nurse practitioner that day back in December 2001, who knows how long it would have been before we would have received a proper diagnosis? When he told me Clay was much more likely to get smallpox than autism, he must not have been aware of the autism incidence rates. If I had known that smallpox had been eradicated, with the last known case in the United States in 1949, but that autism rates were 1 in every 150 children, my decision may have been different. Whether Clay's autism was caused by the vaccinations, the eight rounds of antibiotics, the rotavirus he contracted the fall after his first birthday, or a combination of any of those, I will probably never know. It is futile, at this point, to focus on the cause, when the seconds for his treatment are imminently passing.

But I do know this—Dr. Keller needs to know the facts so that he doesn't mislead any other families. I want to help save others from the pain Clay and our entire family experienced.

My fingers fly over the keyboard, my emotions directly attached. "I hope he reads this letter," I say to myself, taking it from the printer and scrawling my signature at the bottom. Even so, I feel better just sending it to him. I have done my job. And now I can rest easier.

Dear Dr. Keller,

My son, Clay Whiffen, currently three years old, is a former patient of yours. When we brought him in for his well-child appointment on September 14, 2001, we visited with you about our concerns regarding immunizations and autism. You told us not to be concerned because what we were hearing about vaccinations in regards to autism was false. You told us that immunizations were safe and effective. Just as we were leaving, you said, "Clay is much more likely to get smallpox than autism." I thought about it and decided it wasn't worth the risk of Clay getting a terrible disease. Unfortunately, you were wrong.

We slowly lost our son during the six-month period following that visit. Clay no longer called us Mom and Dad. In fact, he never looked at us anymore. He started to scream and tantrum for more than half of his waking hours. He began walking on his toes, not tiptoes, but actually on top of his toes bent over. He stopped playing with his toys, and instead, started lining them all up in a row, or would throw them. If anyone knocked one over in the line-up, he would throw a full-blown tantrum lasting as long as twenty minutes. He started waking up several times throughout the night and had a difficult time getting back to sleep.

All of his behavioral problems made it difficult to take him out into public, so we stayed home most of the day. If we did venture out, he became frightened and would scream until we left. We were sickened our little boy had been taken from us. Dr. Keller, you are a father. Can you imagine this happening to one of your children?

My point in sending you this letter is not to place blame or guilt, or, necessarily, to convince you that vaccines play a role in

ASD. Rather, my purpose is to give you the facts and information regarding autism in hopes of saving other families the pain we have felt. During the past year, I have dedicated countless hours of research and have had conversations with numerous doctors across the country in pursuit of helping my son reach his full potential.

According to the CDC, autism now affects 1 in 150; a decade ago it was 1 in 10,000. There is clearly an autism epidemic, and the numbers seem to keep climbing.

The earlier autism spectrum disorders are diagnosed, the better the prognosis. Please see www.firstsigns.org or www.ucdmc.ucdavis.edu/mindinstitute, which have screening tools that pediatricians and physicians can use to recognize this disorder in its earliest stages. I have enclosed something referred to as the M-CHAT to use as a checklist for autism in toddlers. Hopefully you are already aware of these forms.

I challenge you to become more educated in matters relating to autism, especially since the numbers are climbing at such an alarming rate. The heartache and financial strain it places on families and society is too great to be ignored.

Sincerely,
Leeann Whiffen

Chapter 21

"I have fun today," Clay says, talking out of the side of his mouth in his tinny voice. He smiles his typical crooked smile as he looks up at Brooke. "I went to pet store."

"You did?" says Brooke, purposefully emphasizing "did" in a crescendo.

"With Kimber," says Clay.

"Wow," Brooke replies. "I'll bet that was fun. Let's play with blocks," she says as she finishes reviewing the notes in the logbook.

Brooke gets out the block bucket. They sit quietly, each of them building their castles.

"Oh, look at my castle," says Brooke.

"Look at my castle," Clay says.

"Yours is kind of big. Mine is little," Brooke says.

"Kind of big. Mine is kind of little." Clay says.

Brooke says, "Say, 'Yours is kind of little.'"

I grimace as I watch the monitor. He still struggles with pronoun reversal.

"My mom's name is Joan," says Brooke.

"My mom's name is Leeann," says Clay. Then he says, "My mom's name is Kathy." Kathy is Kimber's mom.

Brooke ignores his response.

She is fantastic at making work play and play work. Brooke is gifted. Clay can't tell the difference when he is in a session with her. She converts most of the programs to a game or craft. Clay is drawn to her happy, enthusiastic, yet disciplined attitude. She is magical in how she stretches him to learn. She is able to get him to do tasks that he has never done before. His reactions and attitude with her prove that he wants to do well. Instructors like Brooke are priceless in an ABA program.

"What are you building, Clay?" she asks.

"You're building a tall, tall tower," Clay replies.

"Say, 'I'm building a tall, tall tower,'" Brooke says.

"I'm building a tall, tall tower," Clay repeats.

"Hmmm," says Brooke. "That will be so cool. I hope it doesn't fall over."

Pronouns. We have to teach him how to use pronouns correctly.

Brooke takes out the photos enclosed in a plastic sheet. Lately, he has trouble remembering his preschool classmates' names. He calls all of the boys Preston, the name of one boy in his class. Noticing Clay's struggle, Miss Cindy takes photos of each child in the class and gives them to me. He reviews the photos in each session.

Brooke quizzes him on each member's name. He gets them all correct.

I stop folding the laundry for a moment and put my hands on my hips as I watch and listen intently at their dialogue. Here is a three-year-old boy going back through the various developmental milestones that he missed. As he has progressed and developed, I've witnessed the rebirth of my son. When he speaks, he sounds like my twenty-month-old nephew. He has the same intonation, sounds, everything. He is progressing, and I am watching it live. Day-to-day. Step by step. This small boy is slowly coming out of his world and into ours.

Sean grows frustrated by the constant tax law changes and interest rate fluctuations that have an impact on solutions he offers his clients, and explores ideas to start a different business that will provide better for our overwhelming financial needs. He and his partner settle on a company that provides services for the automotive industry. He is still able to maintain his tax planning company on the side to a lesser degree, and focuses the rest of his time and energy on starting his new company. I try not to think about the stress involved with starting up a new company so that I can focus on Clay's treatment.

We talk about it on the way to church the next morning. I ask how his plans are coming, but stop him when he starts getting too detailed.

"I guess the bottom line is, we're going to be able to meet payroll over the next few months, right?" I ask.

"Yep." He sighs. I see a worry in his eyes.

I grab his hand. "We're going to do this. I believe in you."

We sit down on the oak bench for the service. The light flickering through the window curtains catches my eye. I watch the shadows move back and forth with the branches on the tree outside. For the first time in months my thoughts aren't completely shrouded in Clay's development. Like the gaps between the branches on the tree, I can finally see through the fear.

I squeeze Drew's hand and whisper "I love you" in his ear. I watch as he folds his third and fourth finger down and sticks out his thumb, first finger and pinky. Then he holds his sign up toward me. I smile.

The speaker makes his way to the pulpit and begins talking.

Clay says, "Mama, read book." I pick him up and put him on my lap and whisper the story to him in his ear.

"Dog, dog. Ruff, ruff," he says in a loud voice. He points to other objects in the book and talks about them. His animation and expressions fascinate me. He points to the ball and looks at me excitedly. "Ball, no, okay," he says in his high-pitched voice.

The man in front of us turns around and stares. After what seems like a full minute, he finally turns back to face the front. Clay begins chattering loudly again.

"Talk softly," I whisper in his ear. "Match my voice."

Clay doesn't yet understand volume control. His volume is either loud or louder.

"See bah in grass. Mama, see bah. See bah. See big, reh bah," Clay says, pointing to a red beach ball in his book. I notice the folds in the man's neck as he turns around again, this time with a scowl on his face, and an audible scoff. I refuse to acknowledge him and certainly don't want to give him the satisfaction of feeling intimidated by his rudeness. I want to scream, *Just settle down and turn around. Don't you know? Don't you know that this same child didn't even know who I was? Don't you know how proud I am of my son and that he can even talk? You have no idea what he has been through.*" I shake my head and sigh in disgust. I'm not going to waste my time with this…this jerk.

We endure a long hour with this man looking back at us and staring in disapproval when Clay talks loud and repeats things. Despite my vows to ignore him, his stares puncture my fleeting security and fear seeps back inside. I am just sure he will say some stupid remark. But I'm glad he doesn't. I am wound so tight I would have unleashed some very unkind words. The kind of words you usually don't use in church.

Later that week I get an email from a member of an autism Yahoo! email group with an attachment listed as "autism card." I open an attached word document that has six simple text boxes. Each box is the size of a business card. In each box it reads,

> "**Autism** is a neurological disorder that impairs language development, communication, and social interaction. It is more prevalent than multiple sclerosis, cerebral palsy, or Down syndrome. According to the Centers for Disease Control, 1 in 150 school age children have autism."

I open the second Word file attached to the email. It is the backside of the card. It reads,

> "Part of his treatment and therapy is to bring him out in public and expose him to things that are difficult for him, like sounds, people, and activities. **Please be sensitive to our situation**. This is a very debilitating disorder with which we struggle every minute of every day. Thank you for understanding."

I have been bothered that I can't just blow people off who make rude comments or gestures. I want them to be more educated, more tolerant, and more understanding of autism and other seemingly invisible disorders. Now, when presented with unwanted advice sometimes accompanied by looks of disgust, I have something to give them in return without having to use my finger.

I'm sitting at the kitchen table reviewing session material in preparation for the team meeting on Friday. I look over and see Clay standing in the middle of the living room. He is looking up at the light on the ceiling with his head cocked to the side, his eyes are squinted—almost all the way closed. Then he places his hand over his left eye, a stim I had observed other autistic kids do before. I feel like someone has kicked my feet right out from underneath me, landing me directly on my backside.

"Clay!" I snap, grabbing his arm.

He jerks out of his trance and looks toward my voice.

"Look what I found…" my voice softens, "Harold the helicopter."

I have never seen him do that before. I rummage through my mind trying to remember any recent supplement changes or treatment adjustments we've made.

I discuss the eye squinting with Trisha the next day before her session. "You know, Leeann, he's also putting his hands in his mouth a lot lately," she says, concerned. "I have to prompt his hands down almost constantly." I glance over at him and see two fingers hanging out of his mouth.

Later, Brooke arrives for a session. She accompanies Clay to preschool every Tuesday and Thursday morning. I confront her right as she walks through the front door.

"How's he doing at school? Has he done anything weird with his eyes lately? Does he look at lights or cover one eye… anything like that?"

Brooke looks to the side, then back at me. "No. Nothing that I can think of," she says. "I'll watch him close. I have noticed that putting his hands in his mouth is becoming a problem."

"I wonder if he's having anxiety about something," I say. "Let's just make sure we keep on top of it and redirect." I feel myself tense up. I've never seen him display these types of behaviors before.

The next day I arrive at Clay's preschool to pick him up, but

Brooke is already gone. She leaves the preschool notebook in Clay's backpack for me to read. I pull it out and start reading, "He's grabbing other kids' toys a lot and isn't about to give the toy up, even when he sees the other child is angry. He seems to be demanding of Miss Cindy, interrupting a lot. He's not referencing other kids as much. He's having a hard time noticing that the other kids are putting their carpets away after circle time. He had low group participation today. On the other hand, he is joining in conversations around the room. He's strong in receptive language. But, he still seems to repeat words and phrases quite a bit if someone doesn't respond."

For the next few weeks, Clay's obsessive behavior increases. He will only color with black and brown, talks about the Pac-Man Xbox game incessantly, and draws pictures of ice-cream cones—in black and brown, of course. He is repeating words and phrases and lining up objects again. He starts pulling at his eyelids.

One night, especially discouraged, I drop into bed. I stare at the white ceiling, memorizing the patterns created by the stamped texture. *What if he slips back to where he was before?* After two long hours of microanalyzing every behavior and every possible cause, I slide into a deep slumber.... *I climb halfway up the sheer rock wall. My foot sends a piece of rock tumbling below. I count to five before I can't hear it tumbling anymore. The pine trees below are tiny shrubs so thick I'm unable to see the dirt in between. The river zigzags through the trees like a lone ski path through fresh snow. I struggle to suck in enough of the thin air. Perspiration drops into my eye, forcing it closed. My right foot cautiously slides across the slate, searching for a protrusion. I find a corner to brace it on. My fingers dig into their holds. I grunt, using all my strength to hoist my body upward. Just as I grab the hold with my left hand, my right foot slips off the edge of the rock. I cling to the side of the mountain with one hand, my body left dangling, while I helplessly scramble with my feet to regain my balance. I grasp with all the energy and determination I have left. Again and again I beat the mass of rock with my limbs. Each time, my hand and feet come up empty. I scream out our family motto, "Never give up." Blood trickles down my hand and onto my arm from pounding on the sharp rocks. I cry out in fear and terror, only to hear the lone sound of my shrill voice bounce off the surrounding cliffs. My hope fades as I begin to slide down the mountain. "Never give up," I whisper as I press my forehead on the rock. Suddenly, my scrambling foot brushes a protrusion. My heart jumps. I stabilize my body. The adrenaline rush exits out each limb as exhaustion sets in and I become limp.*

My face is dripping, my pillow marinated in sweat. I watch my chest heave up and down. I try to make out the numbers on the clock. I blink away the blurriness until they come into focus; 2:15 a.m. *It was a dream. It was a dream,* I say over again, reassuring myself.

September 2003. We hop up the steps and past the two cement lion statues, one with a chipped nose, that flank the entrance to Clay's preschool. Miss Cindy's husband greets Clay at the door, just like he does every Tuesday and Thursday morning.

"Hey, little man, put it here," he says, holding out his hand. Clay slaps his hand. "That's right," he says.

His afro-curly hair, brown mustache, and full Santa-like beard spattered with gray top his lanky body. I've never seen him wear anything but his dark gray mechanic's jumpsuit. His name, Bill, is embroidered in red cursive on a white oval patch on the right side of his chest. He looks like he could be the twin brother of the oil painter Bob Ross who used to be on PBS television.

"Holy moly," I hear Clay say as he gets to the bottom of the stairs and enters the preschool room. "That's cool."

"Thanks," I hear a little voice say back.

He must have learned those words from the other kids in his class.

I continue to listen at the top of the stairs.

"Hi, Clay," I hear a girl say.

From Brooke's notes, I know he seems to be making more friends now.

"Hi, Karly," I hear him say.

"Clay, will you lead us in the song today?" asks Miss Cindy.

"Okay."

I smile. I push open the screen door and hear it slam behind me. It is a beautiful day.

The sun bursts through the wood blind slats and onto my face. I blink slowly and deliberately. The ceiling fan comes into focus. I groan as I roll out of bed and walk toward the window. I turn the blinds so that I can see outside. The mountains are a fantastic array of colors, like they have been splashed with all the shades of the rainbow from a blank canvas. I slide open the window and feel the crisp breeze sweep across my face. The smell of fall blows through the screen and into the room. I stand at the window absorbing it all.

Inevitably, the events of the day ahead flood my mind. I throw on a sweatshirt and begin making arrangements, finalizing my eight-page-thick, 10-point font list for Sean for the upcoming DAN! conference in Portland, Oregon. I'm lucky that my parents saved enough money to pay for my round-trip plane ticket.

I continue the morning routine and begin mixing Clay's

supplements. I look at the printed list stuck to the refrigerator, making sure I haven't missed anything.

2 tsp Brainchild minerals
2 tsp Brainchild vitamins
½ tsp Valtrex
1 tsp Amino Support
¼ tsp Vitamin C
1 pckt Coromega
Vitamin E
Folic Acid
CO Q10
Monolaurin (2 capsules)
Aqua Flora
TMG

I squirt them into his mouth. The rubber stopper on the syringe slowly pushes all the way to the end. His lips pucker, forehead wrinkles, eyes squint, and head shakes back and forth as he swallows hard. I notice my own face is unintentionally mimicking his.

The telephone rings. "Hi, Leeann, this is Sherlyn. Are you going to be coming in to the CBC today?"

"Yes, I'm planning to."

"Oh, good. Well, I have a mom who would like to visit with you."

"Sure, Sherlyn, I'll call her when I get in." Pride grows inside me. I love my volunteer work at the Children's Biomedical Center. Many of those moms with whom I visit remind me of myself a year or so ago. It is so fulfilling for me to be there for them through the rough times. It gives my life extra meaning and purpose.

While organizing supplements in the back room at the Children's Biomedical Center, I hear the door chime. A boy talks to his mom in the lobby. His voice is very distinctive, almost robotic. As I listen, I note his intonation is peculiar, and I realize most of the verbal autistic children I have heard speak like this. I wonder if it's because of the way they are taught language, or if it's because of the nature of autism, or how their brain learns the spoken word.

Clay's voice is still high and sing-song sounding, too. We need to work on intonation, but I'm not sure how. In our ABA program, we are mostly teaching Clay a "canned" way to speak. Yes, he knows his birthday, his name, certain phrases, statements, etc. But does he ever talk about things he remembers, or recount events in his day, or make spontaneous comments? Is his language truly functional?

I remember recently reading about a style of ABA called Verbal Behavior (VB). It uses manding (requesting) and tacting (labeling), and teaching a child how to use language more functionally. I ask Sarah about it at our next team meeting. She seems interested and willing to try it, but has no formal training in VB. I find an online VB training manual on the website for an autism school in North Carolina. As I read the information I become more and more excited. It just makes sense. It hits at the very core of learning how to use language to satisfy everyday needs, and more. I ask Trisha, Kimber, and Brooke to read the entire manual so that we can discuss it at our next team meeting.

That night during dinner, Sean asks Drew to say the prayer. Drew begins, "Heavenly Father, we're thankful for this food and for our family. And please bless Clay that the germs in his tummy will go away so he can eat regular food." I squint open one eye and look at Drew. He is looking down at his plate while praying, with his hands cradling his head.

Drew cares so much about Clay. He takes it upon himself to make sure Clay is always treated well by the neighbor kids, and is the first one to help him when he is hurt. He loves his brother. They love each other. It is the kind of bond we all seek to have with someone in our lifetime. The kind that gives meaning to our very existence.

Chapter 22

Trisha walks through the front door smiling. She and Clay are back from a generalization session, in which they take what he has learned inside our house and generalize it to the community.

"Wow, Leeann. What a great session. You're never going to believe what happened."

"What! What is it?" I say, scooting to the edge of the couch.

"Clay was amazing today!" she says. "He was naturally motivated, seeking to please me constantly. At the end of the session, we went for a walk around a large church. We had a really cool experience while we were there. We watched a mother and her son, who looked to be about nineteen years old, come out of the church. As we walked around to the front of the church, they approached us. The woman said to Clay, 'Do you know how beautiful you are?' Clay looked up at her and smiled. Then her son got down on his knees, to where he was eye level with Clay and told him how he was going to bring joy into a lot of people's lives. After he told him this, Clay said, 'Thanks!' I was amazed at the intensity with which Clay listened. Then Clay knelt down, put his head down, and started to pray. The son looked at his mom, the mom looked at me, then I looked at the son. One-by-one we knelt down together, listening to Clay say a prayer. In his prayer, he said thank you for the church, thank you for Jesus, and thank you for my white jeep. We stood up from the prayer. The young man shook Clay's hand. And we went our separate ways. As we walked to my jeep, Clay was pulling on me, asking if we could go inside the church and talk to Jesus."

I sit there not knowing what to say.

"Did he really do that, Trisha? He spontaneously knelt down and said a prayer?"

She nods. "I know. It's one of those things where you had to be there to believe it. He has been doing fantastic lately."

The fund-raiser for the Children's Biomedical Center is a black-tie event. Sean has been working hard as a member of the fund-raising committee to get businesses to donate their products and services. He is accustomed to formal dinners and business meetings. I'm not accustomed to being out of my traditional T-shirt and jeans. I find a dress that I like, call Amy, and have her put my hair in an up-do. I squeeze into some strappy high heels, but I have to practice walking in them. I borrow some cheap jewelry from another friend who sells it out of her home. My legs wobble like a newborn fawn's as I walk down from our bedroom into the living room where Sean is waiting, looking crisp in his black tuxedo.

"Wahoo," Sean says, following up with a whistle. "I won't be able to keep my hands, or eyes, off you all night."

"Are you sure?" I ask. "I feel like I have three eyes. I'm so out of my element. I'm the cowgirl from Idaho, remember? I don't do formals."

"It looks like you're doing one now, and you're doing it amazingly well," he says, grabbing me around the waist and pulling me toward him. His lips graze my neck.

"Trisha," I yell up the stairs. "Will you take our picture? I'm not sure if anyone will ever see me in a dress like this again, or high heels, or, well, my hair all up like this," I say with my hands doing most of the talking. "So we better capture the memory."

I hear a gasp. "Leeann, you look beautiful!" her voice squeaks in excitement. Her hand is over her mouth.

"See," Sean says, poking me in the ribs.

"Let's just get this over with."

I promenade, as gracefully as I can, considering my shoes, into the Huntsman Cancer Center Pointe Restaurant. I am excited about the prospect of the Biomedical Center getting much-needed funds from this silent auction.

Sally, a friend and local autism mom, walks up and starts talking with us. She has been instrumental in making this evening a success. She was responsible for obtaining about 80 percent of the donations on her own. She holds a glass of wine in one hand and makes limitless gestures with the other.

"Sally, it barely started," I say, pointing to her glass.

"I know," she says, slapping me on the shoulder. "Isn't this great?" she cackles.

We are assigned to a table with two local attorneys, an entertainer and his wife, and several others. A local news channel anchor is the emcee of the silent auction. The new video filmed for the clinic, in which we took part, is shown before the food is served. The narrator says, "A silent epidemic is ravaging the future of this country. Every day, eighty more American children are diagnosed with it. Every year, thirty thousand children are added to the list. These children are not dying, but they are losing their lives. It destroys their potential, prevents them from forming normal relationships, and binds them to a future dependent on others. This illness exists in families across the economic spectrum, in every state of the nation, in every race, in every neighborhood. Suddenly, everyone seems to know someone who has a child with autism."

By the end of the film, tears are in the eyes of even the toughest and most powerful businesspersons and community leaders in the room.

At the end of the fund-raiser, Sean and I help take down decorations. I kick off my high heels and relish walking around in just my bare feet. We are hammered, having spent so much time and effort to make this evening a success. I take a stack of folded tablecloths off a table. I place my chin on top of the tall pile so they don't fall. I walk ten feet or so before smashing into a waist-high cart that was just below my line of sight. My feet sweep out from under me and I crash to the floor. The tablecloths fling out of my arms and fly like kites for a brief moment in the air before settling to the ground, scattering all around me. I am laughing so hard I can't stand up. Several people run to me.

"Are you okay, Leeann?" I hear someone say.

"Wow, that looked bad," another voice says.

I sit there on the floor, my knees propping up my arms, in my formal dress, my hair still in an up-do, laughing. Tears flow down my makeup-stained cheeks as my laughing becomes involuntary, shaking my entire body.

"You thought *I* had too much to drink," I hear Sally say.

"You know I don't drink," I say, still giggling while slurring my words together. I wipe the tears away with my arm. Sally sticks her hand out and helps me to my feet. I'm free. Free from the walls of my typical private self. I completely let go. And it feels so good…So good to just laugh.

Before heading home, Sean and I huddle with several families with whom we have become close through the Biomedical Center. When we converse, we mainly talk about our kids, and hardly anything else. I come to the realization that we don't even know their careers or what interests they have outside of autism.

What matters is that we all have one thing in common.

We spend everything we earn, and exert enormous amounts of energy, trying to find and implement new strategies that we hope will solve at least one of the one hundred symptoms our children manifest. We microanalyze every behavior our children exhibit. The hypervigilance is exhausting, and these parents understand the sacrifices that must be made.

They are doing the same thing every day. In many ways, we are closer than family. We know the pains, the sorrows, and the struggles. We know each other in an intimate, emotional way. We know everything there is to know about each child's symptoms, even though in most cases we have never met him or her. In visiting with these good friends, we begin to become aware that, in this fraternity, we're normal.

As the plane descends into Portland, I look out my window and see the city lights illuminating the sky. The light reflecting in the water glistens as the current moves. I'm relieved to finally be here. I have been so busy with Clay's program and talking with other families at the Biomedical Center that I hardly had the chance to prepare for the DAN! conference. At least I had time to get the right arrangements—several of us booked the same flight. Nora, two other moms from Utah, and I will share a room to save on costs. Nora and I sit next to each other on the plane. We spend most of the beginning of the flight talking about our ABA programs.

"How's school going for Dallin?" I ask.

"Oh, he's okay, I guess. We're really struggling with the public school. They just won't seem to work with us. I really want to have an aide in his classroom to help him, but they refuse to let me do that."

Nora is almost twice my age, but looks much older. Her hair is starting to gray in spots, and the lines around her eyes are deep and creased. She looks tired.

She takes off her glasses and rubs her eyes. "I don't know, Leeann. All of this takes so much time and energy. My health is suffering, especially since my car accident. We just found out that Dallin also has rheumatoid arthritis. He is in such pain that sometimes he can't walk. The kids at school tease him, especially at recess. The other day he tried to play with a group of kids and they started laughing at him, pulled his hair, and threw rocks at him. He tells me about what happens and he doesn't know how to handle the situation. He doesn't understand, socially, what to do."

My blood runs hot as I listen to her tell the story. I suddenly remember riding the bus to elementary school one morning when I was about eight years old. A boy sitting behind me started spitting in my hair. I asked him to stop several times and he refused. I clenched my fist and, with all my might, heaved my body around toward him as my fist met his mouth. I hit him so hard I cut my middle knuckle on his tooth.

I've never had patience for bullies.

I am outraged at Dallin's teachers—the adults who have the power to stop the bullying, but choose to look the other way. I anguish for Nora and her son.

I look at her, and she looks at me. There are no words. I turn and look out the window of the airplane.

For the first time, I start to wonder if I am doing the right thing in helping Clay. Never has this thought crossed my mind. What if I help him get well enough to function in everyday life, but he's still not completely recovered? What if he notices he is different from others—different enough that his peers notice and tease him about it? The thought of not being able to protect him bothers me immensely.

"Nora, what does his teacher say about it?"

"Oh, she says that he is the one who instigates it. She has been very difficult to work with. I'm going to have to change schools. I've spoken with the principal and even the administrator. I'm not getting anywhere."

The plane touches down on the runway. The flaps extend from under the wings to aid in slowing it down, causing a roar. "Dang, Nora. I'm sorry." The loudness from the whirling air drowns out my voice. I turn and look out the window.

As we finish up the first day of the conference, the four of us Utah bunkmates walk the streets of Portland in hopes of finding some great food. We walk into a pocket of delicious smells and follow it around the corner, finding ourselves at Duffy's Irish Pub. We gather outside at a table so we can enjoy the fresh air.

The marathon of the conference presentations from the day feels like a herd of cattle stampeding through my head. I can't concentrate on ordering.

I put my menu down on the table. "Jill James's presentation was exciting," I say. "I'm anxious to go home and try some of the supplements she mentioned that will help boost Clay's glutathione." I realize that I'm talking really loud because of my excitement. I spy the couple at the next table staring at me. I scoot to the edge of my chair, put my elbows on the table, and lean in closer. "I mean, what if this raises their glutathione to normal levels and they can chelate themselves naturally?"

Nora nods her head. "Yeah, Dr. James indicated that their behavior and overall well-being improved too."

"Uh-hmm," the other two say in unison.

Not exactly typical girl talk.

The next day, I'm exhausted and I have a fever. I feel like a grenade has been detonated inside my head. My throat is so sore and swollen I can hardly swallow. I know I have strep throat. Again. The pain is localized to one side of my tonsil, like it was the last five times I've had strep this year. "Crap!" I yell from inside the bathroom.

"What?" asks Beth. She is the nurse at the Biomedical Center. She also has a son with autism.

"I'm pretty sure I have strep throat."

"Oh, no. Really?"

"Yep."

"I'll go ask Bryan if he can get you some penicillin."

She returns a half an hour later.

"Well, since he doesn't have a license in Oregon, he can't get you penicillin. But he did say you can take up to four Advil every four hours."

Disappointed, I say, "Thanks, Beth, for your help."

I go to the lobby and purchase some Advil. I take four and return to my room and sleep for an hour. I wake up feeling really refreshed. The Advil dulls the pain, and I am ready to go again. I take the elevator up two floors to the next presentation. As I walk out, I see Jill James. My stomach jumps in excitement, like a young child who has just seen her favorite superhero. She brushes her bangs to the side while talking with another presenter. I look around at the booths until the person with whom she is talking finally leaves.

"Hello, Dr. James," I say.

She whirls around to face me, smiles and says, "Hello."

I reach out and touch her arm. "Dr. James, I'm so grateful for your research and for your interest in autism. It's because of you, and others like you, that we're beginning to figure out the pieces to the puzzle. I am so grateful for what you are doing."

Her head is slightly tilted to one side and her eyes glisten in the light as she listens.

"You know," she says, "it's because of parents like you that researchers like us do what we do every day. Your passion and commitment to your children are unsurpassed. Your son is lucky to have you, Mrs.—"

"Whiffen," I reply. "Thank you," I say, smiling.

I turn and walk down the hall. Through the crowd, I can see Nora several heads in front of me. I quicken my pace to catch up with her.

"Nora, I've been meaning to ask you something. Several weeks ago I received an email from my Yahoo! group regarding this new treatment called RDI. At first I blew it off as being the new treatment choice of the month, but as I started researching it further, I was really impressed with how it addresses the core deficits of autism. This is the only program I have run across that does this, and it sounds fun for the kids. I recently finished reading the book *Relationship Developmental Intervention with Young Children* by Steven Gutstein. Nora, I was floored at this new way of teaching our kids. It really makes sense. It focuses on making the family environment RDI-friendly. Then there are additional activities you can do to reinforce it. It helps them learn nonverbal communication, social referencing, and to be more vigilant in their environment. I want Clay to not only be able to function in real life, but also have relationships and friends. Isn't that really what life is all about? We need each other to enhance our quality of life. It's through our relationships with our friends and families that we are happier and more fulfilled. It gives our lives purpose and meaning. I want that for Clay. And I think RDI will help us get there faster. I want to start it with Clay. What do you think?"

She stops walking and faces me.

"I've been looking into RDI too. In fact, we're going to start Dallin as soon as we can find a good consultant. The only obstacle is there isn't an RDI-certified consultant in Utah. We would have to fly one in from another state." It's quiet for a moment. We look at each other and erupt in laughter. We agree it will cost $2,500 each, plus the cost of her flight and hotel. This doesn't include ongoing consultation. We both have second mortgages and shoestring budgets. Even the clothes we are wearing are several years old.

"What's a few more dollars?" I say, smiling.

"Yeah…right," she says, shuffling her feet. "I think I've narrowed it down to three consultants. There aren't very many around, since it is fairly new. But I found a couple out of Colorado and one out of Oregon. I'll email you the information."

"You know, Nora, it seems to me that Debbie was thinking about doing it for her daughter as well. Maybe we could split the cost. Otherwise, I'm not sure we can afford it."

"Great," she says, her eyes lighting up. "Let's talk to her and see what we can work out."

I make it through the next two days of the conference with four Advil every four hours. My head is full of scientific terminology and research. It all seems promising. The real chore is sorting through and eventually choosing what will benefit Clay the most.

My drive home from the airport is consumed by figuring out how we can afford to start RDI, which seems the most promising choice to add. Sean recently received enough funding to get his new business started. But what if his funding runs out and we are still swimming in debt? We'd go bankrupt for sure.

Maybe I can start working at night. *What am I thinking? That wouldn't even make a dent in our financial situation.*

I'm relieved to pull into the driveway at home. I quietly walk through the door, thinking the boys might be in bed.

I sneak around the corner of the family room and find Sean, Drew, and Clay all with their shirts off. Sean has green marker on his chest and face. He is growling while baring his teeth and flexing his biceps. He picks up Clay, who is squealing with glee, and holds him over his head. Then he tosses him into the beanbag next to Drew, whose squeals dissolve into laughter.

"Oh, you think that's funny, huh?" Sean says. He's trying not to smile through clenched teeth. "Well, then, let's see how you like this!"

"Oh, no. Oh, no!" says Drew, excited with anticipation. "Don't do it, Dad!"

Sean picks him up and throws him into the couch. He leans over him with his arms bent, flexed, and his fists in tight balls, growling.

"All right, who's next?" he snarls, spinning around, now facing me in his Hulk-like stance. He quickly stands up straight and relaxes his arms. His boyish smile spreads until I see his teeth gleaming through. "Hi, honey," he says with innocence.

"Mom's next," Clay yells. "Yeah, let's get Mom! Yeah, yeah!" Drew echoes. The boys run to me, grab me, and pull me onto the couch.

"It's good to be home," I say.

Mark lives five houses down the street from us. He has carrot-colored hair and an impish grin. His head is shaped like Frankenstein, and his ears stick out of the side of his head like quarter moons. Clay and Mark play with each other almost every day. Discovering they both like *Star Wars* was the spark that ignited their friendship. Every afternoon, they head for a backyard, drawing their plastic light sabers to have mock fights.

Mark and Clay are coloring together when Mark's mom calls and says he needs to go home. Clay cries because he wants him to stay. With his sessions consuming forty hours per week since we bumped his hours up in April after his naps began to fade, he hardly has any time left to simply play with other kids.

This seems counterproductive, so I decide to start integrating playgroups three times per week into our ABA program. It will expose Clay to children he may normally not play with, and will help them know where Clay lives for future unplanned play dates.

The next morning I see our family physician. Strep confirmed. It's the sixth time in nine months. My doctor refers me to an ear, nose, and throat specialist, who mentions a tonsillectomy. I immediately remember a friend who recently had one, and how much time it took her to recover. "I just can't do it right now. Not with everything that is happening in my life. There's no way I can take that much time off."

"Well, Mrs. Whiffen, you're going to have to do something. Maybe you need to reduce some stress in your life. Get more sleep, take your vitamins."

"Good idea. Thanks for your suggestions," I say as I hurry out the door.

Two weeks after recovering from strep, I get a serious case of the flu. I scramble to keep the program running smoothly and get the schedule organized. Trisha leaves for North Carolina for a few weeks to be with her family for Christmas. Kimber calls to tell me her schedule for final tests has changed and she won't be able to cover for Trisha the next two days. I hang up the phone and stare at the wall, my forehead pressing against the receiver.

I am so tired. Capitulating to my emotions, I slink straight down and sit on the floor. I hear the crunching of crumbs underneath me, reminding me that the floor hasn't been cleaned in weeks. I haven't been able to keep any food down in my stomach all day. Droplets of sweat appear on my forehead. I rest my head on my arms, propped by my legs, and melt into the floor. I feel a small hand brush my shoulder.

"What makes Momma sad?" It's Clay. I strain to hear and absorb his voice. I take him in my arms and hold him tight. He strokes my hair and my face, looking deep into my eyes.

"I love you, Mom. What makes you happy?" His words magically heal me. A soothing balm only his sweet voice can provide.

How can I pity myself when my son, a miracle, stands before me?

"You make me happy, Clay." I smile at him and kiss his forehead, as it registers that this is the first time he's ever told me he loves me, spontaneously, without me saying it first.

And he means it.

Over the next few days, I think a lot about what Clay said to me and how significant it is. He noticed I was sad. He wanted to help me. He was empathetic. *Empathetic!* Empathy is one emotion that is practically nonexistent in a child with autism. It is one of the core deficits of autism. It is also extremely difficult to teach.

Is this hard evidence of a turning point? Can I finally, comfortably say he is well on his way to recovery? This is the first time I am unafraid to feel confident about his progress. Every day he becomes more and more like his peers.

That evening I go into his room at 11:30 p.m. to give him

his syringe of DMSA—the drug we are using to chelate him. Again I marvel at the metamorphosis that has taken place in Clay over the two years since his diagnosis. All of the sacrifices we are making are well worth the magnificent and stunning progress he had made.

Even if he weren't progressing as much, I would still continue because I vowed to never give up on him. I watch him sleep as the light of the moon glistens off his white hair and silky-smooth skin. I brush his hair to the side with my fingers. I touch his chin, tilting his head up and to the side. I squirt the sulfur-smelling drug, masked with pear juice, into the side of his cheek. I see him swallow. I stand over his bed and marvel at his endurance and persistence.

I watch Clay as he tenaciously rips the wrapping paper off his presents. I smile and laugh. Two home movies begin to play in my head simultaneously in split-screen view—footage from the Christmas before he turned two, and real time. I tap Sean on the shoulder and motion to him to watch Clay. I'm happy that we can share in the spirit of Christmas together as a family.

Clay's eyes widen and his mouth takes the shape of an "O" as he pulls out the new Matchbox Haunted Mansion. "Ooooh," he says as he starts tugging at the packaging. "Let me help you with that, big guy," I say, smiling as I use the scissors to cut the tape on the box. "That's what I wanted, Mom," the words escaping out of his mouth almost in a whisper as he inspects his new toy. "Zzzzooom, vrrrooom," he says. I watch as he drives his cars in and out of the toy. I whisper to Sean, "Compare this to two years ago." We look at each other. We briefly kiss and share a long gaze.

"Today's my lucky day!" Clay shouts.

Chapter 23

At our team meeting in January 2004, I pose a question to Brooke, Kimber, and Trisha.

"What are Clay's deficits?"

"It seems Clay still has a hard time with attention span, focusing, and impulsivity," Trisha says.

Brooke adds, "He also doesn't seem to contribute when in group activities unless specifically asked or singled out. He doesn't look to see what the other kids are doing when he misses an instruction."

"I have noticed that his eye contact has gone down unless I pause before answering him," Kimber says. "He mainly just listens to an instruction and doesn't necessarily look at who is giving the instruction."

"I think RDI will help with all of these issues," I say. "Now we know what we need to work on with him, let's make sure we're implementing strategies into our daily sessions to encourage participation and increase his overall awareness level. I'm in the middle of arranging to have a consultant come and help us implement an RDI program for Clay. I think RDI will fill in the holes we are seeing."

"I'd like to attend his preschool within the next week or so," Sarah says, "It will help me get a better feel for his social behavior and interactions. This will help mold the programs to his current needs. Leeann, I'll send you a written report."

I get Sarah's report in the mail two weeks later. I gorge

myself on the content, as if his whole future hinges on this one observation.

Clay made several attempts to initiate conversation with his peers...Response rate to peers was above 90 percent...Clay demonstrated good imitation of peer play...During circle time, Clay made seven spontaneous comments, a peer made twelve... Clay was somewhat possessive about a toy he set down and was prompted by instructor to share it, which he did...On a few occasions, Clay attempted to ask a peer something and did not have their attention. Rather than tap them on the shoulder or say their name, he kept repeating the same thing over and over.

Summary and Recommendations—Based on my observation of Clay's behavior on this particular day, his play skills were very appropriate in comparison to his peers. If Clay continues to demonstrate this level of play, the instructor should not interact with Clay any differently than she does with other children in the class. Clay's language was very good, but one or two times his volume was low. Clay needs to be taught how to gain another child's attention when he doesn't get it easily on his first attempt. A token system may be an effective way to get Clay to be more attentive in the discussion during circle time. It would be helpful for the instructor to give Clay a proactive reminder to pay attention before the discussion begins, also letting Clay know that if he does well, he will earn a reward. Clay's instructor should begin to fade out of the classroom, where she can still observe his behavior. If Clay continues to do well, I would recommend that he gradually begin to attend preschool unaccompanied. Our goal should be to have Clay attend school independently by mid-March.

I am liberated as I read each word in the report. I lay on the floor in the family room looking up at the ceiling. I glance at the clock hanging on the wall. It is 2 o'clock in the afternoon. I can't wait until Clay gets out of his session in two hours.

Even without starting the RDI, I can see Clay blends in well with other children now. So well, in fact, that the average person would not be able to pick him out of a crowd as being different from his peers. His language and expressions have really blossomed over the last six months. Sarah is confident in how he is doing and amazed at the rate of his progression thus far.

Still, I need to know exactly how he is doing in terms of IQ, social skills, and language. I want him evaluated by a professional…someone who doesn't live with him twenty-four hours a day, who doesn't microanalyze his every move, judging whether or not the way he spun that toy around was appropriate behavior or autistic behavior. What if we have missed something? I schedule an appointment with Dr. Jennifer Gale, PsyD, in Park City. She is one of the most highly recommended pediatric neuropsychologists in the entire state. Her high demand means the soonest appointment we can obtain is three months away.

Nora, Debbie, and I email regularly in search of an RDI consultant. Nora has heard great things about a woman out of Colorado named Mary. From her résumé and interview, it seems she is the best candidate out of our three prospects. We arrange to have her flown in to Salt Lake City for four days for training and assessments. Once we are trained, we'll weave RDI into our existing ABA program and send Mary tapes every two weeks for feedback. All three of our children will get an RDA, relationship developmental assessment, which is required to start an RDI program. The RDA helps give a baseline in planning treatment objectives and developing customized environments for activity frameworks, based upon each child's individual needs.

But first we have our appointment for Clay's neurodevelopmental evaluation.

We're unusually quiet on the way to Dr. Gale's office for Clay's evaluation, an appointment we'd normally be chatty about. There are other things on our mind. Sean's new company has run out of money, and the investors aren't going to contribute any more capital. We're barely able to scrape enough together to pay the $850 to Dr. Gale for this appointment, and we're wondering how we'll ever afford RDI. We have $200 cash left in our checking account and our credit cards are all maxed out. Sean finally phased out his tax planning practice because his new business has been taking so much time. That means we've had no income for months. Instructor payday is tomorrow.

Stress steals Sean's natural, carefree personality and replaces it with a hollow emptiness I've never seen before. The worry is so sickening that neither of us have been able to eat much for days. I'm afraid to talk to Sean about it, because I don't want to escalate his anxiety even more. But we have to figure out what we are going to do. I finally break the silence, "Sean, tomorrow we have to pay the instructors. What are we going to tell them?"

"I just…don't…know." His lips are pressed tight. "Lee," he says, this time softer, "I'm working on it. Let me take care of it. There are potential investors that are really interested and they told me they would have a decision by tomorrow."

"Sean, what if—" I stop myself.

We drive the rest of the thirty minutes resting on my last comment.

When we walk into Dr. Gale's office lobby, we find a giant dollhouse and a white, fluffy stuffed dog on the floor. The dog is as tall as Clay, who goes over and sits on the ball of fur. When Dr. Gale emerges from her office, I see that she's young, with the body of a hip yoga instructor. She welcomes us with a big smile. She's wearing comfortable clothes befitting the natural, upscale Park City style.

"Hello, Mr. and Mrs. Whiffen. I'm Jennifer."

She doesn't refer to herself as "doctor." I like her already. She has a "Rachael Ray" likeability. She shakes each of our hands.

"This must be Clay," she says, kneeling down on one knee.

"Hello, Clay. How are you?"

"Good," he says, looking at her.

"Great," she says, smiling at him. "Let's go in this room. I'll play with Clay and ask you some questions at the same time." She opens the door to the room. It is full of books and toys. Clay's eyes are wide with possibility.

She asks us dozens of probing questions to get a feel for what Clay was like at the beginning of his behavioral problems versus now. She manages to observe and analyze his verbal and play skills while also digesting our information. After we finish in the toy room, Sean and I wait in the lobby by ourselves as Dr. Gale takes Clay in her office for additional testing.

After we spend an hour and a half reading everything there is to read in the latest *Newsweek,* Sean's cell phone rings.

"Well, that's wonderful news," I hear him say. "Let me get the account number."

He gives me a thumbs-up, winks with a grin, and does a groovy dance move. Just then Dr. Gale's office door opens. Clay emerges for a short break and snacks.

As soon as they go back inside, Sean runs to me, grabs me, and lifts me up in an embrace. "We got funding," he whispers in my ear. "We did it." The stress drains out of my limbs and a peace settles in its place.

"No, Sean. *You* did it. You've worked so hard for this."

After another hour, Dr. Gale peeks out of her office door to say she's finished.

Sean and I enter her office.

Clay looks exhausted. "I tried hard," he whispers to me.

"I know you did, sweetie," I say, holding his hand. "You always do."

"Clay, do you want a prize from my basket?" Dr. Gale asks, showing him her basket.

"Okay," he says, running to her. After agonizing over which prize he should choose, he ultimately picks a Kermit the Frog puzzle.

Dr. Gale sits down. Her chair squeaks as she wheels it closer to us. "Mr. and Mrs. Whiffen, your son is an absolute delight." She turns and looks at him in amazement. "Let's schedule an appointment in two weeks for you to review the test results with me."

"Oh," I say, trying to disguise my disappointment. *I thought we were going to get the results right away.* I want to ask her what she thinks, and how did he do. But I refrain.

I know the time will come.

Two weeks later, on a Thursday morning, I cradle Clay's head in my hands and kiss his forehead. I wrap him in my arms and hug him tightly. "I am so proud of you, son. I love you so much. Hey listen, I'm not going to be here for lunch, but Trisha will be here with you and Drew, okay?"

"No, Mom, please don't go."

I crouch down close to him. I look at him deeply and sincerely. I place my arms on each of his shoulders. His big blue eyes look deep into mine, his full cheeks reminding me he is still a small boy.

"Clay, you are my star." I emphasize every word. I feel my throat close off. He continues looking at me in the eyes.

"Mom, you are my triangle."

The room is quiet except for the refrigerator motor whirring softly behind me. I put my hand up to my mouth trying to contain the laugh. He smiles his crooked smile and tilts his head until it touches his shoulder. His smile morphs into a giggle. Then, simultaneously, we laugh out loud—a deep, feel-good laugh right from the belly. We laugh together some more, and I cry, because I am so full of joy. A joy that is so deep it can only be felt when one has finally emerged from the depths of desperation and discouragement.

It's March 2004, almost two years since Clay's diagnosis. I arrive at Dr. Gale's office early. Sean isn't able to make it this time. He has a meeting with the new investors. Starting up his new company has been so time-intensive. I go down the hall to use the restroom. I am a mixed bag of feelings. As I reach for a paper towel to dry off my hands, I take a deep breath before opening the door.

"Hi, Dr. Gale," I say as she brings me into her office.

Hello, Mrs. Whiffen," she says with her big genuine smile. "Please sit down."

I sink into the soft, voluptuous couch, then abruptly sit upright and scoot to the edge of my seat, my elbows folded across my knees.

"Leeann," Dr. Gale begins, "Clay is a charming boy, and I believe the test results accurately reflect his current levels of neurocognitive and neurobehavioral functioning." She takes her notebook from her desk and places it on her lap.

"On the neurocognitive analysis," she continues, "his subscale scores and core domain score consistently ranged from average to above average." I feel a rush of excitement.

"Speech and language skills are consistently within normal limits. Vocal tone, pitch, prosody, and rhythm were adequate. His language composite score fell within average range. Visuospatial and sensorimotor skills were consistently within normal limits. Clay's learning and memory skills were also within normal limits. He demonstrated an age-appropriate ability to shift and direct attention, and to filter extraneous stimuli to acquire information."

I listen intently. Her words are like water to my dehydrated ears. "Clay achieved a memory domain score in the average range. Clay achieved an attention/executive function domain score in the average range."

As she continues speaking, I begin to feel as light as a dandelion seed blowing through the air. Each time she says "average or above average," I want to jump out of my seat and do the victory dance. It is the most emancipating feeling I have ever experienced.

"So, Mrs. Whiffen, findings from the tests suggest Clay's overall level of neurocognitive functioning is consistently within normal limits. His performance across areas of attention and executive function, learning and memory, speech and language, visuospatialization, and sensorimotor functioning ranged from average to well above average within and between these given domains."

I sit there on the couch, thoughts speeding through my head.

"Mrs. Whiffen," she pauses and smiles, "I am happy to tell you that Clay does not currently meet the *DSM-IV** diagnostic criteria for a diagnosis on the autism spectrum. He is well below the cutoff for autism on the ADI-R and ADOS tests."

She goes on to explain her findings in more detail.

**Diagnostic and Statistical Manual of Mental Disorders: Fourth Edition*

The sound of her voice starts to fade, as if she is talking to me while walking away. It's too much emotion for my mind to contain.

"Mrs. Whiffen," she finally asks, "are you okay?"

"Yes," I say as if I'm on autopilot. "I mean, yes! I'm just so, so…happy…full of happiness." I know I'm not making sense, but I can't seem to focus on what to say.

She continues, "Well, in other words, while in contrast to Clay's well-developed neurocognitive abilities, he does demonstrate patterns of relative weakness across neurobehavioral areas of social interaction, pragmatic language, interests, and behavior. However, none of Clay's observed qualitative differences in these areas are significant to the level that he meets criteria for a diagnosis of autism. Clay clearly demonstrates a pattern of social interest in both adults and peers that is manifested by frequent attempts to initiate and respond to joint attention, to share interest with others, to show empathy, and to spontaneously seek to share enjoyment. Clay initiates conversation with his caregivers for no other reason but to engage in social interaction as he participates in varied and spontaneous make-believe play. While Clay is at times preoccupied with his Lego toys, Bionicles, his preoccupation is not encompassing or to the degree that it interferes with his adherence to daily routines.

"It is my professional opinion that Clay's inherent cognitive strengths, atypical [higher than average] level of social interest, and measurable progress to date are factors to suggest that in the future, as his current interventions are faded, Clay could be considered a candidate for placement in a mainstream kindergarten classroom. Such a placement could either be district-based or private, but should boost Clay's exceptional visuospatial strengths."

She stops talking and the room becomes quiet. She looks at me intently.

"Mrs. Whiffen, I want you to know that never in my entire career have I been able to remove an autism diagnosis. I am absolutely amazed at how far your son has progressed. I am honored to tell you that Clay no longer fits the criteria for an autism diagnosis."

I pause and take a breath so deep I feel like I might float. I hold it in for a moment, then let it seep out slowly.

"Thank you, Dr. Gale." My voice squeaks at the end with emotion. I jump up and hug her, then hurry and sit back down, embarrassed by my impulsiveness. While I know he is doing well, I still wasn't prepared for her to say what she said.

"Dr. Gale, we have seen this day many times in our dreams, only it was so far away we weren't able to touch it. To be here… with you…," I say shaking my head. "To be here with you, giving me these amazing test results, is like having my child raised from the dead."

I dance down the stairs to the car with Clay on my hip, his hand in mine. We make the twisty canyon drive home with the windows down and the radio up.

"We're free!" I shout above the roar of the wind. "We're free!"

My tears dry quickly from the wind whipping at my face through the open windows. I look at Clay in the rearview window. The sun illuminates his smile, and his hair flips wildly in the wind.

"Clay, we kept fighting, buddy. We never gave up. We did it!"

I dial Sean's cell phone.

"Sean," I say, still trying to catch my breath. "We did it!" I say again, this time through tears. "Clay lost his autism diagnosis!"

"What? Wow, I…That's incredible, Lee!"

"I know!" Even as the depth of this hasn't quite hit me yet. Pause. "Sean? I…you…all of this…thank you. Thanks for being there even when I was so preoccupied with Clay's treatment. You're always there. You sustain me."

He's quiet. "Thanks, Lee," he says softly.

Next I dial my mom. I tell her the great news.

We spend five minutes in silence crying together. She finally tells me she'll have to call me later when she can talk.

I begin calling more family and friends to tell them. After sharing the excitement with several, I dial the first four numbers of Nora's phone number. Then I wonder how I'm going to tell her. I can't finish dialing. What if she isn't happy for us? How can I share this excitement with her, knowing her son is still suffering? How will she react? Our bonds are cemented, but I am afraid sharing our news might put a crack right down the middle. I stare at the phone. I realize that I can't call anyone except my own family, and friends who do not have children with autism.

One minute I'm energized and happy, and the next I remember my friends and feel guilty. Guilty that my son has overcome a devastating disorder that millions of other kids and their families may have to live with their entire lives. I think of the isolated mothers who have put careers on hold, risked everything they have to help their child, but without the same results. Why can't all of them have this same outcome? Is it okay to be happy that my son is back? Will my friends in the autism community still want to be friends? Will they resent Clay and me?

Two weeks after our Dr. Gale appointment, Mary, our RDI consultant, arrives at the door, and she is completely different than I had envisioned. She is in her early sixties, has short, curly brown hair, and she wears big glasses. I realize within the first twenty-four hours that she is very set in her ways and not easily dissuaded. I'm slightly uneasy—I prefer to mold our programs to fit Clay's needs, targeting his deficits, rather than to follow word for word out of some training manual. But in talking with her more, I see that this is how she was trained under Dr. Steven Gutstein.

"What brings you into this field?" I ask her curiously.

"Oh, well," she says, "I used to be a music therapist and I helped a boy with autism. His mother told me about this RDI program they were going to start. I became interested, and decided to get certified."

"Hmm. Do you like it?" I ask.

"Well, sure."

That night I call Nora.

"How is everything going with Mary?"

"I think she's really good. She seems to really know her stuff."

"I hope we can integrate it into our existing program. It is implemented so different than ABA," I say.

"I think it will be easier once we have some experience running RDI."

"I think you're right." I say. "At least she'll get us started."

"Yeah," Nora replies.

It's quiet.

"Okay, well, I better…," Nora begins.

"Hey, Nora," I say nervously. "I've…been meaning to tell you something."

I'm still arguing with myself over whether or not to tell her. I don't really want to tell her, but I'm afraid she'll find out and wonder why I didn't tell her.

"We had Clay evaluated by Dr. Jennifer Gale in Park City.

She tested him, and he doesn't meet any of the criteria for an autism diagnosis."

It's quiet.

I think I shouldn't have told her.

"Leeann, that's....so fantastic! You must be ecstatic!"

"Really?"

"What do you mean, really? How many of us would give our lives to have that happen? That's just such great news, Leeann. Dallin is doing well. I sure hope we can get him to the point of losing his diagnosis. Wow."

"Nora?"

"Yep."

"Thanks. Your support really means a lot to me."

I decide not to tell any other autism friends. It just never feels right. When word finally leaks into the autism community, most are happy and supportive. Grateful for the renewed hope it gives them. A few are resentful, but understandably so.

Mary spends one morning and one afternoon of the next two days playing various games with Clay for the RDA, to get an idea of his functioning level so that we know where to begin. Then she has me play the same games with him for a final analysis.

We begin by playing a game called "Back and Forth." Clay and I each sit in beanbags across from one another with our arms locked together. I lay back and he pops up. He lays back and I pop up. I start giggling and accidentally snort. Then Clay starts giggling until he gets the hiccups. "Go faster!" Mary shouts. We go faster and faster until both of us are suffering minor whiplash.

Next, she has us play a block building game and neither of us is allowed to talk. We each have a bucket with the same blocks in it. I am the leader the first time around. I pick up a red block and show it to him, making sure he sees it. Then I put it down. He takes out the red block out of his bucket and puts it down. Then, I take out of my bucket a small yellow block. I hold it in the air so he can see it. I stack it on top of the red block. Clay does the same with his blocks. We continue with this game until his block structure looks just like mine and we have used all our blocks. Then he gets to be the leader in the second game.

Next, Mary brings out a pair of handheld drums. She hands me a drum with a mallet, and then hands Clay the same. She instructs me to do a fast, then slow rhythm, while walking around the room playing follow the leader—without words. Clay loves playing the games, especially when it is his turn to be the leader. The RDI activities dovetail our existing program by reinforcing what we are already teaching him, but also emphasize experience sharing in a relationship. The games are also designed to teach him inhibitory control by stopping when I stop, starting when I start, and continuing along with me, and they teach him social referencing, as he is required to watch for the instruction before he begins.

"It has been a pleasure to work with you. I'm pleased with how well Clay is progressing," Mary says when we're done. It sounds slightly canned. "I'll send you the RDA report in the mail. Also, remember to send your VHS tapes to me every two weeks with $50 each time, and I will return my evaluation by mail shortly after. It has been a pleasure." We shake hands.

The next week, I receive the RDA in the mail. I anxiously tear open the envelope and unfold the paper.

Treatment Plan

- *In the RDAs Clay shows he can be a terrific partner who is happy to have a playmate. These are moments you will build on.*
- *Clay is also a strong-willed boy who wants to be the leader.*
- *He shows preference for verbal interactions rather than nonverbal facial expressions and gestures at this time.*
- *He will continue to test you.*
- *Before beginning to play with him, say, "I'm the leader." When he talks about wanting to be the leader during play, have him reference your face, then shake your head no, and point to yourself.*
- *Clay has excellent verbal and communication skills.*
- *You want to minimize the use of words as you begin RDI, and maximize the use of nonverbal information.*
- *Talk to him only when he is referencing your face.*
- *If he verbally interrupts you, shake your head no, wait for him to reference your face, smile, and begin to count again.*
- *Your goal is to have Clay automatically reference your leadership.*
- *If he is disconnected from you, go to him, offer your hands to him, and hold his hands as you smile and shake your head yes. Then, point to where you want him to go, hold one of his hands and walk together without talking.*
- *Consistency, with a firm leader, is the key to success with RDI.*
- *If there is a time when Clay does not follow your lead as you are successfully playing a game, calmly tell him, "Time to change games." When you are using objects, ask him to hand them to you and put them away. Keep your emotions in control during this time. Then decide (1) if he's tired and needs a break, (2) if you've played long enough, or (3) if this is a power struggle.*

- *If it is a power struggle, stop the play, shake your head no, and say to Clay, "I do not want to play with you right now because you are _____, and that makes me feel_____."* *Then you turn away from him, without eye contact, and wait without talking to him. When he approaches you, smile and say, "We're ready to play."*

GOALS
Clay will reference your face and gestures for important information.
Increase Clay's competence.
Clay will coordinate his actions with the Coach.
Clay will experience fun and excitement as a Partner in play.

We integrate RDI activities into our ABA program, which proves to be tricky since they are two very different approaches. I fear that the structure of ABA and the looseness of RDI will conflict, causing confusion and possibly defiance, so I initially decide to do RDI activities in a different room so that Clay understands what we are doing. Clay still has two sessions per day, now at three hours each since he isn't napping anymore. The last hour of each session is devoted just to RDI.

Two weeks later, I dutifully send in my VHS tape to Mary for review. A week later, I get her evaluation. "Add small changes to keep each game interesting, and to have fun. During drumming, Clay accepted the coach's structure and didn't insist on leadership during this session. Exaggerate how you will hit the drum. For example, put your stick up high and look like you'll hit it really hard, but bring your am down and play softly. He asked a couple times if he gets a turn, and was accepting when the answer was no. With the ropes game, Clay is attentive, his body position is very good, and he was referencing the coach as well. I watched you play 'I'm gonna get you" during the transition time. This is a good game to play nonverbally also. It can end up with lots of giggles and fun play.

Mary continues with her observations, but at the end writes, "Make sure to remember to make RDI a way of life. Work it into all your interactions with Clay."

The next day after the afternoon session Trisha and Clay emerge from the schoolroom. "How did it go today, Trish?" I ask.

"He did really well. But he did something kind of weird. In free play he got out the doctor kit and put on the stethoscope and listened to my heart. He put the plastic Band-Aid on my wrist. Then he pulls out the yellow thing that you use to look in someone's ears. He puts it into my ear and says, 'Oh, can you hear the birdies?' And I'm like, 'What birdies, Clay? I don't hear any birdies.' And then he just didn't say anything." She giggles. Her hands are up in the air as she talks. I study her face.

"That's amazing," I say, shaking my head.

"Really, why?" she says.

"Over a year ago, before Clay could really even talk, we went to the pediatrician's office for a well-child checkup. It was that time that he ran away from me and I lost him for a minute or two. Remember me telling you about that day? Dr. Benway put the instrument in his ears to check them. To help put him at ease, she softly whistled in his ear and said, 'Clay do you hear them? Do you hear the birdies?'

"He was there that day in Dr. Benway's office. He heard and he saw what went on. He just couldn't put the connections together in his brain. His personality is still emerging. Now he is able to do that."

I knew it. He has always been in there. Always.

Chapter 24

That night Sean and I lay in bed.

"You're going to think I'm crazy," I say.

"No, I know you're crazy," he jokes. "What is it?"

I elbow him in the side. "I'm wondering if we should go ahead and try to have another baby."

"Really?" Sean laughs. "I didn't think I'd hear you say that for a long time, if ever."

"Well, Clay is doing so well. I think it would be great for the boys to have a younger sibling. It would teach them to be better brothers and maybe to be more responsible. They would have to share the attention. I think having a younger brother or sister would push Clay socially and help him to mature along with his buddies. I've always wanted a bigger family. But with everything we've gone through with Clay, I can't handle a really big family. I can't take on the stress of worrying about another kid having a disability. But if we just have one more, I think I can handle that. I want to know what it feels like to have the real mother/baby bonding experience, you know, a baby without colic. A baby that loves to be held and snuggled. A baby I can comfort. I think the stress and uncertainty will be worth it."

I pause. Sean opens his mouth to say something, but then closes it again. He continues to look up at the ceiling and listens.

"I don't want a huge space in between kids. If we're going to have them, I'd like to have one more soon, and then be done with it. I know this probably sounds crazy coming from me after hyperfocusing on nothing but autism for the last couple of years. But…you know, Clay is getting older and there will already be at least a four-year gap. I'm talking in circles, aren't I?" I look over at Sean. "Are you listening?"

"Yeah," he says.

"The big stickler is that I am really concerned that we may have another child with autism. From my research, we have a one in twenty chance of having another child with autism because we already have one."

"Lee, if that were to happen, you have so much knowledge. You would know what to do. You…."

"No…No, I can't go through this again. Our *family* can't go through this again. I mean…this Clay experience has sucked the energy out of every cell in my body. And we really are lucky, extremely lucky, with the outcome we've had. What if…what if we had another child with autism and I did everything the same, the same treatments that we have done for Clay, assuming we actually were able to come up with the money to do it all, and the child didn't progress like Clay has? Even though there is so much out of my control, I would never be able to let go of the fact that I could recover one of my children, but not the other. Failure is my biggest fear. I would do everything humanly possible with what I know to avoid having another child with autism. I can't see another child suffer. Emotionally I couldn't handle it. But I want another child. Our family isn't complete…yet. It's risky." I pause. "But I think I'm willing to gamble."

"Is there anything we can do to reduce those odds?" Sean asks.

"That depends. Obviously, we don't know exactly what causes autism. It is pretty much accepted, scientifically anyway, that autism has a strong genetic component, coupled with an environmental insult. And we know autism is four more times prevalent in boys than in girls. If we are to reduce our chances,

I have to make sure I stay away from potential environmental insults like heavy metal toxicity, viruses, and anything else that may be harmful to me or the baby in utero. And…," I snicker, "we'll have to have a girl."

"Honey, you are the one who has to bear the brunt of all of it. I'll let you decide what you want to do. I'll support you in whatever decision you make."

I groan. "Really? You don't have an opinion one way or another?"

"Not right now."

I hug and kiss him. "Thanks for being you. Good night."

I love the way he listens to me talk out my worries and fears—even when I don't seem to make sense. He has an uncanny ability to let me work out my own solutions without meddling too much. He knows my inner workings, and I love him for that.

I start taking prenatal vitamins every morning. I am fanatical about eating well, all organic, mostly fruits and vegetables. I have to know that I have done everything within my control to have a healthy baby. I start seeing a physician who oversees my chelation. He prescribes oral DMSA. It's the same prescription we use for Clay to extract heavy metals from his body. I only complete six rounds before having to stop because of low neutrophils, a type of white blood cell that helps fight off infection.

As a result of my low neutrophils, I seem to catch every illness that comes my way. I'm forced to stop chelation until I regain my health. I focus on staying as healthy as possible for as long as possible. And I constantly worry. What if there is something I'm not doing that I should be doing? There are days where the worry overcomes me. I come to terms with the fact that I can't control what happens. I finally admit to myself—there's no sure-fire way to avoid autism. It will have to be a leap of faith.

Several days later, Kimber comes to me one afternoon session and mentions that we are running short on behavioral programs. "He's growing tired of the same programs, Leeann. Does Sarah have any more?"

"I've asked her, but the other day she admitted he is too advanced for what she has to offer him. I'm looking into an agency based out of California called The Center for Autism and Related Disorders, or CARD. From some of my email lists I've learned they have upper-level programs for children, designed to develop theory of mind and executive functioning skills. They also use a more informal approach consistent with the verbal behavior method."

She nods.

"The other day I showed him two foods. I had some broccoli in one hand, and a cookie, his favorite, in the other. I told him how much I loved the broccoli and even bit off a piece and ate it. Then, I asked him to give me my favorite food. He handed me the cookie.

"Part of theory of mind is to be able to understand that others have different feelings than yours and to be able to use this information to make sense of their behavior and predict what they will do next. Executive functioning is the part of the brain that helps plan and organize, and create self-regulation.

"You know how Clay taps incessantly on your shoulder when he needs something, or says your name over and over and over? I think this will help him understand to wait. It will teach him to be interested in others and not just talk about Bionicles or Buzz or whatever obsession he has at the moment."

"It all sounds perfect for Clay," Kimber says. "How soon can we start?"

"I just looked at CARD's website and will be calling them to schedule a workshop in the next couple of days. I'll let you know."

So many of the kids I've read about who finish an ABA program may look indiscernible from their peers, or maybe don't even fit the *DSM-IV* criteria, but still have social deficits. I hope through RDI and CARD, we can get beyond those issues with Clay.

Cost? There it is again. Cost is always an issue. But with the funding coming through, we may be able to make this work. Besides, we won't need Sarah's biweekly services any longer. She has been fantastic, and it will be hard to tell her. I know she will understand though, because it really will be best for Clay. And we have reached the end of her programs. Still, she was the one who first reached Clay, who guided us through the maze of programs to success.

The next day I call CARD and inquire about their services. The woman on the other line mentions there will be three or four months of waiting after our application has been filed. I ask her to send the application right away. We may be able to find enough money by then to at least pay for the initial workshop, which would be nearly identical to our ABA workshop, although we would be learning upper-level programs this time.

In the meantime, I find and hire an instructor who currently works with a family in our county who uses CARD's services. She has several years' experience with theory of mind programs and says she can get us started right away. This will help us form a bridge until we can save enough money for CARD.

My mom phones to tell me that there is going to be a special on ABC national news highlighting a potentially successful autism treatment program. I instantly flip on the television to make sure I don't miss it. The story highlights one child and his family's experience with autism. He is placed in an ABA program and does remarkably well. I watch with familiarity as the program describes a family going through the same basic things that we are. I'm grateful for the awareness it brings to autism. Sean calls our local ABC station and tells them how impressed we are with the story and encourages them to run more local pieces regarding autism.

"Do you mind if I ask your affiliation with autism?" the ABC representative asks.

"I have a son who recently lost his autism diagnosis."

"Wow. Really? Would you be willing to share your story on the air?"

"Maybe. Let me talk to my wife and I'll get back with you."

"Honey," Sean calls after me.

"Hold on," I say, "I'll be down in just a minute."

"What's up?" I ask, walking down the stairs and into the kitchen.

"What would you think of telling our story to ABC4?"

"No." I don't even take a breath. "Remember what we have always talked about? Our ultimate goal, our dream, our hope was to get Clay past this. In fact, that's why we hardly told anyone in the beginning, and that's why we had planned to move after he lost his diagnosis and before he started kindergarten. I don't want anyone to know."

"Okay, okay. He puts his hands up in the air like he has come into contact with someone wielding a gun. "I just thought I would ask."

"Well, don't you feel the same?"

"I just don't know. I mean, we had always planned to do those things, but something inside me tells me we should rethink this. Will you think about it?"

"Yes. But don't be disappointed if I still say no."

The entire evening, I can hear my own voice, inside my head, boldly making the promise I made over two years ago. *If I can get through this, I will do everything in my power to help those families going through a similar situation.* But did I really know back then that we would get this far? Did I really know how tough the decision would be?

"Lee, think of all the families our story may help. Think of the hope it might give to them to share our story," I hear Sean say. He's right. The biggest hope I clung to was that of Catherine Maurice in her book *Let Me Hear Your Voice.* My eyes gobbled up every word as if it were the last. Her children recovered from autism. It gave me the idea that there was possibility for Clay. It opened my eyes to worlds I never thought possible. It gave me direction and hope. Without hope, you are blind, blinded by the darkness that surrounds adversity and disappointment.

I know what we have to do. It is stirring inside me. It is a chance that may never come again. We have to take advantage of this opportunity to spread the word.

My palms are moist. I have a zit on my forehead, and I'm nervous about what I'm going to say. I have always wanted to make a difference—not to live my life for myself, but to have a profound impact on someone, somehow. I want to be sure I am articulate and clear. This is our chance for the silent voices of autism to be heard. I ask Clay for a third time if he wants another snack. I want him to be on his best behavior.

I sit on the chair in the living room going over my notes of what I want to say. Out of the side of my eye I see a vehicle pull in front of the house. I look and see a black minivan with KUTV Channel 4 painted on the sides. I watch two people get out and unload their equipment. I open the door before they even have a chance to knock.

Jennifer, one of the producers of the local ABC news program, interviews me first and asks direct, emotion-provoking questions, "Leeann, what was going through your mind after your son was diagnosed with autism? How do you think his story will help others? At what point did you feel like he was getting better? What do you want to tell all the other parents out there who are going through a similar experience?" As she finishes the last question, I feel like someone has slammed an orange down my throat. I inhale, trying to suck in the tears.

"I would tell them to have hope. That without hope, all is lost. With hope you have something to look to…like a lone light in the darkness. It is something to focus on so that you'll never give up. Don't ever give up."

"That's all I have," Jennifer says, cueing the cameramen to shut their equipment down. "We're thinking it will probably air Thursday or Friday. I'll call you and let you know." She reaches out to shake my hand. The camera lights from overhead makes her eyes glisten.

"Thank you so much for your time. It's because of folks like you that I'm in this business. What an amazing boy," she says shaking her head.

She leaves with her camera crew, and the front door closes. I go to the window and watch them drive off. I am relieved it is over.

Jennifer calls me the next day and says it will air on Thursday night at 10:00 p.m.

Thursday evening comes. Sean and I yawn and pretend to mosey up to our bedroom like every night when we get ready for bed. I plop on the bed and turn on the television with the remote. "Oh, here it is," I call to him, downplaying any significance the news might contain this particular evening.

After it is over, I realize that I was so nervous watching it that I hardly breathed the entire segment. I inhale a deep breath to catch up on the lack of oxygen.

"They did a great job, don't you think, Sean?"

"Yes, I think so too. I'm really pleased with it."

In a silly voice I say, "Can you believe we were on TV!" My voice gets progressively louder as I emphasize the word TV. I hop up on the bed and jump up and down wildly.

Sean furrows his eyebrows. "Everything okay, Lee?"

"Yeah—fine," I say, out of breath.

I notice he is staring at me.

"What! Why are you looking at me like that?"

"It's just…I haven't seen you act like this since before autism."

"Well, it's me, baby—I'm back!"

I launch up one more time and land on my butt next to Sean.

"You know," I say, cuddling up to him, "it's actually kind of fun being silly."

He looks over at me and with a straight face says, "Hmm, I wouldn't know."

I look at him. Then we bust up laughing. I grab his face and pull it toward mine, kissing him. "I love you so much. We've been through a lot, you and I."

I glance to the side, and then back at him.

"I'm so glad I have been on this journey with you at my side. You've kept the hope, you haven't let me get discouraged, you haven't complained about the huge amounts of stress you have been under from all of the debt we're in, and you have totally trusted me and given me the freedom to spend our money, or lack of money," I say, chuckling, "on whatever I felt was necessary to further Clay's development. I love you for that. I am so grateful for you. You are my best friend."

He looks at me deeply and sincerely, "Thanks, Lee. That means a lot to me. Now, why don't you get silly again," he says, with a mischievous grin.

I see Clear Channel on the caller ID. "Hi, Leeann, this is Jennifer Bolton from ABC4 News. The response to your piece last night was overwhelming. People want to know how to contact you and Dr. Jepson. Can I give out your email or telephone number?"

"Absolutely. I would love to chat with people."

"Great, thanks. Also, we received a telephone call from a family with a child recently diagnosed with autism. They expressed how your story gave them hope—hope that maybe their son could get better also. Because of the response, we're going to run a story featuring their family and their feelings on some of the treatments your family used."

"Sounds great! Please let me know when it will air."

"Thanks, Leeann, I really appreciate it."

I put the phone back in its dock. I'm warm all over. Our story made a difference. This feeds my soul more than anything I have ever done. Clay's success story gave parents hope! And the information is helping other families to find treatment.

I shout as if I am the only one around for miles. "Clay, our story gave parents hope!" I leap into the air and kick my heels. He looks at me with his head tilted.

During the next week, our incoming telephone calls are at an all-time high. My email inbox is flooded with new messages.

I speak with one mother over the phone who has seven children. Her last three are triplets, one of which has autism. "I just think he's autistic because I wasn't able to spend the time I needed with him to bond correctly. He didn't get the attention that he needed from me. Children should be with their mothers," she tells me.

The fire crawls around my ears and up into my forehead.

"Look, Bruno Bettleheim came up with the refrigerator mother syndrome theory in the late 1940s," I say. "It has been discounted and disproven over and over again. Please don't blame yourself. This is not your fault."

"Well, but I recently went to a symposium where an African doctor spoke about how Americans and Africans differ dramatically in their approach to handling their infants. African women have their infants strapped to their bodies most of the time until they get to be too big. As our lifestyle becomes more hectic, we are holding our babies less and less."

"Hmm. That's an interesting theory. I've never heard it before. But I want you to understand that you did not cause this to happen to him."

That evening, I catch up on reading the last week's log notes. Drew and Clay are playing with Legos together behind the couch where I'm sitting. When Clay starts playing with one of Drew's Legos, Drew gets mad and hits Clay.

"Drew," I say, "we don't…"

Clay interrupts, "Drew, don't hit me. You need to be nicer."

"I'm sorry," Drew says.

"I'm sorry, too," Clay says.

Then Clay walks to where Drew is playing and gives him a hug.

I look at them and smile. They will never know how many times I've dreamt of them playing together like this.

Chapter 25

Summer 2004. I want Clay to get as much social interaction as possible before kindergarten in another year, and since Miss Cindy's preschool is out until the fall, I find a new private preschool that offers summer classes. There are viewing windows in each of his classrooms. The observer can see into the room, but it is a mirror to the children inside. This makes it easy for the instructor to take notes on his behavior, and to watch his interactions with the other kids.

After school one day, Clay says to me, "Dad, will you…."

"Clay," I interrupt, "do I look like Dad to you? I sure hope not," I joke.

He looks at me, embarrassed, and says, "Well, sometimes you call me Drew. I don't look like him either."

I am stunned into silence. I whirl around and face him. "Well, young man, you are exactly right." I ruffle my hands through his hair.

I go to the calendar to check. July 14, 2004. It is the first day of my missed period. I count twice just to make sure. This is the day I have been anticipating for four months. Attempting pregnancy has taken us a little longer than in the past because we purchased a book called *How to Choose the Sex of Your Baby*. We hoped if we followed all the specific directions on how to get a girl, we wouldn't have to worry as much about autism. We followed the directions outlined in the book perfectly.

I have a pregnancy test all ready for the occasion, so I grab it and go into the bathroom. I reread the instructions, double-checking that it can really detect pregnancy this early.

"Okay, here it goes," I whisper. I can hardly wait the two minutes. I try to peek before the time is up, but I can't tell yet. I watch the second hand tick on my watch, then glance at the stick again. I can't stand the uncertainty. I check again as I hear Sean shuffle his feet outside the door.

"Honey," I say through the bathroom door, my eyes still fixed on the white bar with two parallel blue stripes. I continue to stare at it in my hand as if to make sure I'm not just seeing double.

"We're having a baby!" I explode out the door and jump into his arms, and we embrace. Just like in the movies.

My smile fades and my face turns serious.

"And now the real anxiety begins," I say.

"Not if we don't let it," Sean replies. "Honey, there are a lot of things in life we can't control. I know that's hard for you to imagine," he says sarcastically, "but let's just do all we know how and hope for the best."

"Hmmm. Sounds easy, but it's not," I say, playing with the corner of his collar, "but I'll try."

"I know this will be hard, but I also know it will be good for our family."

In the ensuing weeks, anxiety sweeps through me like a microburst of wind. I cannot settle down. I worry incessantly about the baby, wondering if it's developing normally. I even worry about how my worrying is affecting the baby. I worry about everything I eat. I almost stop eating altogether because I never feel that what I am eating is healthy enough for the baby. I stew. I worry. I can't sleep. I'm plagued by excruciating migraine headaches, but I refuse to take any sort of pain reliever because I worry it might affect the baby. I don't do any sort of exercise because I think it too might hurt the baby. I can't imagine how a developing fetus can survive being shaken and jumbled around in my uterus while I'm trying to stay in shape. My doctor says it's okay to exercise in moderation, but then again, it was a doctor who told me Clay was fine and to stop worrying. I don't know who I can trust anymore. So I research every question until it doesn't make sense anymore, and then I rely on gut feeling.

That Sunday afternoon, Sean and the boys are engaging in a rowdy game with beanbags. They throw palm-sized beanbags around at each other, and then they tackle the person who catches the bag.

I sit on the couch trying to tune them out while I read a book called *The Child's Discovery of the Mind*. Suddenly, a beanbag flies from across the room and hits my three-months-pregnant belly.

"Guys!" I yell, jumping to my feet as if I had been stung by a bee.

"Gosh, knock it off! Can't you see? I'm not playing. You just hit…you just hit me, the baby!" Fury is circling through me so fast I can't spit out the right words to match my emotions. I hurl my book, hitting the wall across the room. "You guys always have to be so wild and unruly! Why can't you ever just sit quietly and read or something?" Drew and Clay are staring at me, their eyes gaping. I'm close enough to see their large, black pupils. I rush upstairs and into my bedroom. I flop on the bed, surprised by my own overdramatic reaction, so inconsistent with my personality.

Eventually, Sean comes up to our room and sits down by me on the bed. He starts rubbing my back and caressing my hair. "Relax, honey. I know you're stressed about the baby." His rubs turn into soft, fingertip tickles along my neck and arms. "You need to realize that you didn't cause what happened to Clay. It wasn't something you ate, or didn't eat. It wasn't because you stressed too much, or not enough. Lee, you need to understand that there are some things you just can't control."

"Please help me to stop worrying," I plead, scaring myself that I am somehow becoming dependent on him for my stability. "Sean, I really feel like if there is something wrong with this baby that it will be my fault, something I have done. I can't go through each day a nervous wreck. I'm probably hurting the baby worrying so much. I had no idea I would have this much anxiety. I'm only three months along; how am I going to last six more months? Then how do I endure three years after the baby is born waiting to find out if all of its developmental milestones are reached on time? Did we make the wrong decision? My thoughts torment me every day. I want them to stop."

July 2004. Sean and his business partner, Lance, hire their first new employee and decide it's time we meet him and his family. Lance, who loves to cook, offers to have a barbecue at his house. He mentions he has a small, above-ground swimming pool and tells us to have the boys wear their swimsuits.

"Oh, it is a scorcher—high 90s today," the voice reports on the car radio en route to Lance's house. "Whew," I say, looking back at Drew and Clay, with their goggles snugly in place. "You boys ready for a smokin' hot day?" I yell to them in the back.

"Yeah," they yell back simultaneously.

I laugh when I see only the outline of their eyes and lips sticking out from around white sunscreen. They laugh when they see me laugh. Their orange floaties bob up and down with energy.

"This is what it's all about, isn't it?" I say. Sean nods and smiles.

As we arrive at Lance's home, we are invited to go around to the backyard. I meet their newest employee and his wife and kids. Their kids are already in the swimming pool splashing around.

Drew and Clay spring up and down on their toes, like they usually do when they are either really excited or really have to go to the bathroom.

"Can we, can we?" Clay asks, pointing to pool.

"Go for it!" I say. They take off running, with me not far behind.

The water in the pool is about four feet deep. Drew can touch the bottom, but Clay tries to touch and it is over his head. Their floaties keep their heads just above the water. They swim and splash around like sea otters.

A half hour passes. I can almost hear the perspiration sizzle as it runs down my forehead. I begin to feel nauseated. I pick up Drew's towel from the grass and wipe my forehead. I look back at Sean, who is by the barbecue talking with Lance and his new employee. I try to signal to him to get me a drink. He doesn't see me.

I search for any type of cover from the sun. There's no shade except under the umbrella on the patio, which is too far from the pool. I finally put a towel over my head.

I imagine guzzling a cold, delicious glass of ice water. I eye the table with food on it and notice a cooler. Keeping an eye on the pool, I quickly walk over and open the cooler. Yes. Water. I take a long refreshing drink. I swallow in a steady rhythm as I quench my seemingly insatiable thirst. I toss the bottle to the side of the cooler and walk back to the pool. I can see Drew swimming around and some of the other kids, but I can't find Clay. I scan the pool over and over—then the yard. Nothing. Panic sets in.

"Sean," I yell, "I can't find Clay in the pool, do you see him? I can't see him. I can't see him." I feel lightheaded. Sean immediately walks toward the pool, searching for any sign of Clay.

"Sean!" I shriek.

Sean breaks into a sprint, jumps over the ladder and into the pool. He emerges with Clay in his arms. Clay is choking and gasping for air. Water spews from his mouth like a fountain.

Sean's arms are wrapped around Clay's white chest. With Clay still in his arms, Sean slumps down the side of the pool and onto the grass. His clothes, socks, and shoes are waterlogged. Clay is still coughing up water, while trying to take a breath. His lips are a light shade of blue, his face washed out. He sinks into Sean's arms.

I take him and put him in my lap, cradling his head in my arms.

"Son, are you okay?"

"I think so," he croaks. I watch his lips pucker and his eyes squint. He puts his hands over his face. He reaches out and wraps his arms around my neck and cries, big heavy sobs. He buries his head into my shoulder. "I didn't mean to," he says.

"What, honey, you didn't mean to what?"

"Take off my floaties."

"Why did you do that?" I ask, shocked that he would do something so ridiculous.

"Because, Drew didn't have his on anymore."

On the way home, I can't stop wondering how soon we'll be able to begin Clay's theory of mind programs. Would that have helped him think to himself, *Oh, Drew took his floaties off because he can touch. I can't touch, so I won't take my floaties off.* He still thinks of situations in one dimension, black and white.

I finally admit the guilt I feel. "Sean, it would have been my fault if he had drowned. I was just so thirsty and nauseated,

and I didn't want to interrupt you to have you get me a drink.
I shouldn't have left the pool, even if it was only for a minute.
I kept my eyes on the pool nearly the entire time. It was just a
few seconds as I was drinking. Only a few seconds."

We've worked so hard to reclaim our son, yet today we
almost lost him completely.

I hear music blaring from the schoolroom. The thumping of
Trisha and Clay dancing above shakes the light on the ceiling. I
run up to my bedroom to watch. They are dancing to the song
"Funky Town." Clay yells into the fake microphone, "Wonchoo
take me to funky toowwwn?" Trisha runs and takes the microphone and sings, "Won't you take me to funky town?" on cue.
She shakes her hips back and forth. Her hands shimmy in the air.
Clay hops up on the table. He stomps his feet to the music, and
then sticks out a leg and twists it around in the air with his hands
on his hips. Then he jumps down and hops around the room.

Later, Trisha walks up the stairs from the RDI session in
the basement. She has a hand up to her stomach, laughing to
herself. Clay is trailing behind her. "What's so funny?" I ask.
She giggles, pointing to him when he isn't looking.

"Hey, Clazy Wazy, why don't you go jump on the trampoline for just a minute, 'kay, buddy?" I ask.

"All right, Mom. Will you come out with me?"

"I will after I talk to Trish."

I watch him run outside to the trampoline. I notice his baby
face is developing into that of a small boy.

"Okay, what happened?" I ask Trish.

"You know how Clay used to be obsessed with Pac-Man, the
colors black and brown, and ice cream?"

Yeeahh," I say, anxious to hear the rest.

"Well, he knows that he can't talk about them in his typical ABA session upstairs, but when we're doing RDI downstairs, Mary says to just ignore it, right? Well, today, we are downstairs in the RDI room doing activities and Clay blurts out as fast as he can, 'Pac-Man, black and brown, ice cream.' Then he looks at me like, 'Okay, Trish, now what are you going to do?'"

I start to laugh, a laugh that eventually turns into one of those deep, rejuvenating belly laughs that you wish you could experience every day as part of a mental workout. Laughter begets more laughter. I find myself unable to stop. "Oh, Trish," I try to catch my breath.

"He's a smart kid, Leeann. He likes to test me, to see what he can get away with."

The next morning, I finish preparing breakfast and call for Drew and Clay to come eat. No answer. I look around and find them downstairs playing Go Fish. I tiptoe down the stairs and peer quietly around the corner.

"Do you have any monkeys?" Clay asks.

"Nope," says Drew. "Go Fish."

"Awwww, mannnnn," Clay says, exaggerating his disappointment.

"Do you have any pigs?" Drew asks.

"Yep, I do. Here ya go." Clay hands over a pig.

I'm impressed that he doesn't get upset that he has to give away his card. I watch for a few more minutes.

"Boys," I finally say in a silly voice, "it's high time you got your fannies upstairs for some breakfast."

Their heads whip around.

"Oh, Mom, you scared us," Drew says. "We didn't know you were there." They run up the stairs to me and we share a big hug together. I kiss the tops of their heads and chase them up the stairs.

The more we make RDI part of how we live, the better response we get from Clay. I spend time making sure things are mostly unpredictable, thinking of ways to spice up the daily routine.

For dinner one night, I set the table with the glasses facing down and the forks turned the wrong way, just to see how Clay will react. As we sit down to eat, he says, "Hey, what happened here?" One day I wear crazy green, glittered glasses, five times the size of normal glasses, to see what reaction I can get out of him. "Mom, why do you have those?" he says. "Let me see." He pulls them off my face and puts them on. I put a sticker on my forehead and talk to him until he notices. He stares at my forehead until he looks cross-eyed. He finally picks it off.

Anticipation, surprises, unpredictability—they all help Clay reference our faces and our body language to figure out what to do next.

I notice Clay using the skills he's learning, even in interactions outside our own family unit. While my sister, Kristine, and her family come over for a visit, her son rams a car into Clay.

Kristine disciplines her son, "Reece, don't do that please, you'll hurt Clay."

When Reece continues to bother Clay with his car, Clay looks at Kristine to see if she is watching, or if she'll get Reece into trouble. He's referencing people's faces like this a lot more now, especially when he's in an unfamiliar situation.

Clay is progressing so quickly through his formal RDI sessions that by the time I send video footage for Mary to review, he has mastered the activities and needs new ones. I'm frustrated with Mary's timeliness in getting us her feedback from the footage, especially since she tells us not to continue without her approval. I feel like we're trudging through mud when we should be skimming across the top of the water. On the next DVD I send, I slip in a sticky note. "Mary, we decided to continue without your approval because he was getting bored with the activities that he's already mastered."

I begin to wonder if we really need Mary. I discuss it with Sean. "I was talking with the instructors the other day at our team meeting. We think that we can take it from here, now that Mary has given us a starting point. We have the book by Steven Gutstein, *Relationship Development Intervention with Young Children,* which has all the activities we need to continue. I'll just make sure I review tape and talk about how we are generalizing it into our home." We decide we can't afford to receive services from both Mary and CARD.

The CARD program is more complex in how it is administered, however. We need a consultant to navigate us through the unfamiliarity of the new program. CARD phones to let me know that things are in order for our initial consultation. I talk to Nora and Debbie about wanting to use CARD's services and ask if they want to split the costs. Nora wants to continue RDI and ABA, and Debbie wants to continue Floortime and RDI. So, I call another friend, Susan, who has also looked into using CARD, to see if she wants to participate with the consultation and split the costs. She excitedly agrees. We book the consultant's flight and hotel for the two-day visit.

The day of the initial workshop, we bring in kitchen chairs and beanbags to cram as many bodies as possible into our small family room. Susan and her husband attend with their instructors, while Sean and I complete the small brigade with our instructors. Lisa, our new consultant from CARD, begins her presentation. The setting is similar to the one when Sarah first came into our home for the two-day ABA training workshop. Yet my feelings are very different now. I'm comfortable with Clay's progress, and my hope is that this will help him even further.

After taking Lisa to her hotel room, I turn the corner on our street and notice a small boy playing in the road. He is talking, but no one else is around. I slow to a crawling speed. He doesn't seem to see or hear me as I approach him. He has no toys. He's simply talking to himself and making motions with his fingers while standing in the gutter. I roll down the window.

"Hi, Jared," I say. No response. I wait for a moment. His mom comes running toward him, waves, then grabs his hand and takes him into the house.

"Mom, what is wrong with him?" Clay asks.

"Honey, that's Jared. You know, from church. He has…" I can't say "autism." "He has difficulties learning, Clay. I want you to always be nice to him, son. Always."

Chapter 26

Twenty weeks into the pregnancy, in October 2004, we have our appointment with the ultrasound technician. The gel is cold on my skin. As the nurse presses the ultrasound wand further into my exposed belly, I wonder if she is pressing too hard. I can feel the baby squirming all around inside.

Oh, how I want a girl so badly. It isn't because I already have two boys, but because of the odds. Autism strikes four times more boys than girls. I want a girl because she is less likely to have autism.

I clench the vinyl sides of the bed with my slippery palms, my eyes locked on the monitor. The paper underneath me crinkles with my every move. Every one of my senses is on heightened alert, scouring the environment for any odd facial expression or sound that could possibly indicate a problem with the fetus. The whooshing noise of the fluids and the baby's heartbeat are the only audible sounds in the room.

"Looking good," she says as if my nervousness is visible. "See the heart." She points to it on the monitor. "There are the four chambers."

My mind eases, my shoulders relax.

"Head circumference looks good." She taps on the keyboard and clicks with her mouse, drawing measurements on the screen.

"All dimensions are within normal range. Do you want to know the sex of your baby?"

"Yes," I say quietly, swallowing so hard I think everyone else may have heard the saliva rush through my throat. Sean squeezes my sweaty hand, then wipes his hand on his dry pants.

"It looks like you have a little boy in there, Mr. and Mrs. Whiffen."

I feel as if the air has been completely sucked from my body. Did I hear her right? I can only hear the sounds of the machines. Sean looks at me with a half smile. He turns to the ultrasound tech.

"He looks healthy so far, right?"

"Yes, he does. Looks great."

I am still in shock. "Will you point out his, um…" my mouth is dry and my tongue sticks to the roof of my mouth. "Maybe it's the umbilical cord between his legs. Do you think?"

She smiles. "Let's see if we can get him to move around a little more so we can take a look at a different angle." She presses the wand into my stomach further and rolls it around. The baby squirms and it feels like he does a flip.

"See that?" she says. "Right there. There it is."

She hands me a Kleenex to wipe off the gel.

I've prayed so hard for a girl. We tried everything in that book that said if we followed all instructions exactly we had an 80 percent chance of getting a girl. How could this happen? I walk out of the room holding Sean's hand. My feet move as if they have ten-pound weights around each of my ankles.

"You think I was worried before," I say to Sean. "I—"

"Lee, stop," he interjects. "You can't do anything about it. Let's just roll with it, and be grateful for what we have, and the baby's health so far."

It's January 2005, and the baby is getting bigger. I plop down on the couch with the boys, putting Clay on what little lap my bulging belly isn't covering. He slides off my knees and to the side.

"There's no room, Mom."

"Sorry," I say, smiling.

"When is the baby coming?"

"In just eight more weeks, can you believe it?"

He giggles in excitement.

I open the book we recently checked out at the library. *The Carrot Seed* by Ruth Kraus. I am sandwiched between my two boys. I open the book and start to read.

"A little boy planted a carrot seed. His mother said, 'I'm afraid it won't come up.' His father said, 'I'm afraid it won't come up.' And his big brother said, 'It won't come up.'"

Clay says, "Mom, the carrot is going to come up. I know it."

"Shhh, let's wait and see," I reply.

I continue, ending with "And then, one day, a carrot came up—just as the little boy had known it would."

Clay looks up at me and smiles. "See, I told you it would, Mom." Clay leans over and pats my belly. "I wonder when we're going to have a little sister?"

I laugh and ruffle his hair with my hand.

"Oh, Clay, I don't know. Maybe never."

He is quiet, thinking about something.

"Now let's get to bed," I say, pretending to chase him and Drew up the stairs as I waddle toward them like an overweight duck.

I finish tucking Drew in bed and whisper our secret.

"Bushel and a peck, bud."

"You too, Mom," he says, flashing the "I love you sign" with his hand. I turn to walk away.

Next, I walk into Clay's room and find him already in bed.

As I pull the sheets and blankets tight up to his chin, I bend down to kiss his cheek.

"Aaagh," he says. "Your girl hair covered up my eye!"

I laugh and say, "Clay, you're my special boy."

"And you're my special girl, Mom."

I walk down the stairs and into the quiet living room. Although my anxiety is less now that I am further along in my pregnancy, I still think constantly about the tiny body inside me. I pray constantly for his well-being and that I am doing everything I know how to ensure his health and proper development. I remind myself that his being born healthy would only be a small victory. I will have to watch his development closely until he is at least two years old. Even then, I know it will not be until his third birthday that I can begin to relax.

The next morning, I amble over to the ringing phone, hoping I can get there in time. I can barely hear Sean on the other line. His voice is weak and he sounds tired.

"I passed out in the restroom a few minutes ago. I'm not feeling well. Can you pick me up?"

"What? How? Who found....The bathroom?"

"Lee, just come pick me up."

"Okay. I'll be right there."

As I pull up to Sean's office, his business partner helps him walk to the car.

"Lance, what happened?"

"He was using the restroom and passed out. He's lucky he didn't split his head open on the sink."

"That's it? That's all we know?"

"Yes."

His face is yellow, and he slumps down into the seat. I take him to the InstaCare physician. My overdue belly makes it difficult for me to get out of our low-sitting car.

After asking us a bundle of questions, the physician suggests we schedule an appointment with a neurologist and cardiologist for further testing.

A couple of weeks later, we see the neurologist. He does an MRI. Everything looks fine. The cardiologist recommends he wear a twenty-four-hour heart monitor. Sean sleeps with the wires stuck to his chest. He returns the monitor to the clinic, and receives a call back the same day.

"Mr. Whiffen, while you're sleeping your heart is often going three or more seconds in between beats. We would like you to schedule an appointment in two days for further testing, including having you wear the 'King of Hearts' monitor for one week."

At the appointment the cardiologist tells us there is a 70 percent chance Sean will need to get a pacemaker. He thinks Sean suffers from bradycardia, a slow heartbeat, causing him to feel dizzy and fatigued. Sean is only thirty-one years old. I wonder how this could be happening to a healthy young man. The man I love.

I drive us home from the appointment. Sean is in the passenger seat. Many of my friend's husbands like to be the ones driving. Sean sits in the passenger seat almost every time because he knows I like to drive. He doesn't have some big ego that needs to be fed, or any other power or control issues. I love him for that.

"What?" he asks. I realize I keep staring over at him.

"Nothing."

That night I lay in bed unable to sleep. I look over at Sean sleeping. My eyes comb over his face. His thick, brown hair, black stubble covering his face and chin, and round earlobes that he says "turn red when it's really cold outside." I gently kiss his lips. I finally drift off. I jerk awake and find it's much later, with only the glint from a streetlight peeking through the blinds. I turn and see Sean in the same position as when I drifted off. I prop up on my elbow and watch to see if he's breathing. His hands are folded over his chest. It's so dark I think I can see partial movement, but even then I'm afraid my eyes are playing tricks on me. I put two fingers on his neck. I feel a slight pulse. I flop back on my side of the bed and take a deep breath and watch the numbers on the red digital clock until the sunbeams dance into our room.

We visit the cardiologist for the King of Hearts follow-up appointment. He asks if Sean has had any dizziness or other symptoms since his last visit. Sean says no.

"Well, hmm. Let's not put the pacemaker in just yet. But if you have more symptoms, dizzy, light-headedness, or fainting, I want you to call me. Then we'll go from there."

I sigh, comforted by the doctor's words, yet still unsure whether he's going to be all right.

I'm now a week overdue, so my OB/GYN schedules the induction for next Monday. It is the same day Sean's new company is having an open house and ribbon cutting cere-mony. I ask the doctor if we can change the day. "Nope," he says, shaking his head, "You need to have this baby."

We check into the hospital that morning. Sean's open house is in two hours. He paces around the room. I finally tell him, "Just go. Please. You don't need to be here watching me in bed. Besides, it will take me a while to dilate."

"I can't leave you here."

"Sean, go! I'll call you when things start getting exciting."

"Okay, but I'll be right back."

Sean barely slides back into the hospital in time for the action. But he's there, and an hour after Judd is born, Sean picks up Drew and Clay from his mom's house and brings them to the hospital.

"Would you like to hold him?" I ask.

Their eyebrows rise simultaneously, as if I had just asked them if they each wanted a $5 bill. They plop down by each other, making a squishing sound on the cheap vinyl chair. Their arms are outstretched. Sean hands them the tiny bundle of blankets.

"Just right. He's just right," Clay whispers. Then he adds, "He's cooler than me."

They stare at him and marvel that his tiny hands clasp onto their fingers.

"Look, Mom. I think Judd likes me," Drew says. His chest puffs out.

After I return from the hospital, while I'm doing my hair one morning, Clay brings his little blue chair up into my bathroom and sits down by me. Judd sleeps next to us in his bouncer. Clay asks me about my makeup and why I would want to paint my eyelashes black. Then he leans over and kisses Judd softly on the cheek.

Chapter 27

Instead of dragging myself into the shower like every other morning, I spring out of bed like a jack-in-the-box. It's August 2005, and today is Clay's first day of kindergarten. I fumble with the buttons on my pajama top. Like the character in the movie *Groundhog Day,* I have lived this day a thousand times in my dreams, since the day Clay was diagnosed with autism.

Now it is real.

I get out of the shower and get dressed. I hear a tiny knock on the bathroom door. I open it and there stands Clay. He is biting his lip. The other side of his mouth is turned up into a smile. I take his hand, but he pulls it away. I know he is nervous, but when I ask him, he shrugs his shoulders and says, "Um, no."

We eat breakfast together as a family, as usual. The crunching of cereal, slurping of milk, and clanking of our spoons against the bowls combine into a melody. I help Drew and Clay get their backpacks on, and we go out the front door together. We walk down the street together with my arm around Drew's shoulders. We are almost halfway there when Clay grabs for my hand. Our hands link together and our story unfolds in my mind. I look at him as we walk together, snippets of major milestones flashing through my thoughts, one right after the other.

"Mom, why are you staring at me?" he asks.

"Because I love you," I say, wondering when and how I will ever tell him what he has endured. He continues looking ahead.

As we get closer to the school, I see more kids swarming than were packed into our last visit to Chuck E Cheese.

"All right, see ya, Mom," Drew says.

"Do you need help finding your room?"

"Nah, I know exactly where to go. I'm in second grade now, remember?"

"Oh, yes," I say with a sly smile kissing his forehead. "Good luck today, honey."

I walk with Clay up to the side of the school and show him where to get in line. I watch as he stands with his back against the school building with his new classmates and teacher. He accidentally bumps into a boy standing next to him. I hear him nervously say, "Sorry." I flutter my fingers in the air toward him. He flashes me the "I love you" sign with his hand. I take lots of pictures.

I watch as he follows the line of new kindergartners into the school. His small body hides behind his large backpack. He shrugs his shoulders up and down as he walks proudly on his way to an unfamiliar world.

I start walking toward him because I forget to tell him, "Use your inside voice, and raise your hand if you have a question. Oh, and, make sure you ask questions about the other kids and what they like to do because other people like it when you ask about them. You'll make lots of friends this way." But I stop myself when I realize I need to let him be himself.

I stay outside the classroom long after the other parents have gone—just in case he needs me. I glance through the window a few times until the teacher sees me and gives me a funny look. I finally decide it's time to go.

When afternoon approaches, I anxiously walk over to the school. I sit on the edge of the curb in the warm sun. I watch the children burst out of the outside classroom door like an army of ants funneling out of their hole.

I hear a kid shout, "Bye, Clay!"

I find Clay and see him waving at a couple of new friends he has made. My nervousness subsides.

He stands among the chaos searching for me. He gets up on his tiptoes, head and chin up, hoping for a better look. His smile droops when he doesn't see me. "Clay," I yell. "Over here!" I wave my arms high above my head so that he can see. He looks toward my voice, smiles, and runs into my arms.

"Hey, buddy. How was your first day of kindergarten?"

"It was good. Real good. Can I have a Popsicle when I get home?"

"Sure."

We get Popsicles out of the outside freezer and eat them together on the front porch.

"Do you want to jump with me on the trampoline?"

"Sure, Mom. That would be great!" He jumps up and runs around to the backyard. "I'll wait for you back here!" he yells.

A few minutes later, I join Clay on the trampoline. We interlock hands and jump in perfect synchrony. We play ring-around-the-rosie and fall down on top of one another. Our hair is fuzzy from the static electricity. We stand up, and Clay reaches for my hand, shocking me with his finger.

"Ow, you silly!" I say, sliding my feet around the tramp in calculated retribution, shocking him with my finger as I pass.

"Ah!" he yowls.

We join hands again. I tell Clay to run around the edge of the trampoline. I rotate with his run. He runs faster and faster, our hands firmly joined until he becomes airborne. I spin him around and around.

"Whoa, Mom, this is awesome!" he giggles. Our eyes lock, and I'm transported back to the early days when we used to dance. We fall down, suffering from the drunklike dizziness.

We are on our backs laughing.

Clay comes over to me and gives me a big kiss and says, "Mom, I love spending time with you."

Today's my lucky day.

Jyl Read Photography

Epilogue

Katie Moss/Peekaboo Photos

July 2008

Clay is a typical third grade boy—not even his teacher knows of his past. Besides excelling in reading and math, he loves nothing more than to see the look on people's faces when he drops down into the full-on splits, something he has been working on during his three-year gymnastics career. On any given day, you may find him in his room jamming with his metallic blue electric guitar, hanging out with friends, or sorting his NFL football cards, Brett Favre being his favorite. He is no longer on a gluten- and casein-free diet and takes just a daily multivitamin. He truly believes that there isn't anything wrong in the world. His pure, optimistic attitude serves as the framework for the family.

Drew continues to be the big brother who is always looking out for Clay. He enjoys writing short stories and drawing. Once in school Clay was asked to write down his hero—he wrote Drew's name. If you see one of them, you'll usually see the other. They're inseparable.

Judd has grown and developed into a typical three-year old. Each milestone and developmental stage reached has been wildly celebrated and sweetly savored. Judd is the first person Clay runs to each day after school, greeting him with a big hug and kiss. Sean and Leeann have decided not to vaccinate Judd until he turns four years old, using an alternative vaccination schedule. This is a decision they didn't take lightly, and it hasn't come without repercussions. At twelve months of age, Judd suffered from a high fever for several days, which was nonresponsive to ibuprofen or acetaminophen. Because he wasn't vaccinated, the pediatrician was forced to rule out meningitis with a spinal tap, since his c-reactive protein blood test indicated inflammation somewhere in his body. After returning home from the hospital after the spinal tap, Judd began looking out of the corners of his eyes strangely, spinning in circles, and pounding on his head with the palms of his hands. The pediatrician was concerned and ordered a CT scan to check for inflammation on the brain, and it came back normal. After seven days, his fever finally subsided, and he recovered with no residual symptoms. Doctors could not identify the cause of his fever.

Sean's company continues to grow, and he remains an amazing father and husband. He enjoys eating mounds of ice cream and playing sports in his spare time. He hasn't yet had to get a pacemaker, and has only fainted once since that first time.

Leeann serves as the Autism Speaks Utah Chapter Advocacy co-chair and is working with state legislators on a bill to provide insurance coverage for autism treatments.

Every night, when Leeann tucks Clay into bed, she tells him, "You are my star." He still answers, "Mom, you're my triangle." One night recently, he surprised her by bucking the tradition. Instead, he said, "Mom, you're my angel."

In Leeann's home office, above her desk, hangs the brush she used to calm Clay before going out in public. It is a constant reminder of how far the family has come, and the work that is still left to do as an autism advocate.

Visit the Whiffens and read their blog: www.leeannwhiffen.com.

Acknowledgments

I must be the luckiest woman in the world to have the companionship of my best friend and husband, whose love and support are limitless and unconditional. You are the loudest fan in the crowd—cheering me on so loudly I can no longer hear my fears. I love you.

My deepest gratitude goes to those families, clinicians, researchers, and fellow parents who have been determined and steadfast in their fervor to research and find answers. It is because of their passion that many of those affected have found their true potential.

I'm grateful for my parents and for the principles they taught me—work hard, find the real lessons in life, and seek that which is truly important. And thanks to my siblings—Julie, Kristine and Jay, Brian, and Blake and Kate for your encouragement and support.

Jodie Rhodes, thanks for taking a chance on me. Your expertise and experience are unparalleled. Shana Drehs, thanks for caring so deeply about this project. Your keen eye helped reveal many hidden treasures.

To Pamela Bartlett, Holly Mendenhall, Tim Robinson, Tina Dyches, Susan Bassett, and Robyn Bergstrom for your friendship, encouragement, and feedback.

To Brandon Storrs, a deep-felt gratitude for your artistic eye and vision in developing and editing the video trailer and photos.

Steve Hawkins and Cohezion, thank you for your friendship and creative contributions in the design and shaping of the website.

Susan, Betsy, Sondra, Laurie, Amber, Emilie, Cheryl, Pam, Cathy, Marie, Laura, Andrea, Teresa, Sherrie, Ali, Megan V., Amy, Yayoi, Holly, Megan H, and all the autism moms and dads everywhere—you are the silent heroes.

Berk and Tami, thanks for setting us on the right course. And thanks to Lorrie, Keri and Fred, and Brett and Shelley for your support.

To Hank and Diane for raising such a wonderful son.

Bryan and Laurie Jepson, we owe much of Clay's success to you. Thank you.

Sarah, Trisha, Andy, Natalie, Kimber, and Brooke—never forget the profound difference you made in the life of our son. You will always be a part of our family.

Resources

Support, Advocacy, Research

Autism Research Institute (ARI)

619–281–7165

www.autism.com

ARI designs and conducts scientific research aimed at improving the methods of diagnosing, treating, and preventing autism. ARI's research findings contain over 40,000 case histories from over sixty countries and are made available to parents all over the world.

Defeat Autism Now! (DAN!), a project of the Autism Research Institute, has regularly occurring meetings for physicians, researchers and scientists dedicated to finding effective autism treatments. DAN! educates parents and clinicians on the latest biomedically based research and treatment interventions for autism.

Autism Society of America (ASA)

1–800–3AUTISM

www.autism-society.org

Autism Society of America increases autism awareness, advocates for services, and provides up-to-date information regarding treatment, education, research, and advocacy.

Autism Speaks
212–252–8584
www.autismspeaks.org

Autism Speaks strives to fund research into the cause, treatment, prevention, and cure for autism while bringing hope to those who cope with the trials of this disorder. They are committed to raising public awareness about autism and its effects on individuals, families, and society.

Families for Effective Autism Treatment (FEAT)
www.feat.org

FEAT includes parents and professionals supporting autism advocacy and best treatment outcomes. Check for a FEAT in your area.

First Signs
978–346–4380
www.firstsigns.org

First Signs advocates early identification and treatment intervention of children with developmental disorders. The M-CHAT, modified checklist for autism in toddlers, is available for download here: http://www.firstsigns.org/downloads/m-chat.PDF

Generation Rescue
www.generationrescue.org

Generation Rescue was formed by parents of children who have been diagnosed with childhood neurological disorders (NDs). Generation Rescue believes autism is an environmental illness and can be treated through biomedical intervention.

Interactive Autism Network (IAN)

www.ianproject.org

IAN is an online project dedicated to expediting autism research by connecting researchers and families. If you would like to be a part of the IAN community, see www.iancommunity.org, to provide feedback and stay up-to-date with the latest autism research.

National Autism Association (NAA)

877–622–2884

www.nationalautismassociation.org

NAA empowers and educates families affected by autism while also advocating for those who are unable to fight for their rights. It gives hope to families that autism is a biomedically definable and treatable disorder. NAA encourages families to never give up in their mission to help their loved ones reach their full potential.

National Dissemination Center for Children with Disabilities (NICHCY)

800–695–0285

www.nichcy.org

NICHCY serves as a hub of information on disabilities in children and youth including research-based educational practices, IDEA, and No Child Left Behind.

Parent to Parent Program

800–651–1151

www.p2pusa.org

Parent to Parent Program links parents of newly diagnosed children with experienced parents for support, advice, and guidance.*

SafeMinds

404–934–0777

www.safeminds.org

SafeMinds investigates and raises awareness of the risks to infants and children from mercury exposure.

Southwest Autism Research and Resource Center (SARRC)

www.autismcenter.org

SARRC provides services and support to children and families affected by autism, while looking for answers to solve the mysteries of autism.

Talk About Curing Autism (TACA)

www.talkaboutcuringautism.org

TACA is dedicated to providing information and resources in helping to support families affected by autism by linking families with professionals. TACA aims to accelerate the time the child receives a diagnosis to early intervention.

---

*Not available in every state.

Thoughtful House Center for Children
512–732–8400
www.thoughtfulhouse.org
   Thoughtful House treats children with developmental disorders through a combination of medical care, education, and research.

US Autism and Asperger Association (USAAA)
www.usautism.org
   USAAA is dedicated to helping individuals on the autism spectrum achieve their fullest potential by providing education, support, and solutions.

Unlocking Autism
www.unlockingautism.org
   Unlocking Autism is an advocacy group that provides a parent-to-parent support hotline.

Online Video, Training, and Reports

Autism One Radio
www.autismone.org
   Autism One was started by a small group of parents in an effort to address education, advocacy, and fund-raising.

Autism Podcast—Autism Research Institute
www.autismpodcast.com
   Defeat Autism Now! webcasts are a project of the Autism Research Institute. The autism podcasts are compiled from presentations given at recent DAN! conferences.

Autism Society of America

Autism 101—A free online course

www.autism-society.org/site/PageServer?pagename= about_course

This thirty-minute course covers the following areas: Introduction to the Autism Spectrum, Overview of Treatment Options, Treatment Assistance, Transition to Adulthood, More Information, and Resources.

Autism Spot

www.autismspot.com

888–317–8074

Autism Spot provides information and education to the autism community through streaming media, videos, blogs, forums, and news pieces.

Dan Marino Foundation

www.childnett.tv

Childnett.tv is a web channel where viewers can watch personal stories and the latest autism treatment therapies, and hear from the autism experts.

F.A.I.R. Autism Media (Foundation for Autism and Information Research, Inc.)

www.autismmedia.org

F.A.I.R. Autism Media provides video interviews of autism specialists, researchers, parents, and speakers from various national autism conferences.

Schafer Autism Report
www.sarnet.org

The Schafer Autism Report is a daily autism newsletter compiled by the monitoring of all the major news sources, websites, and latest research.

Legal

Individuals with Disabilities Education Act (IDEA)
www.idea.ed.gov

Wright's Law
www.wrightslaw.com

Behavioral Intervention

Center for Autism and Related Disorders (CARD)
www.centerforautism.com

CARD is an organization that treats children around the world with autism and related disorders following the principles of Applied Behavior Analysis (ABA).

The Floortime Foundation
www.floortime.org

The Floortime Foundation the makes DIR/Floortime model broadly available in hopes of helping redefine the potential of children with developmental and communication challenges.

The Gray Center
www.thegraycenter.org

The Gray Center helps individuals with autism spectrum disorders to communicate and interact with others more successfully by increasing social understanding.

PECS (Picture Exchange Communication System)
www.pecs.com

PECS is a unique augmentative training package that teaches children and adults with autism and other communication deficits to initiate communication.

Relationship Development Intervention (RDI)
www.rdiconnect.com

RDI focuses on enabling children and youth with autism spectrum disorders to form lasting relationships with family members and society for a better quality of life.

Social Communication, Emotional Regulation, and Transactional Support (SCERTS)
www.scerts.com

The SCERTS Model addresses the core social-emotional challenges faced by children with autism spectrum disorder and related disabilities.

Treatment and Education of Autistic and Communication-handicapped Children (TEACCH)
www.teacch.com

TEACCH is an evidence-based service, training, and research program for individuals of all ages and skill levels with autism spectrum disorders.

Biomedical and Diet Intervention

Autism Network for Dietary Intervention (ANDI)
www.autismndi.com

ANDI was established by parent researchers Lisa Lewis and Karyn Seroussi to help families around the world get started on and maintain an appropriate diet.

DAN! Practitioner List
www.autism.com/dan

ARI's Clinician Registry lists practitioners who provide bio-medically based treatment for children and adults with autism.

GFCF Diet
www.gfcfdiet.com

Diet resource for parents who need support implementing a gluten free–casein free diet (GFCF Diet).

Thoughtful House Center for Children
512–732–8400
www.thoughtfulhouse.org

Thoughtful House treats children with developmental disorders through a combination of medical care, education, and research.

Other Resources

Autism Early Intervention Fast Start Checklist
www.autismcouncilofutah.org/faststartchecklist.htm

This fast start checklist was designed to accelerate early intervention giving the child the best possible chance to reach his/her potential.

Autism Speaks 100 Day Kit

www.autismspeaks.org/community/family_services/100_day_kit.php

"The 100 Day Kit was created specifically for newly diagnosed families, to make the best possible use of the 100 days following the diagnosis of autism. The kit contains information and advice collected from trusted and respected experts on autism as well as from parents of children with autism. There is a week-by-week plan for the next 100 days, as well as organizational suggestions and forms that parents/caregivers can use to help with the paperwork and phone calls, as they begin to find services for their child."

Autism Speaks School Tool Kit

www.autismspeaks.org/school

"The School Community Tool Kit is available for free download and includes content about the features and challenges associated with autism, the strengths possessed by students with autism, and a host of tools and strategies teachers, administrators, and other staff can use to foster an accepting learning environment."

Autism Speaks Social Networking Site

www.autismspeaksnetwork.ning.com

This Autism Speaks networking site on ning.com will provide a venue for members of the autism community to share insights, opinions, and information.

Mariposa School

www.mariposaschool.org/materials.html

Verbal behavior training manual, free to download.

U.C. Davis Mind Institute

www.ucdmc.ucdavis.edu/mindinstitute

"The M.I.N.D. (Medical Investigation of Neurodevelopmental Disorders) Institute is an international, multidisciplinary research organization, committed to excellence, collaboration, and hope, striving to understand the causes and develop better treatments and ultimately cures for neurodevelopmental disorders. Standing shoulder to shoulder, families, scientists, physicians, educators, and administrators are working together to unlock the mysteries of the mind."

Yahoo Groups

www.yahoogroups.com

Search groups: ABMD, chelatingkids2, Thoughtful House Center for Children, GFCF Kids, EOHarm, RDI-List, Verbal Behavior, NIDS, and meta-mito-autism.

Blogs

Adventures in Autism

www.adventuresinautism.blogspot.com

Age of Autism

www.ageofautism.com

Kim Stagliano

www.kimstagliano.blogspot.com

Kim is the managing editor of Age of Autism, contributes to the Huffington Post, and has three daughters on the autism spectrum.

OC Register
www.autism.freedomblogging.com

Recommended Reading

Behavioral Intervention for Young Children with Autism by Catherine Maurice.

Changing the Course of Autism by Bryan Jepson, MD.

Children with Starving Brains by Jaquelyn McCandless, MD.

Healing the New Childhood Epidemics by Kenneth Bock, MD.

Mindblindness by Simon-Baron Cohen, PhD.

The New Social Story Book by Carol Gray.

Relationship Development Intervention with Young Children by Steven E. Gutstein, PhD, and Rachelle K. Sheely.

The Second Brain by Michael Gershon, MD.

Teaching Your Child the Language of Social Success by Marshall P. Duke, PhD, Stephen Nowicki Jr., PhD, and Elisabeth A. Martin, MEd.

Unraveling the Mysteries of Autism by Karyn Seroussi.

Herbert, M. R. "Autism: A Brain Disorder, or a Disorder That Affects the Brain?" *Clinical Neuropsychiatry* (2005) 2, 6, 354–379.

Searchable Online Medical Sources

Medline Plus
www.medlineplus.gov

PubMed
www.pubmed.gov